PERSPECTIVE IN SHAKESPEARE'S ENGLISH HISTORIES

Perspective in Shakespeare's English Histories

LARRY S. CHAMPION

THE UNIVERSITY OF GEORGIA PRESS
ATHENS

Copyright © 1980 by the University of Georgia Press
Athens 30602

All rights reserved

Set in 11 on 13 point Intertype Garamond
Printed in the United States of America

Library of Congress Cataloging in Publication Data

Champion, Larry S.
  Perspective in Shakespeare's English histories.

  Includes bibliographical references and index.
1. Shakespeare, William, 1564–1616—Histories.   I.
Title.
PR2982.C5   822.3'3   79–18175
            ISBN 0–8203–0491–3

Portions of this study in somewhat different form
have appeared previously in *Texas Studies in Language and Literature, Studies in Philology, Journal of General Education, Tennessee Studies in Literature*, and the *South Atlantic Bulletin*. Permission to reprint this material is gratefully acknowledged.

FOR NANCY
KATHERINE, BECKY, AND
STEPHEN

Contents

CHAPTER I

Introduction

IN 1612 THOMAS HEYWOOD in *An Apology for Actors* praised players and authors alike for the beneficial results of dramatized English history; such productions "have made the ignorant more apprehensive, taught the unlearned the knowledge of many famous histories, instructed such as cannot reade in the discovery of all our *English* Chronicles" (London, p. F₃). The aim of these plays, Heywood continues, is to teach due obedience to the King and to reveal by example the "untimely ends" of the wicked and the "flourishing estate" of the virtuous, "exhorting them to allegeance, dehorting them from all trayterous and fellonious strategems." No doubt Heywood had a vested interest in the respectability of the form; by his own claim, in his preface to *The English Traveller* published in 1633, he "had either an entire hand or at least a main finger" in two hundred twenty plays (including at least twenty-three histories and civic pageants). John Green, in fact, challenged him on this very point in *Refutation of the Apology for Actors* (1615), arguing that the liberties taken either to lengthen or to shorten the historical account are shameful and denouncing the ubiquitousness of the "Foole and his Bables."

Even if Heywood's motive for praising history in dramatic form was suspect, however, no one could deny the public's appetite for the general subject. Sixteenth-century England was teeming with histories, both native chronicles and translations of classical or contemporary works. For a nation with an emerging sense of identity and purpose—cultural and political—they were a means both of comprehending and of emulating earlier civilizations, of drawing analogies at the same time instructive and self-enhancing, and of justifying a contemporary monarchical control which, if not edenic, was demonstrably preferable to the bloody internecine struggles it had suppressed. On the one hand then it is not surprising that again and again history is described as a glass wherein one comprehends the present and envisions the future through a proper knowledge of the past and that in most cases the conceptualized pattern is assumed to represent God's hand at work in human destiny. Laurence Sanders, for example, in 1556, probably one year after a suppressed edition of the *Mirror for Magistrates,* developed a historical dialogue between Eusebius and Theophilus which he entitled *A Trewe Mirrour of the Wofull State of Englande.* Similarly George Whetstone set a "simple Myrror" before the English eyes so that they might perceive "the beauties of vertue without flattery, and the deformities of vice in no shadowes" (*The English Myrror* [London, 1586], p. iii), and Thomas Gainsford some years later penned *The History of the Earle of Tirone* as a "mirror . . . to divert [others] from presuming on any power against such a Prince" (London, 1619, pp. A_{2v}–A_{3r}). The heuristic contentions are almost predictable. R. Allott in *Wits Theater of the Little World* (London, 1599, p. A_{3v}) urges his readers to "profit" from reading the "epitomized histories," while Sir Thomas Smith proclaims in *De Republica Anglorum* that history "could not but be a great light unto the ignorant, and no less delight unto the learned" (London, 1583, p. A_{ii}). "There is no more plaine or ready waye to the right instruction of life, than facts doon in former passed years" (*The Histories of the Chronographer Polybius* [London, 1568], p. 1); "to wise writings on earth, a true history may justly challenge a first place" (*A Discourse of the Civile Warres and Late Troubles in Fraunce* [London, 1570], p. A_{iii}); "all Estates have ever favored those, who with their labour, and industrie, and the adventure of their lives, have from other countreys, brought those things which have been of use, and for the good, and profite, of the Commonwealth" (William Jones, trans., *Six Bookes of Politicks or Civil Doctrine* by Justus Lipsius [London, 1594], p. A_{ii}); "these histories doe afford to the knowledge of former times" (James Ware, ed., *Two Histories of Ireland* by Edmund Campion and Meredith Hanmer [Dublin, 1633], p. 2_v); "what can be more profitable (saith an ancient Historian) than fitting on the stage of human life, to be made wise by their example, who have trod the path of error and danger before us" (Henry Peacham, *The Compleat Gentleman* [London, 1622], p. 52).

Nor is it surprising, on the other hand, that the histories dealing with the Lancastrian-Yorkist struggle of the fifteenth century share a common denominator in their conceptualization of the Tudor Myth. Here the record is a familiar one, but one that bears brief reiteration, beginning with Henry VII's commissioning the Italian Polydore Vergil in 1505 to begin a Latin chronicle narrative which ultimately was printed in Basel in 1534 as *Anglica Historica*. Much of his material was incorporated by Edward Halle into *The Union of the Two Noble and Illustre Families of Lancaster and York*, published posthumously in 1548 with the aid of Richard Grafton. Grafton's own massive *Abridgement of the Chronicles of England* appeared in 1562, followed by a *Manual of the Chronicles of England* in 1565 and *A Chronicle at large and meere History of the affayres of Englande* in 1569. Meanwhile, Henry VIII in 1533 had commissioned John Leland to search for materials for a new history; his work, *Laborious Journey and Search,* was expanded and seen through the press by John Bale in 1549. Certainly the culminating work among these prose chronicles was Raphael Holinshed's *Chronicles of England, Scotland, and Ireland,* first published in 1577 and by 1587 including the talents of William Harrison, Richard Stanyhurst, and Edmund Campion. The Tudor historiography furnished material for poetry as well, of course. The *Mirror for Magistrates* was printed eight times within thirty-odd years (1555?–87), and such works as William Warner's *Albion's England* (1586) and Samuel Daniel's *The Civil Wars* (1595) attest to its continuing vogue near the end of the century, a currency reinforced by England's confrontation with the Spanish Armada in 1588.

In a word, historical material—whether catering to the intellect or the emotion, to national patriotism or common curiosity, and whether serving the purposes of rhetorical analysis, religious polemic, or political theory—provided a ready market for sixteenth-century printers. Previous critics, especially during the past forty years, have effectively recounted the importance of this material to the emerging drama as well. Lily Bess Campbell, for instance, described at some length the various forces that created the great interest in history during the century in *Shakespeare's Histories: Mirrors of Elizabethan Policy* (San Marino: Huntington Library, 1947), and Irving Ribner in *The English History Play in the Age of Shakespeare* (London: Methuen, 1965) traced the emergence of the hybrid dramatic form from medieval drama to its ultimate secularization in the work of Shakespeare and his contemporaries. E.M.W. Tillyard in *Shakespeare's History Plays* (London: Chatto and Windus, 1944) established what for years was the unchallenged interpretation of Shakespeare's plays: influenced primarily by Halle's and Holinshed's historical vision, the playwright depicts an historical pattern reflecting in general the operation of God's Providence and in particular the exaltation of the Tudors through God's decision to restore England to political stability and economic prosperity. Subsequent studies such as Derek Traversi's *Shakespeare from Richard II to Henry V* (Stanford: Stanford Univ. Press, 1957), M. M. Reese's *The Cease of Majesty: A Study of Shakespeare's History Plays* (London: Arnold, 1961), and S. C. Sen Gupta's *Shakespeare's Historical Plays* (London: Oxford Univ. Press, 1964) worked within the general constraints of this traditional interpretation. More recent studies, however, have taken an opposing view. Henry A. Kelly, for example, in *Divine Providence in the England of Shakespeare's Histories* (Cambridge: Harvard Univ. Press, 1970) directly challenges the presence of God's purposive direction in the plays, while Robert Ornstein in *A Kingdom for a Stage: The Achievement of Shakespeare's History Plays* (Cambridge: Harvard Univ. Press, 1972) maintains that Shakespeare in no way is attempting to recreate the Elizabethan world picture. Similarly, James Winny's *The Player King: A Theme of Shakespeare's Histories* (New York: Barnes and Noble, 1968), Michael Manheim's *The Weak King Dilemma in the Shakespearean History Play* (Syracuse: Syracuse Univ. Press, 1973), David Riggs's *Shakespeare's Heroical Histories: Henry VI and its Literary Tradition* (Cambridge: Harvard Univ. Press, 1971), and Moody Prior's *The Drama of Power: Studies in Shakespeare's History Plays* (Evanston: Northwestern Univ. Press, 1973) all take issue in a significant way with the earlier interpretations.

The sharp divergencies of opinion among such studies have tended to provoke a renewed appreciation for the genuine ambivalencies in Shakespeare's stage worlds, those of the histories as well as the tragedies and comedies. Moreover the willingness to examine each of the plays on its own merits, rather than as part of a double tetralogical pattern, makes it possible to trace more effectively the development of

4

Shakespeare's dramaturgical skills and to address directly his fundamental dramatic conceptualization of history. Certainly from the beginning of his career he perceived a basic distinction between history
and tragedy. In *1 Henry VI,* for example, he studiously avoids the
dominance of a single figure. Seven of the twenty-nine named characters in the play appear only once; thirteen others appear in five scenes
or fewer. Only Talbot (twelve scenes), Joan (ten scenes), Richard
Plantagenet (eight scenes), Gloucester and Winchester (each seven
scenes), Exeter, Suffolk, Reignier, and Alencon (each six scenes)
appear more frequently; the King himself figures in only five scenes.
No character is on stage for a significant portion of the action, and no
single figure is of predominant interest to the audience. Such a situation is in signal contrast with Shakespeare's early tragic pieces. Titus
Andronicus, for example, figures in nine of fourteen scenes, Romeo
and Juliet in twenty of twenty-four, and Brutus in eleven of eighteen.
Even more revealing is the total number of lines delivered by these
principals—28 percent by Titus (712 of 2,578), 38 percent by Romeo
and Juliet (1,145 of 2,982), and 29 percent by Brutus (708 of
2,457). In comparison, only one individual (Talbot, 377 of 2,675)
speaks as much as 15 percent of the lines in *1 Henry VI:* Joan delivers
9 percent (254), Richard Plantagenet 6 percent (182), Gloucester
and the title character 6 percent (180, 177). Clearly in the apprentice
tragedies, while there may indeed be problems of philosophic balance
and in particular aspects of the dramatic focus, the plot turns upon a
specific figure whose presence lends coherence to the actions of the
various personae.

If Shakespeare gives such early evidence of the structural significance of a single dominant figure in the tragedies, one reasonably
must look beyond the glib explanation that, without a sure sense of
dramatic form, he is setting Halle and Holinshed to stage in his early
histories.[1] Not only is it more reasonable to assume that he is quite
consciously striving for a particular kind of dramatic perspective; it
also seems likely that by fragmenting the focus, and thereby avoiding
a concentration upon any single individual, he is attempting to achieve
a complexity of perspective effectively to accommodate the historical
theme. Probably few would deny the general superiority even of

5

Shakespeare's earliest histories when compared with their dramatic contemporaries. F. P. Wilson, for example, observes that the "dignity and seriousness of purpose" are in "sharp contrast to many of the productions by other hands"; after exposure to the chronicle plays of other English authors, the Elizabethan auditor must have been shocked to realize that "here he is being asked not merely to observe the pageant of history, but to ponder the meaning of man's role in history."[2] At the same time, however, no critic has specifically examined the particular features which Shakespeare apparently drew from previous history plays, his own dramaturgical contributions, and the unique manner in which he combines these features to create his stage worlds and control the spectators' response.[3] If the end results in the *Henry VI* plays, for example, are not Shakespeare's most powerful efforts, they are nonetheless remarkable achievements for the early 1590s, providing even at the beginning of his career an illustration of the essential ambivalence of his dramatic view and of the careful manipulation of the spectator's attitude toward action and characterization which, with increasing effectiveness, typifies his work.

More specifically, some thirty-nine so-called "history" plays probably antedate the *Henry VI* plays.[4] Of this number, including classical, Biblical, neoclassical, didactic, and legendary histories and psuedo-histories, only sixteen are extant. And fully half of them are termed histories simply because the principal characters and the setting are historical or pseudohistorical. *The History of King Leir* (c. 1588–94), for example, focuses not on the national destiny but on the parent whose unwise trust temporarily costs him his throne. Similarly, *The Love of King David and Fair Bethsabe with the Tragedie of Absalon* (George Peele, c. 1581–94) centers on a father's loss of his rebel child. David's own lust for Bethsabe is paralleled in his son's violation of his sister Thamar; in retaliation Absalon, another son, slays Ammon and subsequently raises himself unsuccessfully against David and his army led by Joab. The slighter *John a Kent and John a Cumber* (Anthony Munday, c. 1587–90), though featuring a battle of wits between Welsh and Scottish magicians, is concerned primarily with the proper resolution of the romantic affairs of Marian, daughter of the Earl of Chester, and Sidanen, the daughter of Llwellen, Prince of

North Wales. Even plots dealing with more recent British royalty like *Edward III* (c. 1590–95) or *The Famous Victories of Henry V* (1583–88) still focus directly on an individual man who happens to be, or is about to become, a king. The former is intensely patriotic, building on England's conquest of Scotland and of France, but it gains coherence through the theme of Edward's successful mastery of the forces which oppose his rule, both from within (his lustful attraction to the Countess of Salisbury) and from without (King David and King John). *The Famous Victories,* analogously, is vigorously nationalistic, but the focus is on Hal's maturation from a wild young prince to a seasoned and prudent soldier, wooer, and ruler. *Woodstock* (1591–95) and *Edward II* (Christopher Marlowe, 1591–93) direct major attention to an effeminate and ineffective ruler victimized by his passion and the evil counsel of those who pander to it; again both dramas confront the spectators predominantly with the miseries of the individual, Richard as he suffers remorse for his actions and as the parasites Green, Bagot, Bushy, Scroop, and Tresilian plot secretly to increase their control over him, Edward as he suffers heinous indignities and a death of indescribable pain and horror. Moreover, except for these last two, the plays develop a narrative perspective. That is, without either external or internal devices through which to establish a pattern of dramatic anticipation, the plays engage the spectators' interest at the level of the plot itself rather than at the emotional level through a shared concern for the manner in which a character reacts to or is affected by the action. But, in any case, the consistent thread through all of these stage worlds is the individual focus. That the character is historical and that he is a king admittedly lend a largeness and a dignity to the story, not unlike the typical plot in the *de casibus* concept of tragedy, but these features do not fundamentally alter the sharply limited center of interest.

Other playwrights prior to Shakespeare, however, do broaden the perspective in an apparent attempt to characterize a nation or a particular phase of national development. For one thing the extension of the morality format into political themes involves the use of abstract characters for broad historical purposes. Indeed, political moralities in 1522 and 1525, a political-religious morality in 1540, a Latin political interlude in 1528, anti-Protestant interludes in 1527 and 1553, and twenty anti-Catholic interludes spanning 1533 to 1552 may well represent the first dramatic attempts to gain a dominant historical perspective. Out of this activity comes in 1538 the only play properly to be described as anti-Catholic history, *King John* (John Bale). While the plot line is again purely narrative in nature, the dramatic issue moves beyond John, the only historical figure, in the delineation of a satanic Catholic power. Surrounded by Widow England, Nobility, and Clergy, John defies Rome but is eventually poisoned by those with vested self-interest in the Church Universal.

Later dramatists broaden the perspective without dependence on such abstract personae. Both *The Wounds of Civil War, or Marius and Scilla* (Thomas Lodge, 1587–92) and *The Life and Death of Jack Straw* (1590–93), for example, avoid focusing on a dominant central figure. The spectator's sympathy in the former vacillates between Marius, who, initially favored as general by the Roman populace, is brutally opposed by his adversary, and Scilla, who following his triumphant usurpation of absolute power suddenly is obsessed with thoughts of death and the vanity of human power. Whether provoked by the gods or by man's ambition, the horror of civil strife along with its corrosive effects upon a nation is the major theme of the play. Jack Straw similarly is one of several rebels (Wat Tyler, Parson John Ball, Tom Miller, Nobs, Hob Carter) against Richard II. Juxtaposing the rebels' ill nature and limited mentality with Richard's rightful and beneficent rule, this play too projects, albeit simplistically, a vision of the perniciousness of internecine struggle. *Locrine* (1591–95) organizes the sweep of events depicting the mythical founding of England around a series of revenges. Following Brutus's bequeathing of his new kingdom to his sons Locrine, Albanact, and Camber, the Scythian Humber invades the land and slays Albanact. Subsequent to Locrine's vengeance against Humber—indeed as late as IV, i—appears the flaw which sets vengeance in motion against him, his love for Humber's wife Estrild and his neglect of his own wife Gwendolyn. Through dumb shows, the ghosts of Albanact and Corineus (Gwendolyn's father), and Ate, Goddess of Revenge (as the chorus), the playwright

8

establishes patterns of anticipation for the spectators, and the eighteen soliloquies totaling over three hundred lines are spread among eight characters. *The True Tragedy of Richard III* (1588–94) also features structural devices which predicate a broad, national focus—the ghost of Clarence, Truth, and Poetry as prologue characters to establish the fifteenth-century scene; the citizen as a choric figure at first virtually idolizing Shore's wife, yet spurning her after Edward's death for fear of Richard's wrath; Report, a character to describe the events of Bosworth Field; two messengers, the one to describe the ensuing reigns of Edward VI and Mary, the other to deliver a paean to the current ruler Elizabeth. Clearly this is a play with a marked and significant historical frame. Yet at the same time, with extensive use of the soliloquy through which Richard can pour out his anguish (Richard and his page together deliver ten soliloquies—183 of 2,005 or nine percent of the total lines), the anonymous playwright achieves an effective focus on the central figure and his rise through murder to the throne, infamy, and fearful remorse. More elaborate still is the broad perspective of *The Scottish History of James IV* (Robert Greene, c. 1590–91), involving three levels of perception: a framing action with Oberon, King of the fairies, Bohan, a Scot, and his sons Slipper and Nano; the private levels within the play of James and the villain Ateukin, with whom the spectators share over one hundred lines in six soliloquies and six asides; and the level of all other characters in the story concerning James's marriage to Dorothy, daughter of the king of England, and his lusting after the virtuous Ida, Countess of Arran. The perspective most closely resembling the *Henry VI* plays is that of *The Battle of Alcazar* (George Peele, 1588–89). Presumably to gain multifaceted angles on the historical event, the playwright spreads the dialogue among seven significant characters. No individual speaks more than 14 percent of the total lines of the play. Sebastian and Muly Mahomet speak 14 percent, the Presenter 12 percent, Abdelmelec 11, Stukley 8, Seth 5, and Muly's son 4. The historical struggle, in other words, is seen from various angles (the usurper's, the victim's, the foreign intervener's), and two dumb shows establish anticipated patterns of action. In the final analysis, however, the total absence of

internalized lines combined with a clear distinction between the innocent victims Seth and Sebastian and the villain Muly Mahomet produces melodrama rather than effective drama.

In summary, even though considerably fewer than half of the extant history plays prior to *1, 2, 3 Henry VI* have survived, Shakespeare
in these plays could observe a wide diversity of dramatic techniques,
ranging from the focus on the single figure to the broader focus on
national theme. He could find, on the one hand, a narrative perspective
in which the plot quite literally unfolds for the spectators as it appears
on stage, and on the other hand an anticipatory perspective in which
the spectators are led to expect significant events and thus to share the
emotions inherent in such anticipation and fulfillment. In some instances external structural devices predicate the subsequent events of
the plot; in other instances the devices of internalization (soliloquies
and asides) prompt the spectators to anticipate and experience the action on a more personal basis.

Shakespeare by the turn of the century had written some twenty of
his thirty-seven plays. Though including only three of his tragedies
and fewer than half of his comedies, this number represents nine of
his ten histories. As suggested by my earlier studies *The Evolution of
Shakespeare's Comedy* (Cambridge: Harvard Univ. Press, 1970) and
Shakespeare's Tragic Perspective (Athens: Univ. of Georgia Press,
1976), the years covered by these plays constitute a period of crucial
development in his dramaturgical skills. Like those earlier studies this
essay will concentrate, on the one hand, on Shakespeare's dramatic
perspective in each of the histories, the manner in which he establishes
the angle of vision that most effectively supports his theme, and the
structural devices that he uses to manipulate the spectators' response
to the characters and issues throughout the developing action. As J. L.
Styan has observed, the "first and last values of drama are revealed in
the response of an audience in a theatre, and all else must be secondary and speculative."[5] For all of us subject to the potential distortions
of the textbook and the isolated study, the point bears frequent repetition. At the same time, the study will focus on the general development of this historical perspective. My aim here as elsewhere is to
insist neither on a crude simplicity in his earliest pieces nor on some

narrowly focused progression of excellence. Plays like *Titus Androni-cus* and *The Comedy of Errors* are apprentice pieces only in comparison with his own later work—not, certainly, with that of his contemporaries. Similarly the recent Stratford productions of *Henry VI* have reminded us that those plays are effective in their own right. Moreover certain artistic achievements like *A Midsummer Night's Dream, Hamlet,* or *1 Henry IV* belie any overly rigid evolutionary concept. The one consistent factor emphasized by such an analysis is that Shakespeare is never static as a playwright. Rather than repeating or imitating past successes, he constantly experiments with structure and perspective. In his history plays, from *Henry VI* in the early 1590s to *Henry VIII* some twenty years later, he continually modifies the dramatic design by which to balance the sweep of history with the effective psychology of character.

CHAPTER II

The Search for Dramatic Form:
1, 2, 3 Henry VI

1 Henry VI, like all of Shakespeare's early pieces, has been both much maligned and defended through special pleading. A "Drum-and-Trumpet Thing"[1] with "no dramatic form"[2] to one critic, it is to another "the highest achievement of a flourishing dramatic tradition."[3] For the most part it suffered for years from a kind of benign neglect, a consequence of the assumption that its primary function was to introduce the two historical tetralogies.[4] Recently, however, various counterviews of the Henry VI plays have served as a healthy corrective by encouraging a closer examination of the individual plays as separate dramatic units which, whatever the larger thematic correlations, were conceived as single and complete entertainments for the Elizabethan spectators on a given afternoon. Perhaps, for example, through a richly textured irony Shakespeare is challenging the traditional Tudor concepts of the significant figures in this internecine struggle;[5] perhaps his major dramatic concern is the frustrations of a monarch incapable of rule;[6] perhaps he is directing the blame for political failure on human machination rather than providential direction;[7] perhaps he is depicting characters within the heroic tradition of history—" 'worthy and memorable' deeds presented through 'lively and well-spirited action' " rising to "the level of a moral spectacle."[8] In any case few critics any longer seem to be obsessed with either the question of authorship or the establishment of a rigid chronology.[9] In fact, once the Henry VI plays are examined individually on dramaturgical grounds, the evidence strongly suggests a normal chronological order of composition. While this issue is obviously not my major concern in this study, it does seem undeniable that throughout these three plays Shakespeare becomes progressively more effective in the dramatic ordering of his chronicle materials.

In *1 Henry VI* the playwright builds upon the not inconsiderable historical material described in the previous chapter and the remarkably varied structural techniques set on stage prior to around 1592; in fact the quality of his achievement is most fully realized in the context of what preceded it. Like the authors of *The Wounds of Civil War, The Life and Death of Jack Straw,* and *The Battle of Alcazar,* he establishes a perspective which through fragmentation broadens the focus of the spectators' attention beyond the single historical figure. At the same time like the authors of *James IV* and *The True Tragedy of Richard III,* he makes extensive use of internalized lines to provoke emotional concern. However, Shakespeare scatters this device among several individuals, some choric in function and some, with diametrically polarized perspectives, involved in the principal conflicts of the plot.

England's unstable political situation in the mid-fifteenth century, more precisely, is reflected through a wide variety of characters. Shakespeare utilizes the private remarks of Exeter, Bedford, and Lucy (five soliloquies, 37 percent of all such lines) along with lengthy remarks (seventy lines) of three messengers to provide the coherence for the seemingly diverse political dislocations in the court, among the common people, and on the battlefield.[10] Before the bier of Henry V, whose reign symbolizes the epitome of English medieval power, the English nobility eulogize the fallen warrior-leader; and Bedford, remaining behind as the funeral procession advances, observes that posterity holds only salt tears for the mothers and babes of generations to come. He would especially invoke Henry's spirit to "combat with adverse planets" in order to "keep [the realm] from civil broils" (I, i, 54, 53).[11] His words are interrupted by three messengers who in turn rush upon the stage with news of "loss, of slaughter, and discomfiture" (59). Obviously the establishment of the theme is more important than the messengers' similitude and credibility, else Shakespeare would hardly have the first overtly chide his superiors for "maintain[ing] several factions . . . whilst a field should be dispatch'd and fought" (71–72). Like a seer he warns the English nobility to awaken before the "flower-de-luces" on their sleeves are cropped further. The die is cast seven lines later with a report that France has revolted, crowning Charles as king, and twenty lines later with word that the valiant Talbot has been captured as a consequence both of inadequate support and of English cowardice. In the scope of a single scene, the English political world constructed by Henry V has collapsed. Henry VI, who in no way figures in the action, is not even mentioned until nine lines from the scene's conclusion. Indeed both Gloucester's struggle for power with Winchester and Joan's exploits against the English are set in motion long before the King appears on stage in III, i. The framework, in other words, establishes a vision larger than the role of any single individual; the drama is to depict the movement of representative Englishmen through a period of history characterized by dissension and rebellion both internal and external.

Exeter and Lucy, aloof from the political divisions which swirl beneath them, deliver additional choric soliloquies at points throughout the play far too evenly and effectively spaced to be coincidental (III, i; IV, i; IV, iii; V, i). Even at the moment at which Henry is newly reconciled with Richard Plantagenet, who is "restored to his blood" and inheritance, and at which the young king is advised to travel to France for a ceremonial crowning on the continent, Exeter reminds the spectators that

> This late dissension grown betwixt the peers
> Burns under feigned ashes of forg'd love,
> And will at last break out into a flame.
>
> (III, i, 188–90)

He recalls the "fatal prophecy" that Henry V should win all and Henry VI lose all, desiring only to die "ere that hapless time" (194, 200). Similarly when Henry later has naively plucked a red rose, a visual symbol of support for Somerset in his quarrel against Richard, and in virtually the same breath has appointed Richard "our regent in these parts of France" (IV, i, 163), Exeter again observes how frail indeed are the bonds of such external cooperation:

> This jarring discord of nobility,
> This shouldering of each other in the court,
> This factious bandying of their favorites,

14

. . . [does] presage some ill event.

. . . .

There comes the ruin, there begins confusion.
(188–91, 194)

The disaster materializes two scenes later when Somerset delays send-
ing to Richard a supply of horsemen for the relief of the embattled
Talbot.[12] "The vulture of sedition," as Sir William Lucy indicates,
"feeds in the bosom" of these great commanders; "whiles they each
other cross, / Lives, honors, lands, and all, hurry to loss" (IV, iii, 47–
48, 52–53). The feigned reconciliation is again Exeter's dominant
thought when he first views Winchester in a cardinal's habit:

Then I perceive that will be verified
Henry the Fifth did sometime prophesy:
"If once he come to be a cardinal,
He'll make his cap co-equal with the crown."
(V, i, 30–33)

In the single act in which detached characters fail to provide such thematic statements through soliloquies, Warwick prophesies that the
"brawl" between Somerset and Richard will soon grow to a factional-
ism which will "send between the Red Rose and the White / A thousand souls to death and deadly night" (II, iv, 126–27).

Through carefully placed soliloquies then, Shakespeare has established the fundamental theme which in two distinct ways lends coherence to the welter of activities which make up the plot. In the first
place the various prophetic statements project a resolution possible
only beyond the chronological limits of the individual play involving
the anarchistic civil struggles of Henry VI's reign; Shakespeare's audi-
tors, readily familiar with at least the fundamental pattern of history
which the Tudor myth dictated, could respond to the emotions associated with this larger theme, much as a contemporary American would
respond to the broader emotional implications of a plot set in the early
1860s. Such a view does not assume that Shakespeare from the outset
envisioned a series of plays which would constitute an epic statement
on fifteenth-century British history; what it does affirm is that Shakespeare was working with particular characters whose conflicts of in-

terest represent grave political issues not to be ultimately resolved within the chronological confines of the single play. At the same time, and ultimately more important, these choric statements explicitly project the theme of *1 Henry VI* as an individual drama: the theme of feigned reconciliation or, more specifically, the repetitive design of overt enmity and struggle giving place to a false harmony which covers a festering hatred. These tenuous reconciliations, by forcing the audience's attention to antecedent and subsequent events in time,[13] render the extended pattern of chronological events inevitable. Indeed the major lines of action coalesce in act 5 in a final dominant portrayal of temporary peace and of the forces which shortly will destroy it.

Each of the four distinct strands of plot functions to illustrate this central theme, and in every instance the soliloquy and the aside are employed as a structural device to signal the duplicity to the spectators. The first skirmish to develop, for example, is that between Winchester, great-uncle to the King, and Gloucester, Henry's uncle and Protector of the Realm. This conflict, appearing in four scenes, is carefully modulated; the open hostility rises progressively in intensity to the point of apparent reconciliation in act 5, when Winchester privately disabuses the audience of his peaceful intentions. On three occasions prior to the final act the increasing severity is signaled not only by the mounting verbal charges and countercharges but also by the means by which their dissension is quieted—in turn by the Duke of Bedford (I, i), by the Mayor of London (I, iii), and by the King himself (III, i). One notes also that the quarrel progressively involves a greater number of people and a greater degree of violence, from the mere ten lines of personal exchange, to the physical barring of Gloucester and his men from the Tower by Winchester and his men, to the street rioting and rock throwing by supporters of either side. The private insights most effectively reveal the growing tensions in his power struggle at Henry's court. Winchester in his initial appearance announces in soliloquy his intention to "send" the young king from Eltham and "sit at chiefest stern of public weal" (I, i, 176–77). Later, at the moment of public reconciliation following the general riot, each pointedly addresses an aside to the audience, Gloucester remarking that he fears Winchester offers his hand with a hollow heart (III, i, 136) and Winchester af-

firming that the token is but a dissembled flag of truce (141). Most
importantly, in the final act when no words of hostility pass between
them and Gloucester is busily arranging Henry's betrothal to the
daughter of the Earl of Armagnac, Winchester—his position now
strengthened through his appointment as cardinal—utters a soliloquy
which grimly underscores the inevitably short-lived peace between the
two. Now he will submit to no one, and Gloucester

> [shall] well perceive
> That neither in birth, or for authority,
> The Bishop will be overborne by thee.
> I'll either make thee stoop and bend thy knee,
> Or sack this country with a mutiny.

(1, 58–62)

An analogous strand, which figures in eight of the twenty-seven
scenes as the play is divided in modern editions, is the struggle between the Duke of Somerset and Richard Plantagenet. Involving the
clash between the Lancastrian red-rose and the Yorkist white-rose factions, this narrative thread is to become central to subsequent plays.
In this particular stage world, however, it functions only as another
dramatized exemplum on the theme of political division and the dangers of false reconciliation. Again the plot strand is carefully modulated to the point of intense overt conflict in acts 3 and 4 followed by
a clearly unstable resolution in act 5. Broached in two lengthy scenes in
the second act, the argument is envisioned by Shakespeare as originat-
ing in a testy conversation among lawyers at one of the Inns of Court
involving "nice sharp quillets of the law" (iv, 17), a moment which
Robert Ornstein describes as a "triumph of the dramatic imagination
over the inartistic formlessness of Tudor historiography."[14] The question in scene 4 clearly concerns the legal rights to the English throne,
although—as the participants choose roses to indicate their support
of either Somerset or Richard—the immediate issue is the attainder
against Plantagenet's house, a charge to be reviewed in the next Parliament. Two of Richard's comments, however, point ominously beyond that simple issue: the ambitious boast that his white rose will
"flourish to the height of my degree" (111) and the closing threat
that "this quarrel will drink blood another day" (134). Scene 5 ampli-

17

fies the situation with the dying Mortimer relating to Richard a full
account of the internecine struggle from his cell in the Tower. Richard,
in a soliloquy hinting at King Henry's death, vows either to be "restored to my blood, / Or make my will th' advantage of my good"
(128–29). The ramifications of the argument build in rapid succession
in the subsequent acts. In III, i, for instance, the spectators catch another significant glimpse of Richard; in a brief soliloquy he coyly
refuses to take sides openly in the Gloucester-Winchester dispute,
knowing full well that he will need the support of both factions in
Parliament (61–64). Somerset's continuing rancor is signaled to the
audience in an aside ("Perish, base Prince, ignoble Duke of York,"
177) moments after Richard's title is restored. Scene 4 extends the
argument beyond the two primary antagonists and beyond the issue of
Richard's good name and estate as, in Paris, Vernon and Basset exchange physical blows over the faction of the roses. Parting with mutual threats, they renew their argument in the next scene before the
King himself and in the presence of the two primary antagonists.
Whether prompted by naiveté or attempting a political coup, Henry
reprimands all involved for quarreling over "so slight and frivolous a
cause" and commands them to "be at peace" (IV, i, 112, 115). Even
more ludicrously he places a red rose on his coat while berating it as a
"toy, a thing of no regard" (145) and proclaiming both his kinsmen
as recipients of his love—to Michael Manheim a mark of his utter
failure as a "politician" (p. 84): "And therefore, as we hither came
in peace, / So let us so continue peace, and love" (160–61). The
center clearly will not hold, however; commissioning them as leaders
of his struggles against the French, he seems to lack not the strategy
but, ironically, the Machiavellian fortitude of the first Monmouth, his
grandfather, who advised Prince Hal to "busy giddy minds / With
foreign quarrels" (2 Henry IV, IV, v, 213–14).[15] The explicit consequences of this hollow reconciliation strike quickly. Richard, in soliloquy on the Plains of Gascony, curses "that villain Somerset" for
delaying his "promised supply / Of horsemen" (IV, iii, 9, 10–11);
and Somerset in the following scene accuses York of rash plotting, of
goading Talbot into an "unheedful, desperate, wild adventure" (iv, 3,
7). In the final act the implicit consequences are obvious in Richard's

disdain for the political accommodation for the French, the "baleful enemies" with whom Henry concludes a disadvantageous peace (iv, 120–22, 147–54).

The action involving Talbot and Joan is again an illustration of the central theme of political dislocation and the false reconciliation and feigned amicability inherent in it. Talbot's episode with the Countess of Auvergne, far from being merely a "light episode" (Pierce, p. 42) or a "pointless excrescence,"[16] provides an obvious example. Ostensibly with peaceful intent she invites him to visit her home, but in soliloquy she informs the spectators that the "plot is laid" by which the capture of this "dreadful night" shall make her "as famous . . . as Scythian Tomyris" (II, iii, 4–6). Only Talbot's suspicion that political hatred and projected violence hide behind the flag of truce saves his life, at least temporarily. Both Talbot and Joan are battlefield figures, of course, and each meets death as a consequence of overt enemy action. Nevertheless, their lives clearly are sacrificed to the various forces of agitation which comprise the domestic political chaos. Both lose their lives as a consequence of an arrant betrayal of allies. Each is introduced as a national hero with a distinct Herculean capacity. Talbot performs "wonders with his sword and lance" (I, i, 122), and whole armies gaze upon him (126); Joan is a "holy maid" sent from heaven (I, ii, 51) who, carrying the "spirit of deep prophecy," fights with "the sword of Deborah" (55, 195). Both likewise receive lavish praise verging on adulation during periods when their fortunes of battle are favorable. To a soldier at Orleans, "The cry of 'Talbot' serves for a sword." "Warlike and martial," his noble deeds shine to Burgundy as "valor's monuments" (III, ii, 118, 120). The King himself, recalling Henry V's remark that "a stouter champion never handled sword," rewards his "faithful service" and "toil in war" by conferring upon him the title of the Earl of Shrewsbury and a position of honor in the forthcoming coronation (III, iv, 19, 21). Joan similarly is addressed as "Divinest creature, Astrea's daughter, . . . France's saint" (I, vi, 4, 29). The French commanders will set her "statue in some holy place, / And have [her] reverenc'd like a blessed saint" (III, iii, 14–15) for successfully enticing Burgundy to desert the English cause. Certainly her moment of greatest glory occurs in IV, vii, as she stands over

Talbot's body scoffing at the many titles by which Sir William Lucy addresses the English stalwart: "Him that thou magnifi'st with all these titles / Stinking and fly-blown lies here at our feet" (75–76). Disdainfully she offers Talbot's body to Lucy, lest it "stink, and putrefy the air" (90). At the critical moment, though, both are deserted by the forces for which they fight. Talbot is "bought and sold" (IV, iv, 13), caught in the political feud between Somerset and York. As Lucy observes,

> The fraud of England, not the force of France,
> Hath now entrapp'd the noble-minded Talbot:
> Never to England shall he bear his life,
> But dies, betray'd to fortune by your strife.
>
> (36–39)

Joan's death is no less manipulated, if far less heroic. In soliloquy before Angiers she laments that her "choice spirits" and "speedy helpers" forsake her, even as do her mortal cohorts who flee the field, abandoning her to the English forces: "Now the time has come / That France must vail her lofty-plummed crest / And let her head fall into England's lap" (V, iii, 3, 5, 24–26). Significantly their deaths in the final analysis bring no greater security than the tenuous reconciliations which comprise the ominous resolution of the play. Talbot with the proclamation in his final battle that the "regent hath with Talbot broke his word, / And left us to the rage of France his sword" (IV, vi, 2–3) leaves no illusions concerning the Yorkist peer who will commit treason to undermine the Lancastrian king. And Joan's final words swell to a vicious curse against the general state of England:

> May never glorious sun reflex his beams
> Upon the country where you make abode;
> But darkness and the gloomy shade of death
> Environ you, till mischief and despair
> Drive you to break your necks or hang yourselves.
>
> (V, iv, 87–91)

One further plot strand, occasionally regarded merely as a linking device to part 2,[17] contributes markedly to the spirit of general anxiety in the final scenes. Act 5 opens with a projected peace confirmed by Henry's marriage to the daughter of the Earl of Armagnac, a plan sabotaged two scenes later when the Earl of Suffolk blatantly sacrifices the good of England to his own individual interests. Himself wedded and yet passionately attracted to Margaret of Anjou, he determines to woo her for the King and thus assure her personal accessibility to him. Again it is the soliloquy which clarifies the perspective; Suffolk privately informs the spectators that he "could be well content / To be [his] own attorney in this case" (V, iii, 165–66), that he will "bereave [Henry] of his wits with wonder" of her beauty (195). And it is he who, as a divisive element, speaks the final lines of the play, again in soliloquy, and thus projects the dissension which inevitably will recur: "Margaret shall now be Queen, and rule the King; / But I will rule both her, the King, and realm" (v, 107–8).

Shakespeare to be sure utilizes various motifs to heighten the spectators' interest in particular situations and characters. Without destroying the essential ambivalence of the divisive struggles among the English, he provokes an emotional response to York's cause through the appearance of the dying Mortimer. The aged Earl describes the "loathsome sequestration" to which he has been subject "since Henry Monmouth first began to reign" (II, v, 25, 23) and with his final breath proclaims Richard his heir and the rightful occupant of the throne. Certainly, too, sympathy is momentarily tilted toward Gloucester with Winchester's threat on two occasions to use the power of the Pope (I, iii, 52; III, i, 51); similarly the strongly Protestant audience would surely react sternly to Winchester's secret payment to Rome for his appointment as cardinal and his pompous boast that now he will force his enemies to "stoop and bend [the] knee, / Or sack this country with a mutiny" (V, i, 61–62).

Shakespeare also manipulates the numerous references to God and the heavenly disposition of earthly events in order to gain sympathy for the English cause despite this internal dissension. Henry V was "blest of the King of kings" and fought the "battles of the Lord of hosts" (I, i, 28, 31); Talbot, for whom "God is our fortress" (II, i, 26), "Ascribes the glory of his conquest got / First to [his] God" (III, iv, 11–12). His colors, he asserts, prosper under "God and Saint George" (IV, ii, 55); and when he swears to the dying Salisbury that he will be avenged on the French, a display of lightning and thunder seems to lend supernatural support to the claim. The French, to the contrary, are "conjurers and sorcerers" (I, i, 26). If Joan initially appears as a "holy maid . . . from heaven" (ii, 51–52), she quickly becomes the "devil or devil's dam," a witch and "high-minded strumpet" from hell (v, 5, 6, 9, 12). Even the French praise shifts to pagan images involving Astraea, Adonis, Rhodope, and Darius (vi, 4, 6, 22, 25). The "damned sorceress" (III, ii, 38; see further II, i, 15–18) is also branded a "vile fiend and shameless courtezan" (45) and a "Fell banning hag" (V, iii, 42). Significant too is the juxtaposition of Joan's exit with Margaret's entrance. The one destined to become a source of new dissension among the King and his nobles enters while the other leaves the stage cursing her enemies and condemned as an "enchantress" with "spelling charms" (V, iii, 42, 31). Consider, too, the contrasting style of death for the two national heroes. Joan degenerates into little more than a slut surrounded by fiends of darkness to whom she offers additional blood and even her "body, soul, and all" (V, iii, 22). Denying her mortal parentage and thereby provoking the curse of her shepherd father, she desperately pleads her belly to save her life, implicating in turn the Dauphin, Alencon, and Reignier. Shakespeare in a word uses her death to ratify her association with evil spirits and to nullify through her cowardice any admiration which her military victories might have aroused.[18] Talbot, to the contrary, in his death transcends the intestine political bickering which vitiates the English cause. Reunited with his son for the first time in seven years (both the youth of the son and the length of the separation are manipulated for emotional appeal), Talbot in two successive scenes pleads unsuccessfully for the child to flee to safety (IV, v, vi). The two fight valiantly and in the face of overwhelming odds carve a monument to bravery among the French troops before receiving their fatal wounds: "Poor boy, he smiles, methinks, as who should say, / Had Death been French, then Death had died to-day" (vii, 27–28).[19] Both the scene of reunion with father and son kneeling in embrace and the scene of tragic separation with the dying Talbot holding in his arms the lifeless body of his son are powerful pageantic images which compound the spectators' sympathy for the English cause.

The combination of these diverse plot strands and the significant use of soliloquies within each of them produces a perspective which places the spectator in a vitally important position and carries Shakespeare, in this and his other early history plays, structurally beyond the accomplishments of any previous chronicle playwright. On the one hand, the multiple strands create a sense of breadth but at some obvious expense to the spectator's focus and the intensity of his interest; on the other, the extensive use of internalization tends to encourage the spectator's emotional commitment to the character. Admittedly a number of the soliloquies in the early plays are choric and expository rather than psychologically revelatory—those of Bedford and Exeter, for example, in 1 Henry VI, of Faulconbridge in King John, even the majority of Richard's in Richard III. Even so, an individual character directly addressing the audience, whether struggling internally at a moment of critical decision or merely commenting upon past events and anticipating those to come, provokes a sense of familiarity which at least momentarily narrows the spectators' focus. In any case fully 7 percent (195 lines) of the text of 1 Henry VI is given over to soliloquies and asides. Here again, however, Shakespeare blocks an overly concentrated focus on a single individual by scattering these passages among thirteen different characters. Only Exeter speaks as many as three soliloquies, and he does so in a purely choric role. Characters more central to the action like Winchester, Talbot, Plantagenet, and Suffolk are assigned only two each, ranging in total lines from merely twelve to twenty-one. The titular character delivers not a single private line.

The uniquely rewarding quality of all of Shakespeare's historical drama results from the ambivalence which holds in precarious emotional balance for the spectators the dynamic forces of society, those who would maintain the established order and those who would destroy or rebuild—an omniscient view, in other words, of the paradox that characterizes the human condition.[20] Admittedly the characters of 1 Henry VI are simplistic; in this play built upon a clash between chivalric patriotism and Machiavellian egocentricity, each represents a certain value construct. Yet the plot takes shape not only from the conflict of these forces for political control of the nation but also from their struggle for the sympathy of the spectators who view them from various angles, prompting at least to a degree a response involving both detachment and engagement.

The structure of *2 Henry VI* is in several respects dramatically superior to that of *1 Henry VI*. Again the perspective is fragmented; no individual speaks more than 12 percent of the total lines, and no fewer than five characters deliver between 10 and 12 percent. These figures —Henry, Gloucester, York, Suffolk, and Margaret—represent a continuation of three of the four plot strands from part 1. While there is more extensive use of the soliloquy than in part 1 (8.5 percent of the total lines, 262 of 3,084), once more Shakespeare scatters the internalization, this time among eleven characters, only one of whom speaks more than 13 percent of such lines. Again, no character appears in as many as half of the scenes. The structural features then, like those in *1 Henry VI,* incorporate elements of both engagement and detachment, and the perspective is distinctly broader than that of Shakespeare's contemporary comedies and tragedies. In this play, however, instead of a unity based on action (parallel thematic movement in four plot strands), Shakespeare through two major dramatic focal points achieves a unity based on character—on the fall of Gloucester and the overt rebellion of York. The first is a contained unit of action of major significance to the individual play and the limited time-span it represents, a telescoping of ten years from Henry's marriage in 1445 to the Battle of St. Albans in 1455. The second once more projects beyond the limits of the stage world and suggests the interminable cycle of political struggles which characterizes fifteenth-century British history.[21] Additionally the figure of King Henry, far more significant than in part 1, serves to intensify the ambivalence of the situation: on the one hand, he deplores violence and genuinely strives to achieve peace and harmony for his kingdom; on the other, his innocence and idealism hardly conceal his refusal or his inability to act expediently, whether against wife or political foe, and in the final analysis he cannot escape bearing a major part of the blame for permitting the seeds of envy and ambition in those around him to grow to such monstrous proportions. Finally, Shakespeare utilizes specific plot devices—dreams, omens, prophecies—to foreshadow the events of the plot, thereby establishing a pattern of anticipation which heightens the spectator's tension and response and provides a touch of the architectonic quality to be used so extensively in *Richard III*.

The character of Gloucester provides the dominant focus for fully sixty-nine percent of the action (2,129 lines of 3,084) through IV, i, as marked in modern editions (the text in the folio is undivided). To be sure, each of the individual plot strands is set in motion in the early moments. Suffolk, for example, with much pomp delivers Margaret to King Henry; but, even before the reading of the proclamation of agreement can be completed, dissension breaks forth anew with charges from Gloucester, Salisbury, Warwick, and York that Suffolk has sacrificed both principle and possession. Not only does the daughter of the Duke of Anjou, secretly admired by Suffolk, come to Henry without dowry; the duchy of Anjou and the county of Maine are to be released to her father, and Suffolk is to receive a tax of one-fifteenth for costs and charges in transporting her. Gloucester brands the agreement shameful, the marriage fatal; and York avers that

> France should have torn and rent my heart
> Before I would have yielded to this league.
> . . . .
>
> [O]ur King Henry gives away his own,
> To match with her that brings no vantages.
> (I, i, 126–27, 130–31)

Cardinal Beaufort's virulent passion against Gloucester becomes clearly visible as he attempts to raise a faction against the Protector, accusing him of "smoothing words" by which to "bewitch" (156, 157) those at court and by which, as heir apparent, to take aim at the crown itself. York's ambition also quickly surfaces again. In an aside he comments that he "hath greatest cause" (207) to condemn the terms of the nuptial agreement since the kingdom is rightfully his. Moments later he reiterates the point in a lengthy soliloquy: " 'Tis thine they give away, and not their own" (221). Although for the present he must make a "show of love" to the Lancastrian Humphrey, his opportunity will come:

> A day will come when York shall claim his own,
> . . . .
> Then will I raise aloft the milk-white rose,
> . . . .
> And in my standard bear the arms of York,
> To grapple with the house of Lancaster.
> (239, 254, 256–57)

The initial scene then is replete with dissension, and only the spectator is in a position to realize the full extent. Each of the animosities, uncomfortably dormant at the end of part 1, flares anew with violent intensity. All, however, quickly take focus on Gloucester.[22] For one thing, his Duchess is baldly ambitious. She would have her husband's head "circled" with "Henry's diadem" (I, ii, 10, 7). In private she observes that, were she a man, she would remove those next of kin who are his stumbling blocks; as a woman she "will not be slack / To play [her] part in Fortune's pageant" (66–67), and Macbethlike she would eagerly learn from those who deal in black magic the fate of the Duke's political enemies. Aware of her design, Suffolk and the Cardinal plant an agent in Gloucester's household to tempt her to conjurations involving the political future; calling himself Suffolk's and the Cardinal's "broker," Hume well knows that "Dame Eleanor's aspiring humor" will speed her to destruction and that "her attainture will be Humphrey's fall" (I, ii, 97, 106). And York, who realizes the obvious political advantages of Gloucester's being "fall'n at jars" with the peers (i, 253), personally arrests the Duchess and her cohorts on the charge of treason, even while his own argument with Somerset is publicly renewed, this time over who will have the regency in France. He observes that her plot, "well chosen to build upon," will prove "A sorry breakfast for my Lord Protector" (iv, 6, 75). Queen Margaret herself is fiercely jealous of "that proud dame, the Lord Protector's wife" and lives to "be avenged" on the "base-born callot":

> She vaunted 'mongst her minion t'other day,

The very train of her worst wearing gown
Was better worth than all of my father's lands,
Till Suffolk gave two dukedoms for his daughter.
                    (I, iii, 76, 82, 83, 84–87)

So intense is Margaret's hatred that she boxes Dame Eleanor's ear for failure to retrieve her fallen handkerchief. Later, sentenced to banishment for her offenses, Eleanor longs only for prison and death. While sparks of ambition remain ("Methinks I should not thus be led along, / Mail'd up in shame. . . . I am Duke Humphrey's wife, / And he a prince, and ruler of the land"), her final moments offer a warning to her husband to beware "the axe of death" which hangs over him, the bushes "lim'd . . . to betray [his] wings" in the persons of Suffolk, York, and Winchester (II, iv, 30–31, 42–43, 49, 54).

Overt hostilities also focus increasingly on Duke Humphrey himself. Queen Margaret is especially vocal, convinced that King Henry is but a "pupil still / Under the surly Gloucester's governance" (I, iii, 46–47). Considered by H. M. Richmond the source of the blight which spreads throughout England (p. 39), she goads her husband about the "strangeness" of Gloucester's "alter'd countenance," the majesty with which he "bears himself," and his "stiff unbowed knee." As one near the King in descent, he is dangerous and should be barred from "your royal person" and "your Highness' Council": "Take heed, my lord, the welfare of us all / Hangs on the cutting short that fraudful man" (III, i, 5, 6, 16, 26, 27, 80–81). His sale of offices and towns in France should, she exclaims, cost him his head (I, iii, 135–37). According to Buckingham he uses the law as a rod (133); according to Somerset he is profligate with the public treasury (131). When King Henry observes a high-flying falcon, Suffolk is quick to apply the symbolism, observing that Gloucester's hawks tower high because they "know their master loves to be aloft" (II, i, 11).[23] He charges the Lord Protector in general with the ruin of the Commonwealth and the enslavement of its people (I, iii, 124–27) and in particular with the responsibility for his wife's "devilish practices" instigated "to frame our sovereign's fall" (III, i, 46, 52). And, albeit on vague charges, he arrests Gloucester for high treason, committing him to the Lord Cardinal until his day of trial for "twit[ting] our

27

sovereign lady here / With ignominious words" (178–79). York accuses him of accepting bribes in France, of failure to pay his own troops, and of devising strange tortures for offenders, and the Cardinal fears that even permitting him to speak will encourage "treason's secret knife" and cool the zeal of those who support Henry (174–77).

Individual quarrels, in other words, are subsumed in the general hatred of the Lord Protector. What becomes increasingly obvious to the spectator, however, is that those who oppose him are motivated by a crass and selfish aspiration for power. Consequently the Duke of Gloucester emerges as a powerfully sympathetic figure; as his destruction becomes increasingly inevitable to the spectators, he assumes the simplistic tragic pattern of the unflawed hero trapped and eventually murdered by his evil companions. A mythic figure who symbolizes "the ultimate in a cultivated man,"[24] he is what Riggs calls the "type of Renaissance governor whom humanists like Ascham and Elyot saw as supplanting such medieval *chevaliers* as Talbot" (p. 119). Sympathy for Gloucester is developed not only through the sporadic comments of objective characters and the obvious self-interest of those who oppose him, but also through his own actions and decisions which consistently reflect a virtuous and patriotic individual. York, as we have noted, is the first to state unequivocally that he but awaits the proper moment to move against Humphrey in his own behalf. The soliloquy, namely Hume's description of his employment to prepare a trap for the Duchess, is also the device a scene later for revealing the crafty designs of Beaufort and Suffolk; and Suffolk assures Margaret that once the bait is taken and Humphrey's power broken, she alone "shall steer the happy helm" (I, iii, 100). Again in act 2, when York reiterates his claim to the throne and receives a pledge of support from Salisbury and his son Warwick, he acknowledges the necessity of snaring "the shepherd of the flock, / That virtuous prince, the good Duke Humphrey" (II, ii, 73–74). Criticism from all quarters swells in act 3 as Margaret accuses Gloucester of an adamant pride which should bar him from Henry's Council, Suffolk accuses him of prompting his wife to her devilish practices, Beaufort charges him with devising tortures for small offenses, and York claims that he appropriated to himself money collected for payment of troops in France.[25] Gloucester not only fully answers each of their charges but also directly warns the King that the political ambitions of his enemies will not cease with his death:

> mine is made the prologue to their play;
> For thousand more, that yet suspect no peril,
> Will not conclude their plotted tragedy.
> . . . .
>
> Ay, all of you have laid your heads together—
> Myself had notice of your conventicles—
> . . . .
>
> And wolves are gnarling who shall gnaw thee first.
> Ah, that my fear were false, ah, that it were.
>   (III, i, 151–53, 165–66, 192–93)

Objective reinforcement of these perceptions of Gloucester's essential virtue comes from several directions. Salisbury, for example, in the midst of bickering about the Lord Protector by Beaufort, Somerset, and Buckingham, observes that those who criticize him speak from pride and ambition:

> I never saw but Humphrey Duke of Gloucester
> Did bear him like a noble gentleman.
> . . . .
>
> And as we may, cherish Duke Humphrey's deeds
> While they do tend the profit of the land.
>   (I, i, 183–84, 203–04)

The petitioners before the palace in I, iii, appear because they believe that Humphrey will pass their way. He is "a good man" from whom they may expect a fair response to their supplication "the Lord protect him" (4–5). Instead from Suffolk and Margaret they receive only a blunt rebuff and the threat of arrest. Perhaps it is King Henry himself who provides the most persuasive observations. In the face of treasonous charges against Gloucester, he affirms his uncle's innocence: "The Duke is virtuous, mild, and too well given / To dream on evil" (III, i, 72–73).

> My conscience tells me you are innocent.
> . . . .

> Ah, uncle Humphrey, in thy face I see
> The map of honour, truth, and loyalty.
>
> (141, 202–03)

Following Gloucester's murder, the King eulogizes the nobleman's untainted heart and his conscience uncorrupted with injustice (III, ii, 232ff.).

It is above all the consistent pattern of Gloucester's actions which in the eyes of the beholder establish him as the central figure of sympathy and interest. For one thing the spectators in the opening scene are prone to agree with Gloucester's evaluation of the terms of Henry's wedding arrangements which seem so disgraceful in sacrificing everything England has fought for in France. So too they can only admire him for admonishing his wife to "Banish the canker of ambitious thoughts" (I, ii, 18); is she not the "second woman in the realm," and would she "still be hammering treachery, / To tumble down" both herself and her husband? (43, 47–48). While he shares the sorrow and ignominy with sweet Nell as they meet for the final time in the public street leading to her imprisonment, his tears represent no compromise of principle or integrity. Two scenes seem designed primarily to reflect Gloucester's sound judgment. In I, iii, he is willing to recant publicly his recommendation concerning the regency of France; although he originally supports York for the position, he quickly agrees for the good of the country to support Somerset when Peter's charge against Horner breeds suspicion about Richard. Wisdom of an altogether different order is evidenced in the Simpcox affair at St. Albans when Gloucester, perceiving the fraudulence of the claim of past blindness and present lameness, exposes the impostor and his wife and turns them both over to the beadle for public punishment. While Gloucester is quick to strike back at his own critics, he never fails to recognize the ultimate authority of the crown. In a word there is not the slightest hint of personal ambition in the Lord Protector, whereas those around him seem to be motivated by nothing else. Like Talbot in part 1, Gloucester is heroic without pride, and his destruction, like that of his counterpart on the battlefield, graphically emphasizes the extensive political corruption which surrounds him.

Gloucester thus provides the focus of interest for two-thirds of the

play. Following the murder in III, ii, Henry makes his one decisive
move in banishing Suffolk (thereby prompting a remarkably erotic
dialogue between Queen Margaret and her lover);[26] and both Beaufort and Suffolk are given death scenes in which the figure of the Lord
Protector looms large—as an element of conscience in the case of the
Cardinal, as a figure of popular appeal to the commoners in the case
of those who dispatch Suffolk.[27] Admittedly, however, Gloucester is a
one-dimensional character whose tragic potentiality is limited to the
sense of waste in the destruction of virtue, and probably for that reason Shakespeare never again places such emphasis upon a simplistic
figure. Yet even in this instance, the playwright avoids the flagrant
melodrama which would result in a conflict of monolithic good and
monolithic evil. For one thing, no single individual functions as the
antagonist; the force which opposes Gloucester is diffuse, spread over
ten characters no one of whom is preeminent. Both Margaret Webster
and Sir Barry Jackson comment on the difficulty of producing the play
because of this diffusion, but more apt, I believe, is J. P. Brockbank's
assertion that Shakespeare reflects the individual "caught up in a cata-
clysmic movement of events for which responsibility is communal and
historical, not personal and immediate."[28] For another thing, as the
spectators observe the full context, it is virtually impossible to place
total blame on those adversarial figures. The king himself, as a consequence of his failure or inability to act, is indirectly responsible for
much of what happens; compounding this destructive passivity is the
fact that the Lancastrian assumption of royalty is hotly disputed—
indeed, II, ii (like II, v, in part 1) is inserted to establish a strong
Yorkist claim to the throne.

Henry in IV, ix, exclaims with at least a touch of the histrionic that
he does not relish the throne, that royalty was thrust upon him before
he was out of the cradle. There is doubtless more than a little psychological insight in such an observation, but to focus on the conditions
which made him king is to neglect the pattern of his own behavior
which has rendered him a failure in that office. Obviously Margaret's
quip about Henry's paralyzing religiosity ("all his mind is bent to
holiness. . . . I would the College of the Cardinals / Would choose
him Pope and carry him to Rome," I, iii, 55, 61–62) is intended more

as a snide condemnation of the absence of masculine assertiveness than as deference to his pious nature. Similarly she later accuses him of being "Too full of foolish pity" to make intelligent political decisions (III, i, 225). Indeed, time and again he fails to act decisively at critical moments which could have arrested the cancerous growth of ambition in those around him. He offers no public recognition, for instance, of the demeaning terms of his marriage agreement with Margaret; to the contrary, while Gloucester, York, and Warwick complain bitterly of the loss of all in France which was bought so dearly with English blood, Henry rewards Suffolk, the author of the covenant, with a knighthood which only adds insult to injury. Henry's naiveté with Simpcox is additional evidence. The possibility of fraud never enters the king's head; his only concern is that God be praised for the miraculous cure of blindness. Also unrealistic are his actions in the face of a threat to his own life by a ragged band of murderers led by the archrebel Jack Cade; he would send the holy bishop to counsel with them: "For God forbid so many simple souls / Should perish by the sword" (IV, iv, 10–11). More seriously, he is idle at key moments when decisive action is vital. In I, iii, he fails to indicate a preference for the regency of France; once he states that between Somerset and York "all's one to me" (102), he speaks not another word while permitting the argument between the two to assume serious proportions; likewise he does nothing to allay the animosity between Eleanor and Margaret when the queen boxes the Duchess of Gloucester's ear for refusing to pick up her handkerchief; nor can he react decisively to Peter's charge of treason against Horner, turning to Gloucester for a solution ("Uncle, what shall we say to this in law?" 203). Again in II, i, he is unable to control the argument building between Beaufort and Gloucester which culminates in a challenge to the death. Clearly he is aware of the nature of their private comments (see, for example, lines 43, 48, 53–56), but he fails to act in a manner so as to command their obedience. His performance as ruler is grossly negligent in III, i, in which, apparently without his foreknowledge and certainly without his concurrence, the Lord Protector is accused of high treason by those he knows to be bitter enemies to Gloucester; failure to act in this instance —or, more specifically, his comment to them to do "what to your wis-

doms seemeth best" (195)—invites the plot which leads to Gloucester's murder. How pathetic then is his comment, too little and too
late, to "proceed no straiter 'gainst our Uncle Gloucester / Than from
true evidence" (III, ii, 20–21) when, within six lines, he is to be informed of Gloucester's death. His action several scenes later is politically stupid, if not outrightly deceitful. In IV, ix, he sends word to
York that he will agree to remove Somerset from the court, whereupon
York dismisses the army that has been in position to march against the
King. Yet when York arrives at court, who should be standing near
Henry's side but Somerset. Little wonder that York should exclaim:

> False king, why hast thou broken faith with me?
> . . . .
> King did I call thee? No; thou art not king;
> Not fit to govern and rule multitudes,
> Which dar'st not, no, nor canst not rule a traitor.
> (V, i, 91, 93–95)

Clearly it is Henry who prompts York openly to take arms against him,
though his final words in fleeing from the rebellion ("Can we outrun
the heavens?," ii, 73) again reveal how impervious he is to the fact
that to a large extent he is the molder of his own destiny.

Henry is an ambivalent character, to be sure. On the one hand, the
spectators despise him for his inability to govern the passions and the
ambitions of those who surround him. On the other, they tend on
occasion to admire him for a passivity provoked by religious concern.
If he is an utter failure as a king, there is a pious idealism in the man
which prompts a sense of respect. In the context of the stage world,
the character functions in a more complex manner than most critics
have previously acknowledged. Manheim may indeed argue that Henry is "the one king who has the capacity to rule well," that not Henry,
but everyone else, is out of step.[29] But in reality, as E. W. Talbert observes, "the attributes of vigor and Christianity are divided between
York and Henry, instead of being combined, as was necessary for effective rule."[30] Shakespeare seems to be especially interested in the
implications of a character who performs "a strong part weakly."[31]
In a word, the force antagonistic to Gloucester—a highly ambivalent

network of actions and interactions—results from the combination of Henry's incongruous inactivity and the movements of the various figures whose evil natures are directly nourished by it. If the force of good is simplistic, the force of evil surely is not, and the resulting struggle is far from melodramatic.

As the character of Gloucester provides the focal point of dramatic interest for over two-thirds of the action, the character of York dominates the final portion. Following Gloucester's death, he emerges as the single figure sufficiently powerful to control at least temporarily the diverse forces which have plunged the kingdom into chaos. While obviously the spectators view critically his move to usurp the crown, they also inevitably see him as a kind of retribution against Henry and the forces which his failure to rule has produced. York is the single figure of significant internalization, delivering forty-eight percent of the soliloquies and asides in the play (126 lines compared to the next highest figure of 35 lines or thirteen percent), and this intimate familiarity prompts the spectators to develop an emotional interest in him. The preparation for this rapport and for York's dominant position in act 5 is carefully designed. We have noted previously his major soliloquy in the opening scene in which he frets over the terms of Margaret's betrothal and sets his eye on the day he will be able to claim the crown which is "his own," his "right" (239, 244). Upon Somerset's report of the loss of France, he mutters in an aside that he "will remedy this gear ere long" (III, i, 91); and in a soliloquy of more than fifty lines he expresses delight that his assignment to repel the Irish rebellion will provide him the opportunity to raise an army:

> My brain, more busy than the laboring spider,
> Weaves tedious snares to trap mine enemies.
> Well, nobles, well; 'tis politicly done,
> To send me packing with an host of men:
> I fear me you but warm the starved snake.
>
> (339–43)

He shares further his intentions to use Jack Cade of Ashford to raise a rebellion in the name of Mortimer: "By this I shall perceive the commons' mind, / How they affect the house and claim of York"

(374-75). From all such activity he hopes to bring the "golden circuit" to rest upon his head.

Even though York does not assume a dominant position until acts 4 and 5, his presence earlier is never forgotten—in his argument with Somerset over the regency in France in I, iii; in Peter's charge of high treason against Horner in I, iii, and II, iii (the specific charge is that Horner accused Henry of being a usurper since Richard Duke of York is rightful possessor of the English crown); [32] and above all in the long discussion with Salisbury and Warwick in II, ii, which methodically establishes the legality of his claim by tracing the lineal descent back to Lionel, Duke of Clarence, third son of Edward III. With his opportunity to garner manpower in III, i, also comes the possibility, through his journey to Ireland, to avoid the rush of events subsequent to Gloucester's murder which leads Beaufort to a death-bed repentance and Suffolk to banishment and death.

York's influence in the final scenes has two effects. First, as the spectators are aware, he is responsible for Cade's rebellion, which registers remarkable progress among the commoners and thereby reflects the pervasiveness of the disorder Henry's passivity has permitted to grow within his kingdom. This material surely has its grave side, "moral and social anarchy" reflecting the "very antithesis of God's plan" and invalidating through travesty the normal ties of kinship. [33] But on stage the action is also humorous, as in Barnardine's refusal to die in *Measure for Measure* or the bear's dining on Antigonus in *The Winter's Tale;* Cade is "a Saturnalia taken in earnest," a caricature combining nonsense with sharp social satire. [34] The execution of the clerk Emmanuel for knowing how to write his name, the slaying of the two Staffords and the dragging of their bodies behind a horse, the striking down of a fellow soldier for calling to "Jack Cade" rather than "Lord Mortimer," the beheading of Lord Say because he constructed a grammar school and speaks Latin and of James Cromer merely because he is Say's son-in-law—such deeds combine the grotesque humor of the incredibly naive blusterer Cade with the genuine reality of the violence and destruction sweeping the land. Indeed the macabre humor of the rebellion is aptly characterized by juxtaposing

35

the horror of Say's and Cromer's heads stuck on poles and forced to kiss with Cade's pompous proclamation of his edict that every girl who wishes to be married must "pay to me her maidenhead" (IV, vii, 122).

Second, as the commoners' uprising in the name of Mortimer subsides, York returns to England and immediately instigates rebellion among the nobility. The climactic battle, as Robert Y. Turner observes, is shaped in the play from York's point of view (p. 12). In a soliloquy opening act 5 he assures the spectators that he comes from Ireland to claim his right and to rescue the crown from "feeble Henry's head" (2); in his eyes there is no question of cunning, deceit, or Machiavellian manipulation—it is the throne which lineally is his due: "Ring bells, aloud, burn bonfires clear and bright / To entertain great England's lawful king" (3–4). Even so, he apparently would have been content to support Henry had not the king practiced flagrant duplicity in his pledge to remove the Duke of Somerset from his presence. As the rebellion assumes definitive form, York again insists upon his legal right to the throne: "heaven created [me] for thy ruler" (V, i, 105); his sons Edward and Richard are Henry's "betters in their birth" (119); "we are thy sovereign" (127); "I am thy king" (143). Salisbury, along with Warwick, concurs: "in my conscience [I] do repute his Grace / The rightful heir to England's royal seat" (177–78). Again the situation is highly ambivalent. Henry does wear the crown, and he does avow unswerving allegiance to God. Yet York's claim to the throne is at least as valid as his; moreover Henry is dangerously deficient in the qualities of effective leadership and in a sense is merely reaping the results of his earlier failure to exercise both public and domestic control. York is the lone powerful figure to emerge from the disordered political situation, and through his soliloquies he holds an emotional fascination for the spectators. In the battle of St. Albans, which comprises the final scene, the king's party is routed and his own power firmly established. The action concludes with York's proclaiming his determination to pursue Henry to London where the intent is to "call a present court of parliament" (25).

Significant also is Shakespeare's first extensive use of structural devices which are to become increasingly important in his subsequent works: omens, prophecies, or other similar events which both increase the excitement of the moment and architectonically heighten the dramatic tension by establishing a pattern of anticipation. In comparison with their counterparts in later plays they may be too straightforward to create anticipation of genuine dramatic impact,[35] but they do provide an obvious method for unifying the narrative events of the plot. These omens are rather methodically spaced through each of the five acts: Gloucester's prophecy, following his refusal to read publicly the terms of Henry's betrothal to Margaret, that France will shortly be lost (I, i, 146); his dream that his staff of office is broken and that the heads of Suffolk and Somerset are placed upon the broken ends (ii, 25ff.); the Duchess's dream of sitting upon the throne, with Henry and Margaret kneeling before her (36ff.); the witch's prophecy of the fate of Henry, Suffolk, and Somerset (iv, 30ff.); Margaret's pernicious comparison of Gloucester's ambition with Henry's falcon which towers high above the others (II, i, 10); York's prophecy that Beaufort, Suffolk, Buckingham, and Somerset, in seeking Gloucester's death, shall find their own deaths by rendering themselves subject to him (ii, 75–76); the Duchess of Gloucester's admonition to her husband, as she leaves in banishment and disgrace, to be aware of "the axe of death" which political enemies hold poised over his head (iv, 49); Gloucester's dire warning to Henry that his arrest will but permit the gnarling wolves to attack the King no longer protected by the shepherd (III, i, 192); Suffolk's desperate remembrance moments before his murder by "Walter" Whitmore of an earlier calculation that he would die by water (IV, i, 35); the Queen's grim private vow to think only on revenge for Suffolk's death (iv, 3); and young Clifford's assertion, in the face of present defeat by York's forces, that "we will live / To see their day, and them our fortune give" (V, ii, 88–89). Each of these prophecies, with the exception of the last two, accurately projects future events in the play; the last two point ominously to the future beyond act 5.[36] The pattern of such moments can hardly be coincidental; indeed, the oft cited curses of Queen Margaret in *Richard III*, which provide a virtual outline of the action, function no more methodically.

Whatever the order of composition, structurally *2 Henry VI* is a significant advancement over part 1. While a series of fourteen falls, from Horner and the Duchess of Gloucester in act 1 to Clifford and Somerset in act 5, relates the play loosely to the *de casibus* tradition, the internal organization of the plot carries it beyond such a seriatim progression.[37] Shakespeare's intention in *2 Henry VI*, as in part 1, is not to focus intensely on a single protagonist but to project the dramatic story of a nation during one of the tragic moments of her history. At the same time, Shakespeare achieves a more effective dramatic coherence by centering the action on two individuals, and his dramatic sense leads him directly to involve the spectator in the value judgments central to the drama. Either a melodramatic delineation of good and evil or a narrative with no concern for interior movement of character results in a virtually passive audience whose interest is escapist or merely curious in nature, the result perhaps of admiration for the ingenuity of a well-made plot. In such cases the characters are pawns who serve the necessities of story; their existence is synonymous with and constrained by their function. In the case of Gloucester and York, however, the spectator's response is not simplistic or static. Gloucester, himself blameless, is caught up in a struggle with various adversaries whose villainy in part is attributable to the king himself; York, in one sense destructively ambitious, in another sense purges the court and addresses the political dangers of the power vacuum created by the king's passivity. The central figure in the design is Henry, whose ambivalence is carefully modulated to provoke a complex response in which the spectator must sit in final judgment on both the characters and the ambiguous situations prompting their actions. As one of Shakespeare's recent editors has observed, the play possesses "the dramatic virtues of construction—continuity, tension, proportion, pace— which no playwright before Shakespeare had succeeded in uniting with a good sense of what interests an audience."[38]

While it would admittedly be naive to assume the great majority of spectators at a performance of the *Henry VI* plays either in Shakespeare's day or ours to be totally oblivious of the disastrous events of

the impending reigns of Edward IV and Richard III, one can attempt
to measure Shakespeare's structural progress between these dramatic
points only by viewing the three plays as separate and independent
creations, whatever the larger thematic correlations. Nowhere is the
playwright's development more crucially evident than in the delineation of the title figure through the three plays. Ancillary to the action
in part 1 and strikingly ambivalent in part 2, Henry is emotionally the
central figure in part 3. In part 1, as we have observed, he as a character is virtually an irrelevancy. A mere infant as the conflicts which
constitute the plot take shape, he finally appears in act 3 as a youth of
"tender years" attempting unsuccessfully to placate the growing animosities between Winchester and Gloucester; in IV, i, he seems totally
unaware of the surging passion behind the symbols of the white and
red roses; and in V, i, he agrees, though his "years are young," to a
projected wedding with Margaret of Anjou. The action of the play
would not be seriously altered if he were omitted altogether. His role
in part 2, on the other hand, is significant both physically and emotionally. The play at first glance appears to have a melodramatic simplistic
protagonist in Gloucester and a villain in York, but Henry cuts a figure
of genuine ambiguity and thereby conditions the spectators' response
to each. Gloucester struggles against those whose villainy accrues directly from the King's passivity;[39] York, while he may be ambitious,
represents the only visible hope for law and order. Henry's incongruous inactivity serves as a catalyst for the destructive forces in the play,
but since there is a pious idealism in the man which prompts a sense of
respect, the spectators' response hovers between admiration and disgust.[40] In part 2, then, Henry is a complex character who provides the
ambiguity for the action. The title role is even more significant in part
3, in which Henry is the sole figure with whom the spectators can iden-
tify emotionally and in which his total repudiation of both sides in the
Lancastrian-Yorkist struggle suggests a kind of wisdom honed in adversity and brings him to the verge of effective tragic development. If
the spectators sit in awe of the superhuman Machiavellian determination of Richard, they pity Henry, perceiving him, for all his flaws, as
something better than that which surrounds him and sensing in him
the universal human condition which copes inadequately with the evil

in its environment and must suffer the consequent waste and destruction.

The meticulous control which prompts and sustains this sympathy for Henry is indicative of the structural achievement of *3 Henry VI*, both in itself and in terms of Shakespearian things to come. The elements of detachment are once more fundamental to the design, with multiple plot lines serving to fragment the perspective and create the sense of breadth: York's confrontation with the king's forces, Henry's struggle with his own conscience and with members of his own party, Edward's amorous intrigues in defiance of his best political interests, and Richard's private aspirations for power. The play opens with York and Warwick in pursuit of Henry, who has fled to London. Once the parties join, Henry, to Margaret's disgust, agrees to bestow his crown upon York and his heirs with the understanding that the Lancastrian be allowed to live out his days on the throne.[41] Such an agreement will not long satisfy either party, and within two scenes warfare has burst forth anew. On this occasion Margaret gains the upper hand, and York is subjected to an ignominious death. As Edward openly declares his designs upon the throne and joins with Warwick to move against Queen Margaret, Henry privately deplores the wanton destruction and bloodshed of the internecine struggle. Within a few scenes Edward promises a crown to Elizabeth Grey in order to slake his own lust, despite the fact that Warwick even at that moment is carrying a proposal of marriage to Bona, sister of Lewis XI of France.[42] Richard meanwhile privately sets his sights on the throne; even as the play approaches a temporary resolution with Henry's murder and Edward's firm establishment on the throne, Richard vows that Clarence's turn is next, "then the rest" (V, vi, 90); his sign of fealty to his brother in the final lines is the kiss of Judas (vii, 33), the fulfillment of his earlier assertion that he "stay[s] not for the love of Edward, but the crown" (IV, i, 126). The action thus moves forward simultaneously on several fronts, reflecting a broad spectrum of the national political malaise and the diseased ambition which it harbors. No individual speaks more than fifteen percent of the total lines, and several characters figure with equal prominence (Warwick, 15 percent; Edward,

14.8 percent; Richard, 13.3 percent; Henry, 12.5 percent; Margaret, 9.6 percent). The soliloquies and asides are again spread over a relatively large number of characters as seven individuals deliver 281 lines (10 percent of the total number of lines, a higher figure than in either part 1 or part 2).

If these elements of detachment contribute to the historical focus of the play, it is in the elements of engagement that Shakespeare registers his significant progress as a dramatist. For one thing, *3 Henry VI* represents Shakespeare's first major accumulation of soliloquies and asides for internal focus, and the result, as Clifford Leech observes, is a "concentrated power" that can be "highly impressive in the theater" (p. 19). Henry and Richard together deliver 185 private lines, almost 6.5 percent of the total lines in the play. By comparison Titus Andronicus speaks only 6 such lines (.002 percent); Aaron, 63 lines (2.4 percent); Talbot in *1 Henry VI*, 52 lines (1.9 percent); York in *2 Henry VI*, 119 lines (3.8 percent). For another thing, as in *Othello* some ten years later, Shakespeare intersects two patterns of internalization: the one character painfully aware of his moral dilemma, the other a cold and calculating schemer devoted entirely to Machiavellian principles. In *Othello* the spectator views the first half of the tragedy primarily through Iago's jaundiced eyes as the opportunist seizes every moment for enlarging his scheme to destroy the Moor; in the last half the spectator experiences privately with the Moor first the agony of jealousy and passion and then the trauma of illumination. In *3 Henry VI* this pattern is reversed as the spectator moves from the morally sensitive mind to that of the amoral schemer. The order is critically significant: emphasis in *Othello* is on the aesthetic resolution of a plot in which— in convenient Aristotelian terms—a potentially noble figure has succumbed to error, in part at least because of his own pride, but has by the end of the play recognized his flaw and achieved a kind of an anagnorisis which bespeaks both the destructive waste and the moral catharsis of tragedy. Conversely, in *3 Henry VI* the final emphasis is upon the rise to power of an awesome and fascinating figure possessed of a maniacal dedication to seizing the throne—a movement which imaginatively casts the reader forward in time and thus reinforces the double sense of time so vital to Shakespeare's historical perspective, the sense of both the moment addressed by the single play and of the events precedent and antecedent.

Richard, more specifically, totally dominates the private passages from III, ii, forward, delivering 116 of the 153 such lines.[43] Even earlier his characterization is firmly established. In I, i, he casts down the head of the Duke of Somerset, whom he has defeated in battle, with the public pronouncement that "thus [he] hope[s] to shake King Henry's head" (20). It is Richard moreover who persuades his father to renew the battle against the Lancastrians. The oath of allegiance to Henry, whereby Lancaster would live out his life as King and bequeath the throne to York at his death, is null and void since it was not spoken "before a true and lawful magistrate" (ii, 23).[44] And it is Richard who, his body moisture quenched by a "furnace-burning heart" (II, i, 80), swears and achieves vengeance against Clifford for York's death (ii, 116; iv, 1–13). Both physical courage and mental agility devoid of moral constraints mark Richard's character from the opening scene, but his initial soliloquy in III, ii, provides the first indication in this play of the ultimate goal to which these traits will be signally contributory. Between him and the "golden time" (127) he seeks stands not only King Edward but also his older brother Clarence and the deposed King Henry and his son; these causes he will "cut off," adding colors to the chameleon, changing shape with Proteus, and teaching "the murtherous Machevil" (193) new tricks to achieve his vision:

> since this earth affords no joy to me
> But to command, to check, to o'erbear such
> As are of better person than myself,
> I'll make my heaven to dream upon the crown,
> And, whiles I live, t'account this world but hell,
> Until my misshap'd trunk that bears this head
> Be round impaled with a glorious crown.
>
> (165–71)

If this is not a detailed modus operandi, it is a general plan of battle, like Iago's "I have't. It is engendered. Hell and night / Must bring this monstrous birth to light" (I, iii, 403–4). The spectators' perspective from such moments gains a new dimension. Every subsequent action they view from the level of privileged information, a view which inevitably produces interest in the character whose perception informs the plot.

Each of Richard's subsequent asides and soliloquies intensifies this personal association. When Edward promises Elizabeth his royal protection and pompously asserts that obedience to the king shall not be questioned, Richard wryly observes that he but bides his time in silence (IV, i, 83). When Clarence joins Warwick in an alliance against Edward, Richard assures the spectators that his "thoughts aim at a further matter" (125). In act 5, standing over the murdered Henry, Richard reiterates the amoral principles which render him such a powerful and efficient agent for destruction:

> I . . . have neither pity, love, nor fear.
> . . . .
> [S]ince the heavens have shap'd my body so,
> Let hell make crook'd my mind to answer it.
> I have no brother, I am like no brother;
> And this word "love," which greybeards call divine,
> Be resident in men like one another
> And not in me: I am myself alone.
> (vi, 68, 78–83)

With methodic callousness he ticks off those already dead—Henry and his son—and addresses his attention to those who still stand between him and the throne. In the final scene it is not Edward's apparent resolution of the political and military struggle but Richard's destructive energy voiced in private remarks to the spectators which dominates the action. While Edward proclaims that he has "swept suspicion from our seat, / And made our footstool of security" (vii, 13–14), Richard, though publicly professing love and obedience to the monarch, privately admits that his "All Hail" is truly translated "all harm" (34).

Admittedly this Richard is a creation of the dramatic imagination. Like contemporary figures such as Aaron, Barabas, Tamburlaine, and later Iago and to some extent Edmund and Iachimo, he is stylized in his commitment to self and power. Yet like Gentillet's Machiavelli he captures the spectators' fancy in his appalling ability to subordinate

43

every facet of his personality to the accomplishment of his self-serving goals, temporarily numbing the viewers' ethical sensibilities with his sinister machinations. More important in the development of Shakespeare's historical perspective, he, as a character through whom the spectators observe and respond to the events on stage, provides a focal point for much of the action. The elements of detachment—not the least of which, as in *Richard III,* is the very stylization which blocks an integral emotional commitment—still operate, to be sure, to maintain a broad perspective, but the additional dimension of characterization provided by clustering a portion of the soliloquies and asides in a single figure adds a dramatic vitality to the abstract design of history.

More prophetic of Shakespeare's mature artistry, albeit dangerous to the historical perspective, is the characterization of King Henry.[45] Appearing in seven of the twenty-eight scenes as divided in modern editions (the F_1 text is continuous), Henry retains a degree of the ambivalence so pervasive in part 2, in that his refusal to assert royal authority fosters political discontent throughout the kingdom. Even so, with the destructive and cynical thrust for power depicted more sharply in the Yorkist Richard and the Lancastrian Margaret than in characters in the previous plays, Henry's moral values come increasingly to command the respect of the spectators. And the resulting tensions border on the genuinely tragic. Since these values cannot survive, let alone prevail, in this stage world of sinister Machiavellian politics, the spectators must watch as this king, who might through earlier positive actions have avoided the situation but whose very moral sensibilities precluded such action, is repudiated by his allies and murdered by his enemies. They watch too as Henry comes "very close to tragedy"; through his moral persistence and his "acceptance of mutability" he seems to achieve a spiritual insight which transcends the physical destruction.[46]

Certainly at first glance the Henry of the opening scene appears to be the same indecisive figure whose passivity so exasperates the spectators in part 2. Described by his enemies as the "fearful" king who "slily stole away and left his men" (25, 3) at the Battle of St. Albans, Henry restrains the Earl of Westmoreland and Clifford, reminding them that York has ample troops and that the city favors him:

> Far be the thought of [slaying York] from Henry's heart,
> To make a shambles of the parliament house!
> Cousin of Exeter, frowns, words, and threats
> Shall be the war that Henry means to use.
>   (70–73)

Henry threatens to unpeople the realm before he would "leave [his] kingly throne" (124), yet within ten lines he laments in an aside that he is lost for further words because his right to the throne is so questionable (134) and that he fears his supporters will desert him (151). At the first sign of the troops who appear upon Warwick's signal, Henry's threat is revealed as mere bravura: "My lord of Warwick, hear but one word: / Let me for this my life-time reign as king" (170–71). As his noblemen depart in disgust, his wife scorns him as a wretched man for his cowardly disinheritance of his son, and the prince spurns his father's request to remain with him. There is no reference here to Henry's acting on ethical or religious principles; he stands on stage at the conclusion of the scene without authority, dignity, or friends.

From this point, however, the king develops to near-tragic stature. In II, ii, still defied by his own wife and allies—indeed prevented further speech by Margaret and requested by Clifford to leave the field of battle—he truthfully addresses the moral vacuum in the atrocities which confront him. York's head on a pole before the city "irks [his] very soul" (6); and to Clifford's eloquent rationalization for such executions, he responds that "things ill got ha[ve] ever bad success" (46):

> I'll leave my son my virtuous deeds behind,
> And would my father had left me no more!
> . . . .
> Ah, cousin York, would thy best friends did know
> How it doth grieve me that thy head is here!
>   (49–50, 54–55)

For the first time also he affiliates himself directly with God, imploring Him to withhold revenge against the English subjects.[47] Most important to this growth are Henry's next two appearances. In a lengthy

45

soliloquy in II, v, for example, there is no question of cowardice or indecisiveness; Henry becomes purely and simply the voice of human compassion against the insanity and wanton destruction of the internecine struggle, and the spectators' emotional commitment is assured. With a molehill for a throne he observes the shifting fortunes of battle—the son who unknowingly has slain his father and the father who has slain his son, each cursing the "butcherly! / Erroneous, mutinous, and unnatural" age which divides families and destroys the very core of civilization (89–90). God, he admits, will ultimately determine the victor, but he would gladly give up his life if it would bring peace to the strife-torn land: "Was ever king so grieved for subject's woe? / Much is your sorrow; mine ten times so much. / . . . Here sits a king more woeful than you are" (111–12, 124). In III, i, Henry risks his life to visit England secretly; and captured with prayerbook in hand by subjects now loyal to King Edward, he asserts that "sour [adversities]" (24) have provided a wisdom not based on earthly prosperity:

> My crown is in my heart, not on my head;
> Not deck'd with diamonds and Indian stones,
> Not to be seen. My crown is call'd content;
> A crown it is that seldom kings enjoy.
>
> (62–65)

The new king's name commands obedience, but "what God will, that let your king perform" (100). This commitment to God's world— along with a genuine insight into the political situation—is confirmed by Henry's final appearances. Once again offered the throne by Warwick in IV, vi, he is thankful to God for his liberty, but he refuses to plague England further with his lack of leadership (21–22):

> I here resign my government to thee [Warwick],
> For thou art fortunate in all thy deeds.
> . . . .
> While I myself will lead a private life,
> And in devotion spend my latter days,
> To Sin's rebuke and my Creator's praise.
>
> (25–25, 42–44)

As he later faces Richard, who he knows will be his murderer, in the

Tower of London, there is no hint of fear, no begging for mercy; indeed he castigates his assailant as "an indigested and deformed lump"
and prophesies that future ages will condemn him (V, iv, 51). Yet
the king seems also at peace with himself and ready to accept the inevitable; even at the moment of the fatal blow his thoughts are not
upon revenge but upon his own sins and God's pardon for his adversary.

Henry then has come full cycle in this play: from the naive and
timorous ruler in act 1 who admits the weaknesses of his title and,
fearing all will desert him, willingly barters his son's right to the
throne in exchange for the promise of his kingship for life, to the
realist who can appraise his own political weaknesses in act 4 and,
somewhat like Richard II, confront his death with dignity and courage
in act 5.[48] This tragic development, which prefigures Shakespeare's
later creations, is far more consistent than that of Titus, whose sudden
emergence into a sophisticated revenger outwitting his adversaries at
their own game is the one thing that the structure—his journey from
arrogance and pride to suffering, ignominy, and madness—will not
support.

Admittedly Henry is not permitted to become such a dominating
force in the play that the historical perspective is obscured. We have
previously noted the multiple plot lines and the scattered use of soliloquies among several characters, structural devices which force the spectators to observe the historical events from a multiplicity of angles.
Juxtaposing Henry's increasing moral sensitivity with Richard's stylized Machiavellianism, depicted through significant private exchange
between the character and the audience, has essentially the same blocking effect. Moreover Shakespeare seems consciously to depict Henry's
murder—potentially the most emotionally profound moment for the
spectators—in abstract, almost ritualistic, terms. Henry, instead of
drawing attention directly to his plight, moments before he is stabbed
visualizes his situation through the filter of an extensive mythological
metaphor, equating himself with Daedalus, Prince Edward with Ica-
rus, York with King Minos, Edward with the sun, and Richard with
the sea.[49] If the analogy evokes moving associations with Henry's dilemma, his sense of responsibility for his son's death and a loving

47

father's tragic loss of his son, and his fatal inability to recognize potential dangers, it also formalizes the murder and abstracts it from reality. So too does Henry's formulaic prophecy which conjures up the image of a metaphysical retributive power at the very moment he is most human.

Even though set within a historical perspective, *3 Henry VI* offers in Henry and Richard far more dramatically compelling figures than any Shakespeare has previously depicted. Equally significant is the fact that the playwright, through an increasingly intense movement between the two major value structures in the play, provides an emotional coherence for the multiple plot strands far more effective than the parallel narrative patterns of part 1.[50] This rotation does not primarily involve attachment to the two political causes; instead, as the fortunes of battle shift, the spectators' sympathy is drawn increasingly to the victims of the struggle, whether Lancastrians or Yorkists. Consequently, sympathy becomes increasingly stronger for Henry, who in both moral and physical terms denounces everything for which the war stands.

Six emotional focal points exist in the play, shifting from pro-Lancastrian (I, i), to pro-Yorkist (I, iii–II, ii), to pro-Lancastrian (II, vi–III, i), to pro-Edwardian (III, ii–IV, iv), to pro-Lancastrian (V, v–V, vi), to pro-Edwardian (V, vii). In the first scene, for example, the spectators hear the Yorkists reporting the death of their adversaries Lord Clifford and Lord Stafford by the swords of common soldiers, and they are repelled by Edward's grisly boast that his bloody sword bears the blood of the Duke of Buckingham, whose beaver was "cleft . . . with a downright blow," and Montague's similar claim that the Earl of Wiltshire's blood stains his battle gear. Even more startling is Richard's tossing down the bloody head of the Duke of Somerset with taunts that it can best speak for him and York's mocking query, "But is your Grace dead, my Lord of Somerset?" (I, i, 18). The tone of the initial scene is disturbing, suggesting not merely that the Yorkists are celebrating a military victory but that they revel in the atrocities which it has spawned. And this suggestion is reinforced two scenes later, from the Lancastrian perspective, as Clifford, permitting no moment even for prayer, stabs York's young son Rutland in a mood of frenzied delight:

> I come, Plantagenet!
> And this thy son's blood cleaving to my blade
> Shall rust upon my weapon, till thy blood,
> Congeal'd with this, do make me wipe off both.
> (iii, 49–52)

When Clifford and Margaret apprehend York in the following scene, they set him on a molehill and place a paper crown upon his head. Tormenting him with the napkin stained with his son's blood, Margaret urges him to "grieve, to make me merry. . . . Stamp, rave, and fret, that I may sing and dance" (iv, 86, 91); after both stab him, he is beheaded and his head set on a pole before the city whose name he bears. The sentiment shifts yet again in II, vi, as Clifford dies and his head replaces that of York. Over the body Clarence, Richard, and Edward deride him with orders to "ask mercy," "repent," and "devise excuses"; Richard would have him live in order to hear the "bitter taunts" (66ff.). Later, as Edward woos Lady Elizabeth, the audience senses a malignant horror and the inevitable destruction of any efforts involving peace and love in Richard's determination to gain "a glorious crown" (III, ii, 171) at their expense. Sympathy is afforded Edward also as he is arrested in IV, iii, and his pregnant wife laments his misfortune in IV, iv. But it converts to horror in V, v, when Edward, with Clarence and Richard, stabs Prince Edward to death in his mother's presence and when Richard in the Tower of London one scene later repeatedly stabs King Henry, mockingly observing that his sword weeps purple tears "for the poor king's death" (63). In the final scene there is perhaps a touch of wry sympathy for Edward, who speaks assuredly of his "country's peace," "brothers' loves," and "lasting joy" (36, 46), even as Richard in asides gives notice that he will shortly "blast [t]his harvest" (21).

Shakespeare thus achieves a degree of artistic ambivalence through a series of scenes forcing the spectator alternately to respond with antipathy to pro-Lancastrian and pro-Yorkist figures. Admittedly the pattern is purely external, based on repugnance to the physical atrocities of war and man's brutality; but it prefigures a structural principle to be utilized more effectively in *Richard II* and *King John*. Moreover this rotating pattern of broken oaths, murders, and betrayals—in conjunction with the general opposition to the internecine warfare voiced by Henry with increasing poignancy and sincerity—produces in the spectators a mounting horror toward the struggle which transcends the concerns or the sympathies of any particular moment. Such thematic unity, providing coherence for the myriad events following the Battle of St. Albans in 1455 and Edward's accession to the throne and Henry's murder in 1471, brings *3 Henry VI* to a distinctive level of artistic achievement.

Two additional features, present also in less advanced stages in either part 1 or part 2, contribute significantly to the structure of this play. For one thing, as Wolfgang Clemen has observed, omens, prophecies, or other similar events both increase the excitement of the moment and architectonically heighten the dramatic tension by establishing a pattern of anticipation.[51] Such plot devices are utilized extensively in part 2. Examples are Gloucester's phophecy that France shortly shall be lost (I, i, 146); York's prophecy that Beaufort, Suffolk, Buckingham, and Somerset in seeking Gloucester's death shall find their own deaths and that Gloucester shall find a means to power (I, ii, 75–76); young Clifford's vow to live for retaliation in kind against those who murdered his father (V, ii, 88–89). These devices are too straightforward, however. The devices in part 3 do not so literally prefigure the events; instead they rhetorically reinforce the theme of political and moral anarchy which results from human brutality and the cycle of retribution which it generates. Warwick, for instance, in I, i, proclaims that the meeting at the Parliament House shall be called the bloody parliament unless York be acknowledged king (39–40), and Northumberland, Westmoreland, and Clifford pledge that York's forces will pay dearly for their earlier victory (93–100); similarly they berate the king for agreeing to York's succession: "In dreadful war mayst thou be overcome, / Or live in peace abandon'd and despis'd" (187–88). In I, ii, York, urged to seize power immediately, vows to "be king, or die" (35). Rutland with his final breath ominously prays that this day will be the height of Clifford's glory (iii, 48); York moments before his death proclaims his curse upon the house of Lancaster (iv, 148, 164): "My ashes, as the phoenix, may bring forth / A bird that will revenge upon you all" (35–36). Richard pledges to revenge both his father (II, i, 87–88) and his brother Rutland (ii, 115–16); and to Margaret's quip that the hunch-back is "Mark'd by the destinies to be avoided" (137), Clarence responds that York's sons "will never leave till we have hewn them down" (168). Following the death of his brother in II, iii, Warwick, along with Edward and Richard, kneels and "vow[s] to God above" to gain a "measure of revenge" (29, 32). The wounded Clifford foresees Lancaster's overthrow (vi, 3), and Richard ominously pledges his intention to "pluck" a crown whether friend or foe stand in the way (III, ii, 195). When Edward takes Elizabeth Grey as queen even while Warwick is arranging a royal union with Bona, Warwick reverses his colors and swears to "revenge [Edward's] wrong to Lady Bona, / And replant Henry to his former state" (III, iii, 197–98); Lewis, likewise, will send "masquers / To revel it with him and his new bride" (224–25). When Clarence and others desert Edward, Richard remains for his own privately announced devious purposes. Young Henry, the Earl of Richmond and the future Henry VII, is sent to safety in France with Henry VI's observation that "divining thoughts" inform him that "this pretty lad will prove our country's bliss" (IV, vi, 69, 70). In the final act prophecy rather than personal vengeance is predominant. Margaret curses the murderers of her son, Prince Edward, predicting that Edward's children will inherit a similar violent and early death (v, 65–67, 82); Henry prophesies that "many a thousand . . . Shall rue the hour that ever [Richard was] born" (vi, 37, 43); and Richard reveals his imminent plans to use prophecies as a device for bringing Clarence down: "King Henry and the Prince his son are gone: / Clarence, thy turn is next, and then the rest" (89–90).

These utterances run the gamut from the warrior's boast to the pitiful and vitriolic last gasp of the defeated, from the anger of the moment to the studied hatred bred of protracted animosity. But with the exception of the final prophecies, which obviously point the spectators to events beyond this play, these devices establish an anticipation of the cyclic struggle for power between the factions of the royal house even while they also rhetorically reinforce the theme of horror and destruction which such ceaseless civil warfare generates. Less prescriptive than the prophecies and dreams in part 2, they assume something of the powerfully suggestive metaphysical qualities of Margaret's curses in *Richard III*.

One last device is perhaps best described as the emblematic scene. It is used only once in part 1, though in apparently the most memorable moment for Shakespeare's contemporary audiences, when the fatally wounded Talbot holds in his arms the body of his dead son. It appears recurrently in *3 Henry VI* and is significant in visually reinforcing the theme of the play. By far the most moving single example is the aforementioned scene, II, v, which graphically depicts the stark hideousness of civil war in a tableau which renders words virtually unnecessary.[52] As King Henry sits on a molehill lamenting the fortunes of war and longing for the simplicity of the swain's happy life, he observes first a son who has killed his father, then a father who has killed his son. The human anguish, which momentarily puts into perspective the fatuity of man's struggle for political power, is aptly addressed by Henry's comment, "O piteous spectacle! O bloody times! . . . Weep, wretched man; I'll aid thee tear for tear" (73, 76). But there are other scenes equally important to the theme of the play. Consider the emblem of political division in I, i, in which York seats himself on the throne while Henry urges him to descend of his own volition and Lancastrian and Yorkist supporters exchange threats and offer to tear the crown from one head and set it on another. In III, iii, King Lewis of France sits upon his throne, attended on either side by those representing the English factions who seek military support. The instability of political support is visualized in III, i, in the keepers who arrest Henry; "subjects but while [Henry was] king," they are "commanded always by the greater gust" (81, 88). And the play's conclusion is thematically powerful, visualizing Edward on a throne he assumes to be secure while his adversary speaks in asides of his present destruction.

In summary, Shakespeare is demonstrably conscious in each of the Henry VI plays of the necessity for a breadth of vision which will effectively serve the historical theme; the political context, itself composed of complex human interactions—far from being merely a background against which an individual's destiny is portrayed—becomes the dominant concern of the play. At the same time he clearly seems to realize that genuine dramatic involvement is founded on compelling characterization, and increasingly he seeks the harmonious blend of those elements of detachment and breadth with those of emotional engagement through depth of characterization. Part 3 centers primarily on two figures, Richard and Henry, both of whom are more complex than the major figures in part 2. Richard's steely determination to rule at any cost, expressed privately to the spectators, commands an awesome fascination, even as Henry's tragic role is afforded full development. Yet the shifting emphases provoking increasing sympathies with the victims of the struggle, reinforced by emblematic scenes spaced throughout the action, establish a theme of political turmoil which transcends interest in any particular individual. Finally, Shakespeare uses specific plot devices—omens, prophecies, pledges of vengeance—to reinforce the theme of moral anarchy and suggestively to foreshadow the events of the plot. Such a structure may be crude in a number of ways,[53] but the Shakespearean virtues are present in embryonic form.[54]

Shakespeare's concern for form is obvious then in his earliest years, the Henry VI plays revealing what R. K. Turner and George Williams describe as the playwright's "steady advance in technical mastery."[55] Equally remarkable is the constant experimentation and the dramaturgical progress registered from play to play, from the parallel plot strands of *1 Henry VI,* to the focus upon Gloucester and York coupled with the genuine ambivalence of Henry in *2 Henry VI,* to the rotating ambivalence and the juxtaposition of antagonistic forces in Margaret and Richard coupled with the use of Henry as a choric figure to give voice to the spectators' alienation from both characters in *3 Henry VI.* In Shakespeare's search for effective historical perspective involving breadth of vision rather than prohibitively intense individual concern, *3 Henry VI* is especially significant in confirming a commitment to a focus predominantly upon character rather than upon action, a commitment which will bear direct fruit in the plays which follow.

CHAPTER III

History as Tragedy:
Richard III, Richard II

THE DIRECTION of Shakespeare's development in *Richard III* and *Richard II* is clear enough. If the three parts of *Henry VI* were written in chronological order—and increasingly critics find no compelling reasons to doubt the fact—then Shakespeare is moving toward a focus upon character. Throughout the three plays he demonstrably aims for those features of breadth which establish the historical perspective, but progressively he organizes his action around dominant personalities. We have observed that in *2 Henry VI* Humphrey, Duke of Gloucester, and Richard, Duke of York, serve as focal points of interest for the myriad events of the plot. Again in *3 Henry VI* two figures are predominant: the demonic Richard, Duke of Gloucester, and the pathetically impotent Lancastrian king. Shakespeare's two Richard plays extend and amplify these last two patterns of characterization with the consequence that the historical perspective is minimized, a fact tacitly acknowledged by twentieth-century critics who regularly include the plays in the study of Shakespeare's development as a tragic playwright. In the conceptualization of the character of Richard III, he was no doubt strongly influenced by the image of the Yorkist ruler inherited from the Tudor Myth, as espoused by Sir Thomas More and Polydore Vergil and transmitted through Grafton, Halle, and Holinshed. In the concept of dramatic form, he no doubt was impressed (probably both artistically and economically) with the dominant stage presence of Marlowe's Titan hero Tamburlaine, whose audacious ambition excited the Elizabethan spectators, and the Italianate villain Barabas, whose Machiavellian monstrosities inspired a deadly fascination. Whatever the reasons, Shakespeare in *Richard III* explores the full implications of the Machiavellian villain-hero introduced in *3 Henry VI*. Instead of taking in a broad sweep of events, he narrows his dramatic vision to those particular incidents which pertain to Richard's gaining and losing the crown. Without a balancing figure such as King Henry in *3 Henry VI*, Richard's character assumes total dominance. Similarly in *Richard II* Shakespeare examines at some length a character like Henry VI brought to center stage. Sensitive and imaginative, flawed by indecisiveness and the lust for self-gratification, woefully miscast in the role of king, Richard is delineated as abominable in his abuses of the royal prerogative and yet genuinely sympathetic in his sufferings as a man. The structure, like that of *3 Henry VI*, juxtaposes two diametrically opposite character types but here Bolingbroke is not as fully developed as Richard, Duke of Gloucester, and consequently Richard II with his tragic potentialities is able to dominate the stage more completely. The Richard plays, in a word, mark a distinct turn away from a historical perspective and toward a focus upon the protagonist, a point from which Shakespeare's maturation as a tragic playwright is convincingly charted.

There are structural features in *Richard III* which suggest a broad perspective, to be sure. Both the large number of speaking parts (over forty) and the numerous settings throughout London (the streets, the Tower, the palace, Baynard's Castle) and throughout the countryside (Lord Hastings' house, Lord Stanley's house, Pomfret Castle, Bosworth Field) reflect from many angles the pervasive political trauma of the period. So too do the numerous curses and the patterns of remorse in the individuals whose fall from prosperity precedes that of Richard. At one time or another, no fewer than sixteen characters invoke through curses God's heavy justice on Richard, eleven in the form of apparitions. Anne, for example, as she laments over the corpse of Henry VI, exclaims:

> O God! which this blood mad'st, revenge his death!
> O earth! which this blood drink'st, revenge his death!
> Either heav'n with lightning strike the murth'rer dead;
> Or earth gape open wide and eat him quick.
> (I, ii, 62–65)

In condemning to misery any wife he might have, she ironically condemns herself—a point not lost on her in act 4 as she reproaches herself anew for growing captive to his honied words.

Most centrally functional is the execration of Queen Margaret in act

1.[1] Her comments in addition provide a means of foreshadowing and anticipating the action of the play. Not only does she prophesy the King's anguished fall, she also provides a virtual outline of the action of the drama. Twice beseeching God to intervene in order that she may accomplish her revenge (iii, 110, 136ff.), she predicts King Edward's death by surfeit, the death of Edward's young son as recompense for the death of her own, the misery of Queen Elizabeth when she shall outlive her present glory, and the premature deaths of Rivers and Hastings. Her curse of Richard specifically invokes heaven's indignation to be hurled down on this slave of nature and son of hell when his sins are ripe. Her imploration that the "worm of conscience" torment his soul underscores Shakespeare's intention to depict a spiritual struggle within Richard. Queen Elizabeth, in act 4, describes Margaret as well skilled in curses and begs instruction on how to utter such pronouncements upon her enemies. Along with the Duchess of York, the three women perform almost ritualistically the Erinyes' functions of scourger and sorrower, the dual role assigned them by Dante. Their mournful wailing and lamentation (which again provides Shakespeare the opportunity to summarize the action to this point) evolves into a harrowing reiteration of curses, now made all the more chilling by the mothers' participation. The Duchess desires to smother her son in the breath of bitter words; she berates herself for not strangling him in her womb, and to Richard's assertion that the heavens should not hear such words, she invokes her most grievous curse:

> Either thou wilt die by God's just ordinance
> Ere from this war thou turn a conqueror,
> Or I with grief and extreme age shall perish
> And never more behold thy face again.
> . . . .
> My prayers on the adverse party fight.
> (IV, iv, 184–87, 191)

Margaret gives thanks to God for enforcing her curses and prophesies of Richard that now

> Ensues his piteous and unpitied end.

56

> Earth gapes, hell burns, fiends roar, saints pray,
> To have him suddenly convey'd from hence.
>
> (74–76)

The ghosts—of Prince Edward (son of Henry VI), Henry VI, Clarence, Rivers, Grey, Vaughan, Hastings, Prince Edward (son of Edward IV), Anne, and Buckingham—also curse Richard's bloody ascent to the throne.[2] Indeed the combined total of thirty-five lines spoken by these spirits who appear in Richard's dream the night before his fatal confrontation with Richmond trigger the spiritual anguish of his final soliloquy. Each apparition, after recounting the usurper's sins, chants his grisly refrain, "Despair, and die!" The spirit of Buckingham, last to appear, charges Richard to die in terror of his guiltiness: "Fainting, despair; despairing, yield thy breath!" (V, iii, 172).

Shakespeare does not question the nature or the validity of the ghosts. These spirits, after all, represent the final stages of Margaret's curse, and Shakespeare is at some pains to establish the credibility of the supernatural machinery of the play. When Richard asserts, for instance, that Margaret's misery is the result of his father's curses upon her, Margaret responds:

> Did York's dread curse prevail so much with heaven
> . . . .
> Can curses pierce the clouds and enter heaven?
> Why then give way, dull clouds, to my quick curses!
>
> (I, iii, 190, 194–95)

A few lines later she proclaims herself a prophetess, observing that her maledictions will ascend the sky and there awake God's gentle-sleeping peace. In the final act Richmond, whose efforts are endorsed by the spirits, is directly associated with God and the enforcement of His will for England publicly and for Richard personally; if Richard is God's scourge, clearly Richmond is His minister. The first brief glimpse of Richmond finds him addressing his followers shortly atfer landing in England, assailing Richard's yoke of tyranny and ordering his troops to advance in God's name. In the lengthy scene depicting the eve of Bosworth Field he prays to God, whose captain he accounts himself:

> Make us thy ministers of chastisement,

That we may praise thee in the victory!
To thee I do commend my watchful soul.
(V, iii, 113–15)

In his final oration he proclaims that God and good cause fight upon
his side. Both Blunt and Stanley, as well as the spirits of Clarence, the
young princes of Edward IV, and Buckingham, bless his efforts in the
name of God. By contrast Richard is consistently associated with sin
and the devil. In the first act alone he is by Anne and Margaret five
times branded a devil; he is the son of hell, a devilish slave, a fiend, a
dreadful minister of hell. In the final act he is twice termed God's
enemy by Richmond just prior to the battle.

Shakespeare paints the national malaise with a broad brush. He
constructs a theologically affirmative stage world in which the omni-
science and omnipotence of the divinity are assumed, even by those
who experience only misfortune and misery, and he depicts a human circle in which the conscience is alive and sensitive to the values
centered on that God. Again the emphasis is upon breadth as Shakespeare preplots Richard's final reflective moments on various occasions
throughout the play by depicting character after character, in the face
of death, turning his thoughts to the state of the soul and the sinful
nature of his earthly life. Grey and Rivers and Vaughan, for example,
assert their innocence and embrace until they meet again in heaven.
Hastings, who refuses to harken to the counsel of Stanley's dream or
the omens of his stumbling horse, repents of the pride which prompted him to court the favor of mortal man more than the grace of God.
King Edward on his deathbed vainly attempts to reconcile the factions
at court, requesting an interchange of love before the supreme King of
kings. Buckingham, despairing for having dallied with the high All-
Seer, calls for the officers to lead him to his block of shame where his
wrongs will reap their just rewards.

In this pattern of introspective moments, Clarence's final scene is
the most extensively developed parallel to that of his tyrant brother.
Like Richard, Clarence has fearful dreams which predict his destruction and, in the reflecting gems mocking the dead bones, underscore
the vanity of temporal power and possession; like Richard, he faces in
his troubled vision the spirits of those whom he has murdered, War-

wick and Prince Edward, son of Henry VI. Like Richard, he despairs
because his sins give evidence against his soul and his prayers cannot
appease God; he is heavy of soul and fain would sleep; he describes
his agony to a companion who attempts to console him. And, like
Richard, he is unable to achieve a full repentance.[3] Of his own spiritual state, the last the spectators hear is that his sins overwhelm the
best efforts of his prayers. His last moments, far from suggesting any
kind of spiritual solace, find him begging for his life, even as he loses
it ignominiously with a knife in his back.

Richard's ending is also passionate. His frenzied cry for a horse on
the battlefield and his refusal of rescue from Catesby with the decree
that he has set his life upon a cast and will stand the hazard of the die
are surely intended to be the actions not of courage but of desperation.[4]
He has not been fatalistically manipulated into fulfilling the final
stages of Margaret's curses voiced at the outset of the play and in the
ghosts' execrations just prior to the battle; to the contrary, he in the
previous scene has clearly repudiated the promptings of his conscience
even as he senses the vanity of human fortune and the inevitable destruction of those committed to it. The spiritual counterpart to his
physical death he asserts with his final commitment to self:

> Let not our babbling dreams affright our souls;
> Conscience is but a word that cowards use.
> . . . .
> Our strong arms be our conscience, swords our law!
> March on, join bravely, let us to it pell-mell;
> If not to heaven, then hand in hand to hell.
>
> (V, iii, 308–09, 311–13)

In addition to the patterned curses and the veritable parade of characters who cross the stage on their journey to violent death, various
choric scenes and foil characterizations broaden the scope of the play.
The scrivener of III, vi, reveals the alarming increase in Richard's
brazen callousness in moving against his enemies and suggests the
mounting apprehension throughout the land. The three citizens of II,
iii, point explicitly to the dangers of a kingdom ruled by a child and
the ripe opportunities for the Duke of Gloucester, who is full of dan-

ger. Richmond, for all his glorification, is significant primarily as the adversary of Richard and as the antithesis of what politically and personally the Yorkist usurper represents. Richard's description of Prince Edward (son of Henry VI) is inserted for the direct comparison which it affords; the sweet, lovely, young, valiant, wise, and royal prince, Richard contrasts with his own halting limp and misshapen body "whose all not equals Edward's moi'ty" (I, ii, 249). Similarly Shakespeare emphasizes the reactions of Edward IV, the second murderer of Clarence, Dighton, and Forrest to the bloody act of assassination, in order to contrast their remorse with Richard's calculating emotionlessness. Edward, shocked to learn that his countermand has come too late to save Clarence's life, recoils in horror when Stanley pleads for the life of a servant charged with murder. Edward exclaims that one will straightway fall on his knees to beg pardon for carters or waiting vassals:

> But for my brother not a man would speak,
> Nor I, ungracious, speak unto myself
> For him, poor soul.   (II, i, 127–29)

Certain dregs of conscience prompt the second murderer to fear the damnation his act will bring; he even attempts to warn his intended victim as his companion strikes, repenting of the deed as soon as it is done and refusing the money for which he has sold his peace of mind (275, 283–85). Both Dighton and Forrest, fleshed villains and bloody dogs according to Tyrrel's report, "Melted with tenderness and [kind] compassion, / Wept like [two] children in their death's sad story" (IV, iii, 7–8). By contrast, Richard asserts that he is happy in the news of the princes' death, and Clarence's death he views dispassionately as the successful completion of a task well planned. His peremptory command by which Buckingham is ordered to dispose of Hastings —"Chop off his head! Something we will determine" (III, i, 193)— provides perhaps the most effective contrast.

If the intent of these structural devices—the curses, the multiple falls, the choric scenes, the foil relationships—is to develop a broad perspective within which Richard will provide the spectators the necessary degree of interest in the individual figure, then the panorama is quite literally obscured by the sheer artistry of Richard's portrait. Richard is admittedly too palpably villainous, a bottled spider, a hunchbacked toad who methodically and, to a large degree, unconscionably wades through blood to the throne, but he fascinates the spectators with the combination of his devilish wit and Machiavellian dedication. For one thing, he dominates the stage, appearing in ten of eighteen scenes as indicated in F_1, and delivering more than 32 percent of the total lines (1,139 of 3,534). Moreover through twelve soliloquies and four asides (179 lines, 5 percent of those in the entire play), Richard provides the eye—albeit jaundiced—through which the spectator observes the action, and the result is a refinement for the popular stage of a Senecan device which in part provides the basis for the development of Shakespeare's tragic perspective. Conversely, of course, such a clustering of private lines obviates the breadth of vision and the fundamental sense of detachment on which the historical perspective of the *Henry VI* plays was primarily dependent.[5]

These soliloquies serve several major structural functions. For one thing, like those of Barabas in *The Jew of Malta* they constantly reflect the unholy vigor and callous zeal which feed Richard's ambition and provoke in the spectators, if not sympathy, an awed appreciation of his boundless energy and vitality. An Aaron moved to the center of the stage, Richard is determined to prove a villain. Not shaped for sportive tricks, rudely stamped, curtailed of fair proportion, cheated of feature, deformed, unfinished, he hates the idle pleasures of peaceful days; his identity must be established, if at all, by the enforced power of the battlefield or of the court, not in the normal affections of the human heart.[6] Just as in soliloquy he broaches the action at the outset of the play, so he concludes the lengthy first scene, still obviously taking an energetic delight in the world for him to bustle in. In the following scene he gloats over his successful wooing of Anne, having no friends to back his suit at all but the plain devil and dissembling looks. Of his ability to sow dissension between the king and the queen's kindred, he inwardly boasts:

> And thus I clothe my naked villainy
> With odd old ends stol'n forth of holy writ,

And seem a saint, when most I play the devil.
(I, iii, 335-37)

Sparring verbally with Prince Edward in the middle of the play, he wryly likens himself to the formal Vice, Iniquity, moralizing two meanings in one word even as he tosses out ominous proverbs in asides: "So wise so young, they say do never live long" (III, i, 79); "Short summers lightly have a forward spring" (94). Assured later that his wooing of Elizabeth will proceed as profitably as that of Anne, he approaches her as a self-proclaimed jolly, thriving wooer.

From first to last then, the soliloquies are utilized to remind the spectators that Richard is possessed of an almost uncanny combination of zeal and shrewdness; like Tamburlaine he becomes more than mere tyrant, informing the stage world with his spirit as well as with his presence.

Of prime significance also is the use of the soliloquy to establish a perspective through which the spectator, by anticipating events, can fully appreciate the manner in which they affect the central character.[7] Step by step Richard informs the audience in advance of his plots against those who in any way limit his power; as early as the first scene he hints that the throne is his ultimate goal, the "secret close intent" which he "must reach unto" (158, 159). At the same time, the soliloquy is a vehicle to exploit Richard's hypocrisy. While the result is not yet the delineation of character on the physical and metaphysical levels Shakespeare is to achieve in the great tragic figures, it moves beyond anything in the earlier chronicle plays. Through Richard's hypocrisy the spectators are drawn into the central character and share with him a rich perspective of dramatic irony. Thus they escape none of the agony as, with the victims' full confidence, he lures Clarence and Hastings to their deaths; to both he is a trusted friend and counsellor, yet to Richard, as he informs the spectators, each is an obstacle in the path of his ambition to be eliminated by means of a trap sprung at the proper time. With an even greater awe they observe his ability to divide and conquer within the court as Elizabeth and her kinsmen receive the blame for Clarence's death. They can anticipate Richard's egotistic joy upon winning Anne even in the presence of the corpse of her murdered father-in-law and while the memory of her murdered betrothed is still green; and they share with him the bitterly comic irony as, with Buckingham's aid, he woos the lord mayor and the populace by walking, prayer book in hand, between two clergymen.

The soliloquy is also of signal importance in Shakespeare's attempt to achieve a philosophic dimension for the play. The tenth soliloquy (IV, iii, 36–43) sets the stage for Richard's first significant failure, his inability to persuade Elizabeth to rally her daughter to his side. It is at this point that the spectators begin to achieve a vision larger than Richard's—to a degree identifying with him as a result of the fascination of his ambitious energy and spirit and to a degree observing him from above as he runs headlong into the net of destruction which both history and his own character have prepared for him. The later Shakespeare will create in his tragedies far more complex double visions through which the spectators will be profoundly involved in the inner struggles of a protagonist with an active and sensitive conscience at the same time they observe the events set in motion by a decision of passion which sweeps him to disaster; in his subsequent Henry plays he will create genuinely ambivalent figures without the sacrifice of breadth of perspective. However, to look backward rather than forward, Richard is Shakespeare's most powerful characterization to date. Although his spiritual struggle is minimal, a double vision results both from the spectators' external familiarity with the historical narrative (a narrative set in the context of a world in which God's ordinance smiles upon the emerging Tudor dynasty and presumes the destruction of Richard's demonic ambition) and from the internal structural features which provide at least a momentary glimpse of Richard's private hell. His last three soliloquies progressively force the spectators to this double vision. In act 4 he establishes the critical importance of his winning Elizabeth as bride, observing that Richmond, his primary antagonist, is aiming at the same prize (iii, 40–43). Hence he is smugly delighted that Elizabeth is apparently a relenting fool and a shallow, changing woman for allowing her daughter to be won in such fashion. But the die is cast for the crook-backed king when Stanley asserts that the queen has readily consented to the espousal of Richmond and Elizabeth. Encountering deceit for the first time, Richard is unable to cope with it, largely because his remarkable successes and his pride have virtually blinded him to the possibility of failure, to the possibility that someone will not acquiesce unquestioningly to his will.

Richard's only extensive articulation of spiritual anguish occurs in his final soliloquy. If Shakespeare ultimately fails to achieve a satisfactory philosophic dimension for Richard through this passage near the end, he has clearly attempted to prepare both the central figure and the spectators for this climactic moment.[8] Even Gloucester's early wit plays somewhat gingerly on matters spiritual. In the third scene, for example, as Margaret with chilling effect pronounces curses upon all responsible for the death of her husband and son, Richard quibbles with her at length, twice attempting to turn the execration back upon her by blurting "Margaret" just at the point she is to name him. On her exit he attempts to change the subject by directing the conversation to Clarence and his murderers, on whom he piously begs God's mercy and pardon. When commended by Rivers for his "Christianlike" attitude, Richard wryly responds in an aside that it was well to conclude so rather than curse himself. This same turn of mind is in evidence again in act 2 as Richard, following King Edward's death, feigns sorrow while requesting his mother's blessing. From the Duchess of York, who earlier accused him before Clarence's children of deceit and villainy, Richard receives a curt benison which prompts his aside:

> And make me die a good old man!
> That is the butt-end of a mother's blessing.
> I marvel that her Grace did leave it out.
> (ii, 109–11)

On several occasions the sardonic humor builds upon references to heaven, hell, blessing, and curse. While it would push the text too far to assume that Shakespeare intends to reveal an inner torment beneath this facade of wit, the spectators can hardly fail to notice that such thoughts are never far from Richard's mind.

In IV, ii, the agitation is certainly genuine as Gloucester for the first time is unable to conceal his emotion from those around him. Even as in soliloquy he reacts with angry indignation to Buckingham's hesitance to murder the young princes (24–26), Catesby observes to another that the King is angry and gnaws his lip. A few lines later

Richard informs the spectators that Buckingham shall no longer be privy to his counsel, after which he orders the astonished Catesby to rumor it abroad that his wife Anne is gravely ill. His subsequent soliloquy, though he swiftly tempers himself to the task at hand, signals briefly his growing desperation and loss of confidence in his "uncertain way of gain":

> But I am in
> So far in blood that sin will pluck on sin.
> Tear-falling pity dwells not in this eye.
>   (IV, ii, 63–65)

The tenor of these lines is supported by other incidents throughout the play, such as the king's addled confusion in dispatching Ratcliff and Catesby when he first hears that Richmond is landing and that many throng to the shore to welcome the invader, or his striking the third messenger, or the report of his frequent nightmares by Anne, who asserts on two occasions that she never slept a quiet hour with him because she was continually awakened with his timorous dreams.

If these moments are skillfully performed, the spectators are by no means unprepared for the spiritual despair voiced in Richard's final soliloquy. Starting from his dream, he desperately berates coward conscience for afflicting him; his flesh trembles; he recognizes himself as a murderer and a villain and, Faustus-like, would fly from himself. His conscience has many tongues as his sins throng to the bar proclaiming him guilty. In a remark reminiscent of his earlier desire for his mother's blessing and his subsequent affiliation with Buckingham, he laments that no creature loves him; nor will any pity him when he dies. So powerful are the effects of these moments that he for the first and only time openly admits his fear to another, informing Ratcliff:

> By the apostle Paul, shadows to-night
> Have strook more terror to the soul of Richard
> Than can the substance of ten thousand soldiers
> Armed in proof and led by shallow Richmond.
>   (V, iii, 216–19)

Richard III's character, in a word, is overwhelming. His energy informs the action of the play as the spectators' fascination builds upon a strange combination of horror and humor. As Robert G. Hunter recently has observed, Richard is the efficient first cause of his tragedy, a tragedy created in action.[9] Richard is Shakespeare's first character to be infused with a significant internal dimension throughout the full range of the play, a consequence not only of the numerous asides and soliloquies but also of their combination with the supernatural machinery which anticipates both his external and internal struggles and the seriatim sequence of characters who, in their own moments of truth, provoke the spectators' attention to the metaphysics of Richard's personality. To this end Shakespeare has made significant alterations from the several sources he presumably utilized. In none of them does Margaret, who actually died in 1482, return to England after she is ransomed. In none is Hastings imprisoned at the instigation of his enemies at court, the queen and her kinsmen; and in none does he naively miscalculate his fortunes with Richard just prior to his condemnation. The details of Clarence's murder are borrowed primarily from Halle's description of the murder of the two young princes, previously dramatized both in Legges's *Richardus Tertius* and the anonymous *The True Tragedy of Richard III*. Admittedly, Shakespeare does not basically reshape his central figure; he inherits the tradition of a guilt-ridden Richard in whom vaulting ambition has o'erleaped itself and whose mind, according to Polydore Vergil, was "enflamyd with desire of usurping the kingdom, partly was trubblyd by guiltynes of intent to commyt so haynous widkedness." Halle describes Richard's dream before the battle as "a punccion and pricke of his synfull conscience" in which he "sawe diverse ymages lyke terrible develles which pulled and haled hym, not sufferynge hym to take any quyet or rest." In *The Mirror for Magistrates* these devils have become "All those murdered Ghostes whome I / By death had sent to their untimely grave"; and in *The True Tragedy* Richard relates to Lord Lovell that the "ghosts of those whom [he has] slaine in reaching for a Crowne" come gaping for revenge, whether he wakes or sleeps. But if Shakespeare does not create his Richard whole cloth, he is the first actually to dramatize the ghosts and to provide them the extensive dialogue by which they function as an extrapolation of Richard's conscience. In none of the sources does Shakespeare find the elaborate Machiavellian strategy which the soliloquies provide in methodically mapping out Richard's designs on the throne, or his nervous blessing on Clarence's murderers lest he spiritually indict himself, or his anxious concern for not receiving his mother's full blessing, or his frenzied anger when Buckingham balks at the command of murder.

The True Tragedy anticipates, to be sure, the moral sensitivity of the Yorkist usurper. At one point in that play a page describes the deep sigh and fearful cries that come from the depths of Richard's heart. On three occasions Richard himself bemoans the kingdom gotten by murder of his friends; he fears the severe judge and for a brief moment would repent and appeal for mercy to a righteous God; the horror of his bloody practice strikes terror to his wounded conscience. Twice his comments point beyond his physical death: though his enemies would kill his body, yet shall they leave a "never dying" mind; having spoken his final words, he asserts, "What more I have to say, ile make report among the damned souls."

Shakespeare's dramatic contribution, in relation to *The True Tragedy,* is one of subtlety and refinement. The earlier play contains not a single line of soliloquy, Richard's remorse being voiced not in the inner recesses of the human spirit but in open conversation with those about him. Furthermore the Richard of *The True Tragedy* is a relatively simplistic character, fluctuating throughout between the poles of temporal ambition and spiritual anguish. By contrast, Shakespeare's Richard is at the outset a dedicated and calculating Machiavel whose slow erosion of self-confidence will eventually precipitate the frenetic disillusionment of his final soliloquy; only then does he overtly admit his fear to another, even as he falls victim to the despair which controls his actions on the battlefield.

Apprentice qualities are admittedly not difficult to find. It may well be, for example, that the presumed inevitability of Margaret's curses tends to diminish the impression of Richard's free will, as does the consistent barrage from the surrounding characters of images equating him with the devil. By the same token, Richmond, God's captain, is highly stylized, as are several of Richard's victims such as the young princes and Anne. Even the ghosts, which function as a metaphysical device by which we gain insight into Richard's soul, lose impact through extension into the dream of Richmond; with the rhetorically balanced condemnation of Richard and praise of Richmond, the apparitions become too obviously a stage device for ordering the final events of the play. It may well be also that Shakespeare is guilty of redundancy, that the moral design comes close to being tedious at times as Margaret's prophecies in act 1 are reiterated in act 4 with the help of Elizabeth and the Duchess of York and as the spectators view the seriatim destruction of nine characters, each of whom to some degree recalls the design of the action.[10] And it certainly is true that Richard is not a totally convincing tragic character in comparison with Shakespeare's later figures. Like Titus, he at no point reflects a concern for the consequences of an act before he commits it, and his momentary remorse is relatively superficial, the result more of fear than of contrition or spiritual insight.[11]

Admitting all such deficiencies, the construction of *Richard III* is an exceptional accomplishment; indeed the play in all probability was Shakespeare's first major stage success.[12] It is not at all surprising that in his early years in London he turned his efforts to chronicle material so much in vogue, but the strong historical traditions imposed certain inescapable limitations. Shakespeare obviously was not free to depict Richard as a sympathetic and misunderstood ruler; the basic political facts of the recent past which weighed so heavily upon the present could not be altered beyond reason; Richard's defeat clearly had to carry the conviction that an era of greater stability was ushered in, establishing on the throne a ruler of finer moral sensibilities and of larger capacity to unite the many factions of a divided kingdom; consequently the final scene had to emphasize Richmond's assumption of power rather than Richard's loss of life and any tragic implications inherent in it.

Shakespeare was free, however, to shape the events concerning Edward IV, Edward V, and Richard III to the life of a single figure. He was free to emphasize Richard's thirst for power and the physical infirmities for which the Machiavel was determined to compensate. He was free to treat the various incidents so as to give the impression of mounting tension resulting from an ambition which was never sated, to reveal the moments at which such obsession cost Richard control both of others and of self, to depict in the king's moments of weakness his fear of the moral order he had violated. Above all, he was free to infuse the action with dramatic tension by placing in conflict Richard's towering ambitions and the cosmic irony of the historical fate which dooms him to ignominious defeat. Both the curses and the pattern of remorseful falls underscore the philosophic dimensions of the play by emphasizing in turn the macrocosmic divine control and the microcosmic spiritual reflection preceding death. Thus are established the environment for and the anticipation of Richard's spiritual anguish triggered in the final soliloquy.

Whatever the play's flaws, Shakespeare has consciously shaped his material to create a villain-hero of consuming interest, and he has achieved this complexity of character at the expense of his broad perspective in *1, 2, 3 Henry VI*. History at this point has become a contextual scenario in which Shakespeare explores the rise and fall of a single titanic individual whose actions assume tragic dimensions because the spectators, despite the providential frame of reference, are encouraged to believe that Richard's spiritual anguish betokens a condition ultimately determined by the exercise of his free will. The progression toward such a dramatic conception of history has been steady throughout the three earlier plays. For a moment, as it were, the development of Shakespeare's historical perspective has become one with the earliest stages of his tragic perspective. Not until after *Richard II*, and then only with material from British as opposed to classical history, will the separate exploration continue.

Richard II like its predecessor is fundamentally a history play, as that term was so ambiguously used in Shakespeare's day. Published in F_1 as *The Life and Death of King Richard the Second* and positioned as the second entry in the "Histories," it obviously takes its place among the several stage pieces which reflect Shakespeare's continuing interest in the formative years of English government and the consequent nature of English society. Certainly in one sense the focus, like that of the earlier Lancastrian plays, is upon matters of national rather than individual moment. The spectators watch the abuses of the royal office breed a discontent that spreads infectiously; even if no actual warfare is depicted, they nonetheless sense the horror resulting from a kingdom divided into two armed camps. Appropriately the scenes are scattered across the land (Gloucestershire, Coventry, Wales, Bristol, Pomfret Castle, Windsor) and across London (Lancaster's home, the royal palace, Ely House, Westminster, a street leading to the Tower). And appropriately the *dramatis personae* is again quite large, with over thirty speaking parts representing the full social spectrum, from the stable groom and gardeners at one end to the King and Queen at the other. The final scenes of the play direct primary attention not to the fate of the individual fallen ruler but to the affairs of the kingdom and the importance of maintaining the stability of civil order during a traumatic transfer of power.

Yet, having said all of this, one must admit that conceptually *Richard II* is more nearly tragedy than history. Interestingly, the five quarto editions prior to the folio bear the title *The Tragedie of King Richard the Second;* and without question the action is structured in such a manner that the spectators' interest is centered on Richard, either in sympathy or disdain, for the vast majority of the time. Although he is essentially a static character, he provokes an impression of near-anagnorisis in his soliloquy at Pomfret Castle; measured against Titus and Richard III before and Romeo and Brutus after him, he represents a genuinely significant stage in Shakespeare's development as a tragic playwright. As in *Richard III* the historical perspective and the tragic perspective are again fused at this stage of Shakespeare's development, and the breadth of focus so consciously achieved in the *Henry VI* plays is sacrificed to that consuming interest in character integral to the Elizabethan tragic vision. Like Richard III, whose soliloquies carry the spectators through the various stages of his overreaching ambition and thus force them to anticipate his destruction at Bosworth Field, Richard's characterization points inevitably to his confrontation and deposition by Bolingbroke and to the necessity of his extermination in the name of King Henry. At the same time, this Richard is dramatically more interesting than his earlier namesake. The Yorkist king who wades through blood to the throne which is his obsession is limited in dramatic appeal. Like Tamburlaine he can feel only hate and greed. The spectators, consequently, can never fully perceive the human being beneath the Machiavellian cloak; they cannot share from within the full range of human emotions which in the tragedies will produce pity as well as fear. Richard II, by contrast, is a man for whom pity—if not terror—comes easily, both because of the poetic eloquence which stylizes his suffering and turns it into a "thing of beauty" and because of his own capacity for sorrow.[13] Granted, most of this sorrow is self-pity. Nonetheless there are moments when the emphasis on his suffering blinds us to the woeful shortcomings as a king which precipitate his downfall; moreover he has at least fleeting moments of concerned affection for those around him who share his fate.[14] For the spectators then there is an emotional dimension in Richard II which Richard III does not possess and which the narrative inconsistencies in Titus never allow to develop. The full tragic experience is not yet realized, to be sure; there are no final insights which produce wisdom concomitant with destruction and death. By the same token Richard lacks something of the physical stamina and the demonstrative assertiveness against his adversaries which we come to expect in Shakespeare's tragic protagonists (and which Marlowe was able to depict somewhat more effectively in Edward). But Shakespeare's overriding concern for the relationship between character and spectator is clearly emerging.

For our present purposes, the most significant measure of this concern lies in the structural experimentation. In *Richard III* the protagonist is developed from within; despite the rigidity of character which constrains the degree of success, Richard III's numerous soliloquies and asides do compel the spectators to relish the savor of victory and suffer the agony of defeat through his eyes. Perhaps consciously, Shakespeare traces a different path in *Richard II* in which the protagonist delivers only a single soliloquy moments before his assassination.[15] Here the character is developed from without, but the dramatic focus is still sharply upon the single figure. A procession of characters emphasizes at one moment Richard's heinous mismanagement of his office coupled with his moral lassitude, at another moment the sanctity of the kingship which forbids a subject to oppose the divinely ordained monarch, and at still another moment Richard's personal distress. The

71

result is a powerful ambivalence in the figure of Richard. God's vicar on earth capable of evoking the aura of mystery which surrounds medieval royalty as envisioned by an Elizabethan audience, he at the same time is thoroughly decadent in his self-centeredness; intent upon catering to his personal pleasures, he lacks the vital concern for the security of his kingdom as well as the masculinity and decisiveness which characterize an effective leader.

To compound the ambivalence, Bolingbroke's development as a foil character is more powerful than that of Richmond in the earlier play. Whereas Richmond for all intents and purposes is not introduced until the fifth act, Bolingbroke figures in the play from the opening scene, and his eventual struggle with the king is inevitable by the end of act 1. At the same time Bolingbroke is not, like Richmond, a monolithic figure of virtue acting as the hand of God rendering justice to a tyrant and bringing peace to a strife-torn land. Not only is he a political usurper against God's anointed; his own motives are ambiguous from the beginning. The spectators are never able flatly to condemn him for moving in defense of his inheritance and in defiance of the parasites who surround Richard; on the other hand, they are unable to make a significant emotional commitment to a character whom they perceive but dimly as one who, whatever the justification, defies the moral and political values established in the play. As a result they are drawn back to Richard, both in sympathy and in disdain.

Richard, in brief, is clearly Shakespeare's most complex character to date.[16] In a sense he is an extension of the sensitive figure woefully miscast in the role of king characterized in *3 Henry VI;* if Richard's overt abuses of the royal prerogative strike the spectators as more contemptible than Henry's passivity, so too his sensitivity and sense of hurt provoke a greater compassion. Moreover, whereas Henry shares the focus with the Machiavellian Duke of Gloucester, Richard is the sole dominant figure, and he provokes an emotional concern far beyond that of the Lancastrian ruler. Even so, as with Romeo and Juliet, it is a concern developed and controlled primarily from the outside, not—as later in Brutus and more powerfully in Hamlet—something generated by a profound introspection. It is the result of setting a dissipated king in the religiopolitical context of divine right, of juxtaposing to him an ambiguous figure who seems to possess all the monarchical traits which the ruler lacks, and then of surrounding them with numerous characters who in a variety of ways repeatedly call attention to the king's dilemma.

The authority of God is flatly assumed in the play. The hand of divinity operates directly through His anointed, and this relationship is alluded to time and again by Richard and his supporters and tacitly acknowledged through King Henry's "guilt of conscience" in the final scene. Bolingbroke, admittedly, defies the political power of the king. But he is no Richard III who delights in evil for its own sake; nor does he, like Iago or Edmund, ever challenge the power of heaven. To the contrary, he refers to his divine soul and to God's grace, and he later ascends the throne in God's name. This value structure is further enforced through the elaborate emphasis on knighthood, an order founded in service to God and King, as both Mowbray and Hereford frequently reiterate.

It is not surprising then that Richard's position as king by divine right is not at issue.[17] The complexity of the play arises instead from the manipulation of the spectators' attitude toward Richard the man. In the opening scene, for example, their first impressions are of a king who attempts with dignity and equity to moderate a vicious quarrel between two of his subjects, Mowbray and Bolingbroke.[18] Before the conclusion of the scene, however, the seeds of suspicion are sown concerning Richard's complicity in the murder of his Uncle Gloucester, the Protector during his minority, and the remainder of the act confirms this royal involvement. Thus Richard's character is intentionally sketched slowly in the initial scenes. Only after the favorable impressions are registered are the flaws revealed, at first obliquely, then directly, even as the spectators confront a specific defense of the royal prerogative along with the first hints of Bolingbroke's possible ulterior motives.

The key to Shakespeare's ambivalence in this first act is the figure of Thomas Mowbray, Duke of Norfolk, a character who has posed an enigma to many a commentator on the play. The problem centers primarily on Mowbray's response to Bolingbroke's assertion that he is responsible for the death of Thomas, Duke of Gloucester:

73

For Gloucester's death,
I slew him not, but to my own disgrace
Neglected my sworn duty in that case.

(I, i, 132–34)

Perhaps, it has been suggested, Norfolk means that he has failed to
reveal a plot against Gloucester's life, or to protect him from physical
danger, or to avenge the murder immediately, or to report fully his
knowledge of the murder. Or possibly the passage is intentionally
vague and ambiguous, a part of Shakespeare's design in blurring Richard's involvement with the debate, at least during the first scene.[19]
Obviously the significance of this or any other passage is subject to the
determination of the individual actor or armchair reader. The actor
may delete the lines altogether or deliver them in a manner which fails
to provoke any reaction from the auditor. On the other hand, he may
choose by well-placed pauses and assertive glances at both Bolingbroke
and Richard to provide striking dramatic emphasis. So delivered,
Mowbray's words need not be explained away as vague or as a loose
end which is further evidence of Shakespeare's early work. To the contrary, they are pivotal to the developing relationship between Richard
and Mowbray and, more important, between Richard and Bolingbroke. As a small but significant modification of Holinshed's account,
the lines reveal Shakespeare's growing determination to mold the material of the *Chronicles* into the stuff of drama.

To be sure, there is no open proclamation of Richard's personal
commitment or involvement in Bolingbroke's accusations concerning
Gloucester's death.[20] In the following scene, however, the widowed
Duchess of Gloucester pointedly accuses Richard of responsibility for
her husband's murder and urges Gaunt to seek vengeance and justice,
to which Gaunt replies that he may not lift an angry arm against God's
minister. Thus when Hereford and Mowbray meet for their duel in
scene 3, the spectator, aware of the possible alliance in murder between Mowbray and the sovereign, now will rivet his attention on
Richard's treatment of Mowbray and the King's attempts to maintain
in public an image of equity and objectivity.

Since the protatical emphasis in *Richard II* is clearly the crucial

74

struggle between Richard and Bolingbroke, a struggle which takes final shape from Bolingbroke's unlawful return to England in open defiance of Richard's proclamation of banishment, one of Shakespeare's principal objectives in the first act is to make dramatically credible the scene in which Bolingbroke is banished. Holinshed obviously provides the lead with the description of the struggle between Hereford and Mowbray, but he is altogether silent concerning Richard's specific motives for moving against them. The historian says only that the King "waxed angrie" when Hereford first stated his charges against Mowbray, a remark vaguely suggesting latent antagonism between Bolingbroke and his King. As for the defendant, Mowbray does not in Holinshed reply to Hereford's charge of responsibility for Gloucester's murder; he at no time invokes the King's name in self-defense. He simply denies that he has misused eight thousand nobles from the King's treasury in failing to "pay your people [soldiers] of the town of Calais" (Richard Hosley, ed. *Shakespeare's Holinshed*, New York: Putnam's, 1968, p. 69). When later pronouncing eternal banishment upon the Duke, Richard asserts that Norfolk "had sowen sedition in the realm by his words" (p. 73) and that the troops in Calais had indeed not been paid. Both points Shakespeare apparently rejects as unsuited to a scene in which the focus must remain sharply on the developing relationship between King and cousin.

Shakespeare, in short, must provide the motivation for the banishments at the same time he draws clear lines of contention between the two principals. It is not sufficient for Richard to banish Bolingbroke (as well as Mowbray) merely for the refusal to be reconciled by royal mandate. Richard must come to believe that Bolingbroke already is directly challenging the power of the throne and "undermining [his] authority and the very basis of his survival."[21] The banishment of both must be integral to this growing conviction.

The most obvious motivation is provided in the brief scene following the banishment. Even as the King decides to sell the right to taxation and suggests that Gaunt's death will result in additional funds to underwrite his war in Ireland, Bolingbroke clearly emerges in Richard's mind as a personal foil. In conversation with his courtiers, Richard decries the audacity of "high Hereford" and demands to know how much of an emotional show there was at the parting. He scoffs, with obvious jealousy, at Hereford's

> courtship to the common people,
> How he did seem to dive into their hearts
> With humble and familiar courtesy.
>
> (I, iv, 24–26)

The more significant point for the present discussion is that Shakespeare subtly but firmly establishes the grounds for this dissension through the character of Mowbray and his "enigmatic" lines in the first scene. Richard, in other words, is by no means suddenly obsessed with Bolingbroke's personality in scene 4; he is merely giving verbal expression to an animosity which has been growing and festering since the opening moments.

The turning point in the relationship between Richard and Mowbray—and in turn between Richard and Bolingbroke—is Mowbray's choleric retort that he did not kill Gloucester, but in that case neglected his sworn duty.[22] Richard, at the outset presumably unaware of the charges Bolingbroke is to bring against Norfolk (even Gaunt tells the King that he has not been able to sift the argument), acts with magnanimity and grace as he addresses each of his subjects, warmly calling Bolingbroke cousin at the same time he observes that it will take a serious matter indeed to provoke a thought of ill in Norfolk. When Bolingbroke states his charges against Mowbray, Richard retorts, "How high a pitch his resolution soars!" (I, i, 109). While he may indeed suspect at this point that the attack is really leveled against him, he is careful to maintain his posture of objectivity, assuring Mowbray that the hearing will be fair despite Bolingbroke's royal kinship. Mowbray, however, pushes the issue to the critical stage with his reference to sworn duty; with more gall than discretion, he appears overtly to implicate the King as ultimately responsible for the murder, a fact which a significant reaction from Richard can make indelibly clear. To make matters even worse, he then roundly protests the King's efforts to silence the whole matter before it gets out of hand:

My life thou shalt command, but not my shame:
The one my duty owes, but my fair name,
Despite of death that lives upon my grave,
To dark dishonor's use thou shalt not have.

. . . .

    . . . Take but my shame,
And I resign my gage.
     (I, i, 166–69, 175–76)

Mowbray assumes no doubt that Bolingbroke, realizing where his charge now falls, will not dare pursue the issue further. This, of course, is Mowbray's cardinal error; his unbridled tongue will shortly cost him perpetual banishment. Richard speaks not one kind word to the duke after this moment. He is furious when Norfolk refuses the royal reconciliation. Likewise at the lists in Coventry, when Mowbray formally requests the King's blessing prior to his encounter with Bolingbroke, he receives only a curt two-line response: "Farewell, my lord, securely I espy / Virtue with valor couched in thine eye" (I, iii, 97–98). In contrast Richard, mere moments earlier in reaction to his cousin's request, descends histrionically from his platform and embraces Bolingbroke in his arms, a gesture not present in Holinshed. Surely the response to Mowbray is no "touch of affectionate approval,"[23] but instead a sharp rebuff delivered with a cold and formidable stare. A few lines later Mowbray is facing the heavier doom of an exile from which he is never to return, a turn of events that seems abrupt only to the spectator who has missed the significance of Richard's reaction to Mowbray's careless words and the growing alienation stemming from that instant. Mowbray, apparently having acted as virtual henchman for the King, may well claim that this sentence was "all unlooked for from your highness' mouth" and that he has deserved better, but it is hardly likely that the irony of his final words—"Within my mouth you have enjailed my tongue"—is unintentional on either Shakespeare's part or the duke's.

Mowbray's words are, of course, no less critical to the relationship between Richard and Bolingbroke. For from this moment, if not from the outset, Bolingbroke's charge of murder extends to the King, and he now realizes that his refusal to throw up his gage (and thus retract his charges against Norfolk) Richard must now take as a direct affront to the royal prerogative, indeed as treason itself. The King's subsequent blessing for Hereford at Coventry is a rather obvious attempt at overcompensation for the sake of the public image. But what follows should surprise no one. Bolingbroke's banishment is as dramatically credible as that of Mowbray, even without the subsequent scene (4) in which Shakespeare draws the more specific foil relationship between the royal cousins.

The narrative from Holinshed which describes Richard's abuse of royal power and Bolingbroke's illegal return from banishment with demands arising from this abuse is not, in the particulars leading to this situation, primarily concerned with either focus or motivation. Through Mowbray's words Shakespeare molds this material to create the interest in character and the conflict of the individual wills which are essential to effective drama. As C. H. Herford in his edition of 1899 was among the first to observe, the playwright in devising Mowbray's reply draws on two additional passages from the *Chronicles,* one before the actual encounter between Mowbray and Bolingbroke and the other following it. Holinshed reports that when Mowbray first received instructions to do away with Gloucester, "the earle prolonged time for the executing of the kings commandment, though the king would haue had it doone with all expedition" (2:837). The historian later records that Sir John Bagot, at his trial following the deposition of Richard and the assumption of power by Bolingbroke, reported that Mowbray claimed he had not murdered Gloucester, that "he had saued his life contrarie to the will of the king, and certeine other lords, by the space of three weeks" (3:5). In both passages Richard's guilt is clear; in fact, in the latter passage Shakespeare found the words of Mowbray which he has transferred to a crucial moment in the play. As a consequence, Mowbray's actions are made functional to the development of Bolingbroke's personality and the early suggestions of the extent of his ambitions, and the banishment of both Mowbray and Bolingbroke is given credible motivation in terms of the growing hostility of Richard.

By the end of act 1, then, although the balance of sympathy by slow degrees has been tilted against him, Richard is a thoroughly ambivalent character. Through the remainder of the play various characters pull the sympathies of the spectators first in one direction, then in the other.[24] In four further scenes, for example, the dominant emphasis is on Richard's flagrant abuses of office. The strongest condemnation occurs in II, i, as the dying Gaunt proffers his counsel to a king whose will mutinies against reason and whose shameful conquest of England has resulted in his leasing the nation like a tenement or pelting farm. He proclaims Richard to be sicker than he:

> Thy death-bed is no lesser than thy land,
> Wherein thou liest in reputation sick,
> . . . .
> A thousand flatterers sit within thy crown,
> . . . .
> Landlord of England art thou now, not king.
> (II, i, 95–96, 100, 113)

His finishing thrust names Richard directly as murderer of his brother Gloucester. The charge is confirmed by York thirty-eight lines later as, in the face of the king's seizure of Gaunt's place, coin, revenues, and moveables that rightfully should descend to Bolingbroke, he decries the monarch's violation of the law of primogeniture by which Richard himself holds the throne. The nobles too in the same scene reproach Richard for a host of ills ranging from the flatterers who insinuate themselves into his favor to the grievous taxes which burden the people. In the following scene, York as Lord Governor of England bemoans the sick hour that Richard's surfeit has made, the tide of woes as the nobles flee and the commons grow cold; torn between duty to his sovereign and love for his kinsmen whom the king has wronged, he openly comments on the king's responsibility for Gloucester's death, preferring such a fate for himself to his present misery. Bolingbroke in scene 3 voices similar charges against the ruler who plucked the rights and royalties from his arms. Similarly in IV, i, Richard's complicity in political murder is flatly assumed as the nobles quarrel among themselves over who wrought noble Gloucester's death "with the king" (3–4).

79

At the same time in eight of the fifteen scenes of the last four acts, the conversation of secondary characters diverts the spectators' attention from Richard's faults. Both York and Carlisle, for example, continue to stress the religious nature of the royal office which renders immediate judgment on rebel and rebellion alike.[25] At Berkeley Castle York denounces Bolingbroke's unlawful return to England as deceiveable and false to the anointed king, just as later at Flint Castle he warns his nephew to take not further than he should from the sacred king because the heavens are over their heads. The strongest affirmations of divine authority are voiced at Westminster Hall at the moment Bolingbroke informs the courtiers that he will ascend the regal throne. The Bishop of Carlisle proclaims Hereford a foul traitor, as is any subject who dares give sentence on his king,

> the figure of God's majesty,
> His captain, steward, deputy, elect,
> Anointed, crowned.   (IV, 1, 125–27)

At the same time the characters who observe his anguish and misery compel the spectators to pity the king who seems so unaccustomed to suffering. The queen's affection on three occasions underscores Richard's finer qualities. Apprehensive for his safety in Ireland, she makes a guest of grief in recompense for bidding farewell to her sweet Richard. This grief intensifies six scenes later as she is forced to overhear the gardeners converse of her husband's deplorable state. And it is most poignant during her final meeting with her lord in the streets of London. She is her true king's queen, he her fair rose, her map of honor, her most beauteous inn; on parting from her husband and her king, she strives to kill her heart "with a groan." Northumberland, one of his most outspoken opponents, is touched at Flint Castle by the king's sorrow and grief of heart. Certainly the most gripping moment is York's tear-filled description of Richard's ignominious plight in Bolingbroke's victory procession in London, in which there was no man to cry "God save the King" and no joyful tongue to welcome him home. When dust was thrown upon his head, only with smiles, the badge of patience, did he manage to combat the tears of grief. The

groom in the final act reflects a similar affection in visiting his erstwhile master in prison to voice his anguish over Bolingbroke's riding
during his coronation parade on roan Barbary, the horse on which
Richard so often rode.

Shakespeare thus develops a kind of choric commentary in such a
manner that he forces the spectators to view Richard as rightful king,
dissolute reprobate, and suffering man. The character at the center is
also vocal about his woes, and interestingly enough his comments help
to maintain the ambivalent tensions. The audience tends to react in
sympathy to his outspoken grief, both because of the natural tendency
to sympathize with pain either emotional or physical, when it is intro-
spectively depicted on stage, and because of Richard's magnificent gift
of poetic utterance. Certainly the spectators react sympathetically to
Richard's almost parental concern for his native land as he returns
from Ireland in III, ii. He salutes the dear earth, greeting it like "a
long-parted mother with her child" who eagerly mixes her tears and
smiles. But respect wanes with his naive assumptions that nature will
protect him and with his comparison of himself with the sun whose
rising in the east Bolingbroke will not be able to endure.[26] So also they
are stirred by his wrath when he believes that his attendants Bushy and
Green have defected, and touched by his grief when he discovers they
are dead. They are stirred by his lyric eloquence as he determines to "sit
upon the ground / And tell sad stories of the deaths of kings" (155–
56). But the moment turns sour when, in despair and refusing to defend his title or his kingdom, he announces his intention to go to Flint
Castle and there to "pine away." The situation is similar in III, iii.
Richard's initial posture in confronting Bolingbroke is firm and admirable as he demands the obedience due to the lawful king and stresses
the sacred nature of his office. But just as he often "begins with a
strong denunciation only then to weaken and give in altogether,"[27] he
capitulates in sentimentality before Hereford has to demand anything,
glibly comparing himself to "glist'ring Phaeton" and calling for night
owls to shriek where mounting larks should sing. Again later, in Westminster Hall, the spectators' sympathy goes out to the oppressed ruler
who so poetically can express his grief and his disdain. To compel him
publicly to read his list of grievances is cruel, however wise politically;

when forced to insinuate, flatter, and bow, he indeed seems painfully out of character; to demand that he personally hand over the crown is to render his grief most poignant even at the moment Bolingbroke's fortune is at its height. Ultimately, however, he sacrifices full sympathy through his histrionic display of self-pity. The dignity of suffering is transformed into maudlin sentimentality when, for example, he claims that his eyes are so full of tears that he cannot see, then examines his face for deeper wrinkles now that sorrow has struck so many blows, afterwards dashing the mirror to the ground even as he declares that thus sorrow has destroyed his face.[28]

Through each of these scenes Richard's poetic eloquence is undeniable, but the moments of excessive sentiment tend to hold the spectators at arm's length, limiting their sympathetic engagement with what otherwise could be construed in the protagonist as a kind of wisdom gained through adversity. He may perceive at least dimly that kingship provides only a hollow crown in which man has but a little scene to monarchize, that he should be as great as is his name, that in considering the course of his downfall he must brand himself a traitor with the rest. But the full impact of such potential insight dissolves in tears. So also do his final pronouncements just prior to his death, though here Shakespeare certainly brings the protagonist as close to an anagnorisis as Brutus and far closer than Titus, Richard III, or Romeo. Here too the spectators' rapport with Richard is most nearly complete as in his lone soliloquy—his single performance without an audience—he muses on the many roles which a person is forced to play in life. Overhearing discordant music, he compares his own life to broken time and unkept proportion, admitting that he had no ear to recognize the true time: "I wasted time, and now doth time waste me" (V, v, 49). Although from this point he again laments excessively the sighs, tears, and groans that mark his present time and although he dies with the conviction that his soul will mount and that his seat is on high, the moment is not without power; coupled with his anomalous moment of physical valor as he slays two assassins before receiving his fatal wound, the scene elevates Richard as close to tragic stature as any figure in Shakespeare's early plays.[29]

One of the fundamental necessities of maintaining a delicate ambivalence in the protagonist is that Bolingbroke must not, for artistic as well as political prudence, emerge as a clear villain, thereby casting the audience's sympathy totally upon Richard despite his flaws.[30] Certainly by the end of act 1 the worst possibilities are established— though through the biased mouth of Mowbray, who warns that the king will to his sorrow discover all too soon Bolingbroke's true nature. Moreover the gnawing question of timing lingers in the back of the mind when, within 130 lines of Gaunt's death and 118 of Richard's seizure of the Duke's estate (the same scene in F_1 and in all modern editions), Northumberland announces that Bolingbroke with a large group of supporters is returning to England in defiance of banishment. Shakespeare seems through the telescoping of time almost consciously to be clouding Bolingbroke's claim, voiced later by Northumberland, that his coming is but to claim his own dukedom. As A. C. Sprague aptly observes, Shakespeare "with the chronicles before him, . . . must have been aware that Bolingbroke's weeks were becoming hours."[31]

But the possibility of villainy never becomes a certainty, as it does with Mortimer in *Edward II,* both because the ambiguity of motive is sustained throughout and because Bolingbroke, the foil of the king, possesses those qualities of pragmatism and leadership so painfully lacking in Richard that they tend to be accepted as virtues almost without question. Admittedly, Bolingbroke's first words on English soil sound strange for a man of limited ambition; he promises recompense for his friends as his fortune ripens with their love and as his treasury grows richer. Without anyone's questioning his right to do so, he swears to weed and pluck away the king's parasites; and two scenes later he seizes the royal prerogative of execution, judiciously washing their blood from his hands by a public reading of their crimes in misleading Richard. He is careful, though, to send a statement of allegiance to Richard at Flint Castle. The offer of peace, to be sure, is conditional. He demands his estate, else a crimson tempest will stain the fair land. For the second time, Northumberland reports that Bolingbroke swears his coming is only for his lineal royalties. But Richard gives all, in effect, and Bolingbroke is not forced to reveal his full motive; he becomes the king's captor without the need for explanation.

In the final acts Bolingbroke displays the specific qualities of leadership which Richard lacks. By permitting no one to accept a challenge pending a day of further trial, he firmly contains the developing quarrel among his nobles so reminiscent of the struggle which Richard at the outset bungles so badly. Unlike Richard, he decisively puts down a budding rebellion, rendering immediate judgment on the conspirators among the nobility. He gives evidence of political sagacity sorely absent in his predecessor. On the one hand, he accepts the necessity of condemnation though his heart rejoices—in the perfunctory banishment of Sir Pierce of Exton moments after Richard's assassination. On the other hand, he also realizes the pragmatic value of selective mercy though his heart thirsts for vengeance—in his not forcing Richard to read publicly the scroll listing crimes against the people or in his pardon granted to Aumerle for the sake of his aunt as well as his cousin.[32] Interestingly enough, in suppressing the Oxford conspiracy the Lancastrian policy ends for this play (if not for history and for Shakespeare's future chronicle plays) the increasing agitation against the royal office—from the Duchess of Gloucester's powerless defiance, to the nobles' conspiracy in Bolingbroke's usurpation. The sanctioned king obviously could bring no peace and order to his realm; for Bolingbroke, though he publicly pays judicious token-attention to a guilty conscience, and perhaps for the spectators as well, victory and stabilization appear to be ample justification for the outrage done upon the spirit.

Shakespeare, in short, effectively creates a chameleon in the character of Bolingbroke; a reading of his actions at any one point depends upon one's momentary attitude toward Richard, to whom he is the direct foil. The spectators may have the uncomfortable impression throughout the play that he actively seeks the crown, but it is difficult at any given moment to measure the extent of his ambition simply because any overt action on his part is to a degree the result either of inaction or of political folly or mismanagement on the part of the king. Thus though their relationship with Bolingbroke constantly shifts, it is always Richard who determines that relationship. More effectively than Richmond, Bolingbroke is the shadow against whom the principal figure is illuminated.

In establishing the perspective for Richard's ambivalence, Shakespeare includes numerous passages which create for the spectators a pattern of anticipated action. This material is by no means as heavy-handed as in *Richard III,* in which Margaret's curses at the outset literally outline the events to come and the spirits of Richard's victims appear in the final act to recapitulate the incidents and announce Richard's imminent overthrow. Although still repetitious and on occasion artificial, such passages in *Richard II* are for the most part more effectively integrated in the action, "more subtle, less obtrusive." [33] Most significantly, they serve a more varied function, at times enriching the ambiguities of Bolingbroke, at times anticipating from various angles the decline and fall of Richard, and at times strengthening the philosophic dimensions of the play. The ambiguity concerning Bolingbroke, for example, is sharpened by Mowbray's prediction that his true colors will shortly be revealed (I, iii, 204–05) and by Richard's observation that, when Bolingbroke returns from banishment, it will not be as a friend (iv, 20–22).

Far more extensively, the anticipatory devices prepare the spectators for Richard's ill fortunes. Both uncles emphasize the flaws which will lead to destruction. The dying Gaunt flatly proclaims that the king's rash, fierce blaze of riot cannot last; his vanity like an insatiate cormorant will soon prey upon itself. York's warning is directed to Richard himself, who invites untold dangers upon his head and loses countless followers by appropriating Gaunt's estate. More emotionally charged are the queen's intuitive apprehensions just prior to news of Bolingbroke's return concerning some unborn sorrow, "ripe in fortune's womb," that is approaching her (II, ii, 10) and Bagot's ominous conviction a few lines later, on parting from Bushy and Green, that the three shall never meet again. Two further passages are admittedly more artificial. In II, iv, the Welsh forces loyal to Richard refuse any longer to await his return from Ireland because of withered bay trees, meteors, a pale moon, and whispering prophets—various signs which forerun the death or fall of kings. Richard's glory crashes to earth "like a shooting star"; his "sun sets weeping in the lowly west" (21). More elaborate still is the scene in which the queen overhears the conversation of the gardeners at Langley. Here certainly Shakespeare sacrifices credibility for the sake of an extended comparison of Richard with an incompetent gardener whose failure to root away the noisome weeds and to prune the fast-growing sprays has produced his "fall of leaf." Though too contrived, like Margaret's curses, this scene positioned midway through the play does glance both backward to Richard's misuse of the royal office and forward to the deposition and death which will be its consequence.

In the last half of the play Shakespeare on four occasions directs the spectators to an anticipation of the War of the Roses which Richard's overthrow ignites. At Flint Castle Richard himself first mentions the pestilence which shall strike the children yet unborn and unbegot if usurping hands are lifted against his crown. Twice the Bishop of Carlisle lends the dignity of religious office to a similar prophecy. At the moment of Bolingbroke's ascension at Westminster, he declares that if Bolingbroke is crowned the "blood of English shall manure the ground, / And future ages groan for this foul act" (IV, i, 137–38). And he reiterates the point following the coronation: "The woe's to come; the children yet unborn / Shall feel this day as sharp to them as thorn" (322–23). Finally, Richard voices the same concern to Northumberland as he is being conveyed to the Tower, predicting that the Earl will shortly not be satisfied with half the kingdom, that the time shall not be many hours of age before foul sin will gather head and new rebellion spread corruption through the land.

These passages obviously fortify the religious dimensions of the play because they suggest God's ordinance beyond Bolingbroke's successful usurpation. That is, though the violation of religious sanction wreaks no disaster within the scope of the play, the spectators are assured that God's inexorable justice will ultimately prevail. The prophecies also enable Shakespeare to set the play within the fifteenth century political-historical context with which his spectators were familiar and, as recent criticism has suggested, to allow those in the audience to draw certain analogies between Richard's reign and that of Elizabeth.[34] Thus these anticipatory devices function within the play to heighten the tension and to suggest the power of heaven inextricably bound to the kingship; they also function beyond the play to broaden the scope of the issues and thereby provoke a richer emotional and intellectual response.

It is likely also that Shakespeare, now preparing his fifth play involving the War of the Roses, was coming to envision at least dimly the dramatic treatment of Henry IV and Prince Hal.[35] If so, these passages serve the additional function of providing narrative links with the work to follow; and while this matter is not in itself pertinent to the study of his historical perspective, it does further reflect the growing concern for structural control in the early plays which is central to my study. Certainly the prophecies anticipate Henry IV's struggles to consolidate his power at Shrewsbury and at Gaultree Forest. As various critics have noted, Henry's first mention of his unthrifty son in V, iii, anticipates Hal's legendary wildness which is to be more extensively developed in the future play: " 'Tis full three months since I did see him last. / ... Inquire at London, 'mongst the taverns there" (2, 5). The remainder of this scene, however, most critics would explain away as immature, even unintentionally ridiculous. Quite probably the playwright, though without total success because the relationship remains vague, was attempting to anticipate Hal's equally legendary true repentance. For at the very moment in the scene when King Henry remarks that he sees some sparks of better hope in his son, indeed within two lines, Aumerle bursts into the king's chambers asserting his abject repentance for his part in the conspiracy against the new king. Proclaiming fealty to Bolingbroke, he begs for a pardon on his knees and swears that his heart and hand were not confederate in his earlier treasonous plotting.

Aumerle's action has every justification within the individual stage world of *Richard II*. The father's discovery of the son's conspiracy against Bolingbroke provides a basis for the display of York's fierce loyalty to the crown despite his abhorrence of the method by which Henry ascended the throne; Henry's pardon of Aumerle reveals his disposition to mercy as a means politically of consolidating the power of his command and personally of atoning for the guilt he harbors concerning the deposition of Richard. Nevertheless, it is difficult to assume that the juxtaposition of Aumerle's present repentance with Henry's expectations of a future repentance in Hal is mere coincidence.

There is, moreover, an analogy between the reaction of York and

87

that of King Henry in the following plays. The extent of this analogy suggests that the dramatist in *1 Henry IV* was quite conscious of the link provided in this earlier scene of *Richard II*. In each he constructed a twofold contrast between father and son. First, the parent is envisioned as loyal and efficient, the son as treacherous and digressing; second, the father fears that his reputation, his ambition, and his estate will be destroyed through the actions of his offspring.

In *Richard II,* Aumerle's disloyalty is described in Henry's words to York:

> O loyal father of a treacherous son!
> Thou sheer, immaculate, and silver fountain,
> From whence this stream through muddy passages
> Hath held his current and defil'd himself!
> Thy overflow of good converts to bad,
> And thy abundant goodness shall excuse
> This deadly blot in thy digressing son.
>
> (60–66)

In the initial scene of the following play, Henry proffers a similar denunciation of his own son: "I . . . See riot and dishonor stain the brow / Of my young Harry" (84–86). Later he condemns Hal's low desires grafted to the greatness of his blood. References to Hal's base inclination, his disloyalty to his ancestors, and his alienation from the hearts of the court and princes of his blood suggest parallels with the earlier condemnation of Aumerle.

More important to the dominant conflict between father and son in *Henry IV* is the analogy suggested by York's fears that Aumerle's deeds threaten to destroy the father's reputation and Henry's similar apprehensions in the later play.

> So shall my virtue be his vice's bawd,
> An' he shall spend mine honor with his shame,
> As thriftless sons their scraping fathers' gold.
> Mine honor lives when his dishonor dies,
> Or my sham'd life in his dishonor lies:
> Thou kill'st me in his life.
>
> (*Richard II,* V, iii, 67–72)

It can hardly be coincidental that Henry, in lamenting Hal's delinquency, draws upon precisely the same figures of the son motivated by the desire for the father's gold and the father's symbolic death in the son's misdeeds.

> See, sons, what things you are!
> How quickly nature falls into revolt
> When gold becomes her object!
> > (*2 Henry IV,* IV, v, 64–66)

> Give that which gave thee life unto the worms,
> Pluck down my officers, break my decrees,
> For now a time is come to mock at form.
> > (116–18)

Branding Hal his nearest and dearest enemy, Henry is convinced that the future reign will be unguided and rotten.

Shakespeare therefore in the final act is apparently anticipating specific events in his next chronicle play, just as in the predictions of civil strife he is mindful in general of the eighty-six years being covered in these plays and is making his spectators mindful of the ultimate price of usurpation. As in *Richard III*, he is constantly providing the narrative guideposts to achieve coherence of plot by arousing in the spectators anticipations concerning both theme and character which the action will then satisfy. He is also obviously attempting to establish a double vision by which the spectators will experience Richard's dilemma sympathetically in part at least and at the same time sit in judgment on him as they perceive the forces of power which his failures allow to emerge and the subsequent destruction they will wreak in the context of history. Admittedly Richard has several rhetorical flurries when action is virtually suspended and drama suffers despite the poetic eloquence; admittedly Richard never achieves true tragic insight. In his soliloquy in act 5, however, the spectators are compelled to believe that he is bordering on such wisdom. Like Edward II, he is remarkably engaging despite his deeply flawed nature. Indeed among Shakespeare's protagonists he is the first whom the spectators seem to know thoroughly and consequently to care about emotionally. While this

familiarity does not arise from a delineation of the inner man, there is
—as in *Romeo and Juliet* and, more importantly, *King John* and the
Henry IV plays—a significant structural achievement in the perspective resulting from the numerous angles and attitudes from which they
are invited to view him. Significant also is the skillful manipulation of
Bolingbroke as an antagonist whose motivations remain sufficiently
ambiguous not to force the reader into a firm judgment on him and
in turn on Richard. Whereas Marlowe makes the spectators almost
oblivious of Edward's faults in drawing them to pity the king's physical torments and to condemn the heinous ambition revealed in Mortimer, Shakespeare is able to maintain a delicate balance throughout the
play, keeping ever before the audience both the best and the worst
in Richard's personality. Equally important, through references to
Bolingbroke's ultimate destiny, Richard's downfall is accommodated
within the philosophic context of the play. With its emphasis on a
protagonist of potential merit who freely engages in decisions and
actions which violate the values established in the stage world and
in turn produce waste and destruction, both individual and general,
Richard II points directly toward the major Shakespearean tragedy to
come.

Shakespeare at this point in his career is around thirty years old, and
in all likelihood he has written three histories and one tragedy prior to
Richard III and *Richard II*. The last scenes of *Richard II* without question reveal his continuing interest in the chronicle materials, specifically in Henry's struggle between conscience and ambition as he attempts
to consolidate his authority throughout the kingdom and in the escapades of a seemingly defiant and irreverent heir apparent with characters from London low-life. At the same time, the structure of the
Richard plays suggests a growing conceptualization of tragic form,
with primary attention directed to the fortunes of a single individual
instead of to several figures whose combined activities and conflicts
reflect the fortunes of a nation. Shakespeare in *Richard III* and *Richard II* has moved significantly toward his profound tragedies characterized by a singularly restricted emotional focus; certainly it could not
be anticipated that in *King John* and *1 Henry IV* he would again
move toward a distinct historical perspective incorporating drama-

turgical elements from both the earlier Henry plays and the Richard plays while through Roman history developing in *Julius Caesar* an individual tragic focus unencumbered by expectations of broad historical moment and overtones of a recognizable providential guidance.

CHAPTER IV

The Maturity of Perspective:
King John, 1, 2 Henry IV, Henry V

DATING *King John* from external evidence is simply impossible. We know only that the play, first published in F₁ 1623, is noted as Shakespeare's by Francis Meres in 1598; the first recorded performance is at Covent Garden in 1737. Although a minority view, which holds that *The Troublesome Raigne of King John* (published in 1591) is dependent on Shakespeare's play, argues for 1590 or earlier, internal evidence has led the majority of Shakespearean critics to suggest 1594–1596.[1] The structure of the play, considered in terms of Shakespeare's developing historical perspective, strongly supports a date between *Richard II* and *1 Henry IV*. *King John,* in fact, occupies a pivotal spot in his handling of material from the English chronicles.[2] Following the composition of *Richard II* a conscious bifurcation seems to occur in Shakespeare's dramaturgy. In *Julius Caesar* he continues to develop the focus which leads directly to his major tragic achievements, a focus involving psychological analysis and the internalized protagonist. Brutus, like Richard II before him and Hamlet and Othello after him, confronts an ambiguous situation requiring decisions and commitments which cost him his life even at the point of his greatest sensitivity to the true nature of things. If Brutus's illumination is insignificant in comparison with that of Hamlet and Othello, he like them engages the spectators through soliloquies and asides in the intensely limited focus upon the spiritual agony of what Harley Granville-Baker terms the "war within himself."[3] Shakespeare in *Julius Caesar, Hamlet,* and *Othello* continues to explore the dramatic potentialities of dynamic characterization, of figures who ostensibly develop and mature and whose insights grow more perceptive as a direct consequence of their experiences in the course of the five acts.

In the *Henry IV* plays (1597–98) and *Henry V* (1599), all probably written within two years of *Julius Caesar,* Shakespeare on the other hand essentially returns to the broad perspective and the skeletal characterization of *1, 2, 3 Henry VI.* But there are major differences, for in these plays he combines multiple plot lines with an emphasis upon character ambivalence to achieve richer and more provocative interactions than are to be found in the earlier Lancastrian stage worlds. Without creating figures who, like the tragic protagonists, dominate the spectators' interest by their development, he achieves a level of genuine human complexity by carefully manipulating and modifying the spectators' angle of vision. Hal they see at one moment as a crass manipulator of his Eastcheap companions, at another as an affable young man with a remarkable capacity for good humor and the blustering acquaintance who epitomizes it, and at yet another as a soldier possessed of a splendid courage and magnanimity on the battlefield; Falstaff they view as a fat parasite, as a boon companion in fun, and as a philosopher who loves life above all else including honor and reputation. King Henry at one moment is the public figure carefully calculating the political ramifications of every word; at another he is the remorseful father who senses that his son's profligacy is the "hot vengeance and the rod of heaven" sent to "punish [his] mistreadings" (III, ii, 10, 11). Hotspur too is at one moment a veritable Mars on the battlefield, at another a braggadocio, at another a husband and companion well matched in spirit and wit. In *2 Henry IV* key figures—Henry, Hal, Northumberland, and Falstaff—are depicted from a variety of angles that prohibits a simplistic response from the spectators. *Henry V* establishes a broad historical perspective through multiple plot lines, diverse settings, static characterization, and a chorus which unilaterally directs attention to the theme of national patriotism; at the same time, another structural pattern works in subtle opposition to the first and ultimately renders untenable a monolithic view of the young king's character. A brief but significantly placed soliloquy in which Henry gives voice to spiritual anguish and concern, a constant focus upon the king resulting from the diverse manners in which the surrounding characters view him, the consistent interweaving of thematically related episodes which divide the spectators' attention between allegorical abstraction and character analysis—such are the structural devices whereby Shakespeare lends to the characterization a degree of depth and dramatic vitality foreign to the *Henry VI* plays.

King John appears to be the play in which Shakespeare commits himself to the development of this powerfully ambivalent perspective combining the elements of depth and breadth, of engagement and detachment, which will ultimately produce *Henry IV* and *Henry V*. On the one hand, he simultaneously develops several plot lines or central issues, scatters the settings across two nations, and utilizes uniform or nondynamic characterization—structural devices designed to broaden the spectators' vision beyond any single figure or single chain of incidents. On the other, his design forces the spectators to observe each of the major issues from a wide diversity of views with the result that these issues (if not the principal characters, as in *Henry IV*) assume an ambivalence that provides a genuine human dimension for the play.[4] Imposed upon this mixed response to each of the principal concerns of the play is an independent pattern of shifting sympathy for the characters themselves, a pattern which, albeit broader, is reminiscent of that which alternates sympathy between the King and Bolingbroke in *Richard II*. Shakespeare, for instance, alternately provokes sympathy and disdain for John through his modifications of *The Troublesome Raigne;* the English King "seems more genuinely heroic in facing down the cardinal and blacker than ever in his relations with King Arthur."[5]

So the perspective in *King John* combines a breadth of vision with a compelling ambivalence toward the action and the principal figures. The structural devices through which Shakespeare establishes for the spectators a sense of historical breadth are readily demonstrated, and in this sense, of course, the play is closely akin to *1, 2, 3 Henry VI*. For one thing, no single character dominates the action either physically or emotionally. The principal figure in *Richard III*, by comparison, delivers well over 30 percent of the total lines (1,127 of 3,599); over 5 percent of the total lines (185) involve him in soliloquies (eleven) or asides (five). Similarly Richard II speaks more than one-fourth of the total lines in his play (738 of 2,755); while his only genuine soliloquy (66 lines) occurs moments before his death at Pomfret Castle, he gives the word-drunk impression throughout the play that he for the most part is talking to himself (or to the spectators) despite the presence of additional characters on stage. Moreover in both plays the great majority of the other scenes focus sharply upon the protagonist through conversations about him—in *Richard III* the conversations of Margaret, Anne, Buckingham, and Richmond; in *Richard II* those of Bolingbroke, Carlisle, Gaunt, York, or the parasites. In *King John,* to the contrary, the title figure speaks only 17 percent of the lines (438 of 2,570). The bastard Faulconbridge, in fact, delivers a larger number (20 percent, 521 of 2,570), though he is by no means so predominant as the central figures of the Richard plays. Four additional characters figure significantly in the action: Constance (10 percent), King Philip (8 percent), Hubert (8 percent), and Pandulph (6 percent). The multiplicity and range of the scene locations also enhance the broad perspective. Ten different settings are employed, seven in England and three in France, with action shifting from England to France and back again to England. The first act, as established in the folio text, depicts both King John and his circle at the English court and King Philip and his circle at the gates of Angiers. Acts 2 and 3 involve a battlefield near Angiers and Philip's tent; acts 4 and 5, set in England, include a battlefield, the Dauphin's camp, John's castle, and Swinstead Abbey. Eight characters speak more than 5 percent of the lines, none more than 20 percent, and the action is spread over ten different settings in the sixteen scenes. Inevitably the spectators' interest is directed, not to single individuals, but to the broad sweep of events characterizing critical moments during John's reign.

Contributing also to this broad perspective is the stationary quality of the major figures. Unlike the dynamic characterization of Richard III (the guilty conscience which subtly erodes his vaunted invulnerability) or the bolder design which permits Richard II through his suffering to gain significant insights moments prior to his murder, the characterizations in *King John* set forth no basic development. John himself, for example, is throughout the action a creature of expedience.[6] At the outset, although he full well realizes Arthur has the better claim, he boldly asserts his right to the throne. Yet when he realizes that a military victory is impossible, he readily agrees to a marriage of convenience between his niece and the French Dauphin, sacrificing all English possessions in France except Angiers to preserve his rule at home. Later, in order to remove his nearest enemy, he secretly orders the assassination of Arthur, but he desperately desires him to be alive when he realizes that he has pushed his barons too far and lost their support. His cry of anguish ("I repent. / There is no sure foundation set on blood; / No certain life achiev'd by others' death," IV, ii, 103–5) is one of his most hypocritical moments; for within fifty-two lines, having regained a degree of confidence, he orders another execution, this time the hanging of a prophet who predicts that the king will surrender his crown on Ascension Day. To the same papal legate he so flagrantly defied earlier he willingly submits his crown in act 5 in order that Pandulph will return it to an English king now perforce subservient to the Pope.[7] After he is poisoned by a monk, John utters not a word of remorse for his conduct; his attention is directed entirely to the burning pain which fatally gnaws him from within.[8] John, though he reverses himself on several occasions, acts consistently on the single principle of political survival.

Faulconbridge also is essentially one-dimensional, his character compounded of almost equal portions of brashness, ambition, heroism, and patriotism. Certain qualities may be predominant at one moment or another but never to the total exclusion of the others, and one finds it difficult to accept without qualification the argument that he grows from a "naive enthusiast following chance to a man of mature insight and ability."[9] It is a tempting position both because Faulconbridge is a fascinating and refreshing figure frequently compared with Prince Hal (for whom a similar development is often claimed) and also because John, like Henry IV, fails to hold center stage in the manner in which Shakespeareans are accustomed by the Richard plays and the tragedies. The Bastard's wry wit and his ambition are directly visible in his soliloquies and asides, occurring only in the first two acts, but his mind is no less agile in his baiting of the Duke of Austria in act 3, his chiding of John for time-wasting lethargy and his dialogue with Hubert in act 4, and his audience with the Cardinal and the Dauphin in act 5. His ambition is evidenced also in his acceptance of John's order to seize money and valuables from the English monasteries to finance the military campaign ("Bell, book, and candle shall not drive me back, / When gold and silver becks me to come on," III, iii, 12–13). His eager report of success in act 4, his efforts to protect the "life, the right, and truth of all this realm" (IV, iii, 144), and his alacrity in pledging support to King Henry in act 5—all such actions smack strongly of a practical concern for maintaining both possession and royal favor. Whatever the interpretation of the critic with leisure to reread and contemplate certain passages, the spectators, judging by the consistency of the characterization, have no reason whatever to infer that the Bastard entertains thoughts of usurpation in V, ii, 37–38, a temptation which (according to these same critics) he withstands and thereby achieves a final stage of maturation.[10] Certainly his heroism and his patriotism are apparent throughout the play: in act 2 in the struggle for Angiers, in act 3 in the battle renewed by papal intervention, and in act 5 in the confrontation with the invading French army.

Hubert too is a uniformly conceived figure; he may act at one moment from fear and at another from compassion, but there is no fundamental growth or alteration in his character. Similarly Pandulph's every move, whether for war or peace, is dictated by his singleminded dedication to Rome; he is, as H. C. Goddard has observed, a "Polonius and Iago rolled into one" (1:144). All of the characters, in other words, like those of the *Henry VI* plays, serve the purposes of the narrative; none assumes an organic nature and calls specific attention to its development at the expense of this broad design.

At the same time, like the figures of the later *Henry IV* plays, the principals are complex, viewed from divergent public and private angles which provoke from the spectators ambiguous responses effectively moving the drama far beyond a simplistic melodramatic design. A vitally important method for developing such ambiguity is the internalization depicted in four central figures through six soliloquies and six asides totalling 5 percent of the text. If the diversity prevents a prolonged restriction of focus, these private moments nevertheless generate a momentarily close emotional relationship between character and spectator. Such a moment occurs with Arthur in IV, iii, as he builds his courage to attempt his escape by leaping from the wall of the castle. "The wall is high, and yet will I leap down. . . . / I am afraid, and yet I'll venture it" (1, 5). Disguised as a ship boy, he implores the ground not to hurt him; mortally wounded, he offers his soul to heaven and his bones to England (10). Just as the pathetic situation renders Arthur most sympathetic at the moment of death, so Hubert gains a brief rapport through the three asides in which he privately struggles against his promise to murder Arthur. He is affected by the "innocent prate" which awakens his mercy (IV, i, 25); admitting that the young boy's "words do take possession of" his bosom (32), he condemns the "foolish rheum" (33) which blinds him from performance of the king's command. So too we privately share John's fear when he realizes his lords have rebelled (IV, ii, 103) and his remorse when he hears of his mother's death (181).[11] In the final act he ruefully recalls, having proffered his crown to Cardinal Pandulph, that the prophet had predicted he would "give off" his crown by noon on that date (i, 25–27). Fully 80 percent of the soliloquies are delivered by the Bastard who, standing for the most part outside the central action, provides a choric commentary which, through the very artificiality of such an intermediary, tends to increase the detachment between the spectator and the central figures.[12] In the first act, the Bastard's private words constitute an ironic commentary on the English and French aristocracies who engage in bombastic counterclaims for the British throne. Himself a new-made knight, he is not "A foot of honor better than [he] was" (1, 182). Now, though, he can "make any Joan a lady"; he can forget men's names with decorum, and after his meal he can suck his teeth and engage in knightly conversation (184, 187, 192). This indeed is "worshipful society"—"Exterior form, outward accoutrement / . . . sweet, sweet, sweet poison [flattery] for the age's tooth" (205, 211, 213). He is not, however, merely a disinterested railler; possessed of a "mounting spirit" (206), he will "learn" in order to "avoid deceit" (215). So too in act 2 Faulconbridge scoffs at the French, who would fire upon themselves by simultaneously deploying their cannons to the north and the south of Angiers (i, 413–14). Hubert's stratagem to save the city by arranging a marriage between the Dauphin and John's niece he describes as a bethumping with words which has given a "stay" to death (455–66). And he clearly recognizes the self-serving interest involved in the betrothal:

> Mad world, mad kings, mad composition!
> John, to stay Arthur's title in the whole,
> Hath willingly departed with a part [the dowry],
> And France, whose armor conscience buckled on,
>   . . . [is drawn]
> From a resolv'd and honorable war,
> To a most base and vile-concluded peace.
>   (561–64, 585–86)

"Commodity, the bias of the world," will inevitably corrupt "all direction, purpose, course, intent" (574, 580). Again, though, the Bastard is not the disinterested moralist; he criticizes such activity because material fortune has not yet smiled on him, not because he inherently opposes it:

> Well, whiles I am a beggar, I will rail
> And say there is no sin but to be rich;
> And being rich, my virtue then shall be
> To say there is no vice but beggary.
> . . . .
> Gain, be my lord, for I will worship Thee!
>   (593–96, 598)

Interestingly enough then, Shakespeare utilizes the type of soliloquy found in both the *Richard* plays. Faulconbridge, like Richard III, addresses the audience in a direct and familiar manner. If he lacks the Yorkist King's sheer delight in malice, he possesses the same sardonic wit and verve. Both characters appear to be more intelligent and more energetic than those around them, and both through private dialogue share this spirit with the spectators. Richard frankly wants the crown, and he disparages those who stand in his way, methodically preplotting the amoral scheme which will lead him to the throne. The Bastard simply wishes to thrive. He has no desire to usurp another's power or wealth, but he is aware of the self-interest which dictates every move, whether personal or national, and he is determined not to be manipulated by others. If Faulconbridge is no devil, he is certainly no saint. His choric function tends to broaden the spectators' focus by creating yet another fictive angle from which to observe the actions on stage, but the character is fascinating in itself, coolly rational like his more villainous Hobbesian counterparts Iago, Iachimo, Edmund, and Aufidius—and far more richly ambiguous than the hypercritical malcontents Thersites and Apemantus. Hubert, Arthur, and John, on the other hand, engage in introspective soliloquies which, like Richard II's, reflect an emotional response to their direct involvement in the action. Their private statements underscore their suffering and draw the spectators' interest to the human dimension of the stage world.

Perhaps the most significant structural feature in *King John* is the thematic organization and the arrangement of scenes in a manner which, by forcing the spectators to view each of these themes from various angles, creates an ambiguity toward the issues themselves and the major figures associated with them. Certainly there is no denying that the narrative thread of the play is broken and discontinuous, the result in most instances of what Shakespeare omits from his source.[13] The struggle between the French and the English for control of Angiers is apparently resolved by a compromise which in itself collapses. The struggle, renewed on English soil, is again settled by compromise, at which point the English king dies by poison. John's earlier attempt to assassinate his nephew fails, but the young Arthur is killed in a fall from a castle wall during an attempt to escape; by this point, though, the king desperately wants Arthur to live because the issue has become central in a developing struggle with his own nobles. The bastard son of Richard I is introduced as a brash patriot; he has two opportunities to display his splendid heroism, and to him are given the ringing final words proclaiming Britain's endurance. As a plot summary these comments are admittedly simplistic, but they do suggest something of the incessant winding and twisting of the narrative. Not even a thematic pattern such as the one Shakespeare employed in *1 Henry VI* (a repetitive design of overt enmity and struggle giving way to a false harmony which covers a festering hatred) seems at first glance to account adequately for the inchoate action. Shakespeare's aim in moving away from the direction of dynamic characterization in *Richard II* is apparently to focus the action on crucial issues, all relating to the rather insidious concept of "commodity"—a self-interest smacking of Machiavellian political cunning. If the concept is curiously nonmedieval, it begins to set the scene for the political philosophy that will provide the basic coloration for the stage worlds of *Henry IV* and *Henry V;* and the accumulation of diverse views of a particular concept moves Shakespeare toward the multiple angles of vision that produce a rich ambiguity and a sense of development for the static principals of those later plays.

The action of *King John* is organized around three basic themes: illegitimacy and John's right to rule, John's action leading to the failure of his rule, and the nation's survival. In each case the complexity of the issue prohibits a monolithic response, thereby increasing the spectators' intellectual and emotional concern. In act 1, for instance, the action juxtaposes two views of illegitimacy, political and physical. Chatillion's opening lines speak of John's "borrowed majesty" (1, 4) and usurping sword (12–13), and his own mother admits that force far more than right makes him king: "So much my conscience whispers in your ear, / Which none but heaven, and you, and I, shall hear" (42–43). John, despite these public and private assertions, is determined to maintain his power with the "thunder of [his] cannon" if necessary (26). Faulconbridge likewise is initially defensive about the charges of his physical bastardy. In the face of his younger brother's charges and the potential loss of his inheritance, he supposes himself the eldest son of Robert Faulconbridge (52); he and his brother, he thinks, are from the same stock (60). Commodity, however, leads him to acknowledge his illegitimacy. For the sacrifice of his father's estate he accepts knighthood and the opportunity for service and advancement at court as the presumed natural son of Richard I. In broaching the play's first major concern then, the early scenes also establish its operative morality. More importantly for our present purposes, act 2 forces the spectator to an ambivalent response to the entire question of John's rule. King Philip of France blasts "the usurpation / Of [Arthur's] unnatural uncle, English John" and his "rape / Upon the maiden virtue of the crown," pledging to "wade to the marketplace in Frenchman's blood" (II, i, 9–10, 97–98, 42) in order to force Angiers to acknowledge Arthur's supremacy. Lymoges, Duke of Austria, also swears never to return home until England "salute[s Arthur] for her king" (30). Arthur's mother, Constance, asserts that John "usurp[s] / The dominations, royalties, and rights / Of [her] oppressed boy" (175–77), and Queen Elinor herself suggests the dubiety of John's claim, not only by her previously noted aside to her son but also by her subsequent counsel for John to accept the proposed marriage between his niece Blanche and the French Dauphin: "[M]ake this match. . . . / For by this knot thou shalt so surely tie / Thy now unsur'd assurance to the crown" (468, 470–71). Other details, on the other hand, qualify this perspective. Elinor maintains that she can produce a legal document (Richard's will, naming John as his heir) barring Arthur's claim. The patriotic tone is sporadically strong in John's pronouncements against the foreign foe. He defies the French demand for submission, offering Arthur more than he can ignominiously gain from "the coward hand of France" (158), and he pleads his lawful rule before the gates of Angiers, mocking the French who threatened to attack mercilessly before he arrived but who now, "amaz'd, vochsafe a parle" (222, 226). The Bastard, too, exchanges occasional words of patriotic defiance with Austria (135–40, 143–46). Even the enemies' reports of England could not fail to stir the hearts of many in Shakespeare's audience. Lymoges describes the country as "that white-fac'd shore, / Whose foot spurns back the ocean's roaring tide," a "water-walled bulwark, still secure / And confident from foreign purposes" (23–24, 27–28). If such a passage of massed metaphors is reminiscent of Gaunt's famous lines in *Richard II*, Chatillion's account of the English soldiers anticipates those of the chorus in *Henry V*:

> Rash, inconsiderate, fiery voluntaries,
> Have sold their fortunes at their native homes,
> Bearing their birthrights proudly on their backs,
> To make a hazard of new fortunes here.
> In brief, a braver choice of dauntless spirits
> Than now the English bottoms have waft o'er
> Did never float upon the swelling tide
> To do offense and scathe in Christendom.
>
> (67–75)

Neither side, in short, lacks appeal, and the ambiguity is heightened by Hubert's claim (albeit one of policy) that Angiers will be loyal to the individual who proves to be the King: "Till you compound whose right is worthiest, / We for the worthiest hold the right from both" (281–82). One, he continues, must be proven superior by a greater power than human choice (332, 363, 368). Arthur himself asserts that he had rather be dead than the cause of such civil consternation (164), and the suffering mother seated alone on the ground, her throne of sorrow, becomes a sympathetic figure quite apart from the military factions. Both sides, moreover, claim God as their ally; John is "God's wrathful agent" (87, see also 283), and Philip fights for Arthur "in the name of God" (106, see also 35–36, 185, 298). As Sigurd Burckhardt correctly observes, the deity "is spoken for by voices which not only contradict each other but repeatedly belie themselves." [14]

John's right to the throne thus is presented in the protasis with a skillful ambivalence based on narrative issues rather than character. While there is no real question of who has the legitimate right, of who is guilty of usurpation, and while a pervasive self-interest is apparent at every turn, Shakespeare nonetheless manipulates the spectators' angle of vision to construct a human situation in which choice is neither romantic nor simplistic. In acts 3 and 4 John engages in four basic actions which culminate in his failure as king. Perhaps only one of his decisions is morally reprehensible, but all are ill timed, and coincidence seems to conspire against him. His refusal of obedience to the Catholic Church presumably occurs antecedent to the action of the play, but the confrontation with the papal legate could not occur at a worse time than the moment of reconciliation with King Philip. Certainly the fates themselves could not have arranged Arthur's accidental death more grotesquely—at the very point John has proclaimed that his nephew lives and when he is so dependent on that life for reconciliation with his barons.

In any event the structure of these scenes, like that of the earlier acts, forces the spectators to observe each of John's actions from more than one angle and consequently continues to develop the rich ambiguities confronting the spectators at every turn. The king's defiance of the Church, for example, is considered gross blasphemy by Philip,

Lymoges, and Lewis. The "heavy curse from Rome" places "in jeop-
ardy" all such rebels against the "faith" (III, i, 205, 346, 263). Cardinal Pandulph charges John with spurning "the Church, our holy
mother" (141) and enjoins Philip to oppose him as "champion of our
Church" (255).

> [John] shalt stand curs'd and excommunicate,
> And blessed shall he be that doth revolt
> From his allegiance to an heretic. (173–75)

Constance has reasons beyond faith, of course, for supporting Pandulph's efforts to block the alliance between France and England.
While she urges Philip to renounce his support of John so that thereby
"hell [will] lose a soul" (197), her primary concern is that Arthur
will gain a kingdom (187).[15] John, to the contrary, denounces the
"meddling priest" and the "juggling witchcraft" which extracts "tithe
or toll in our dominions" (163, 169, 154). He maintains that he is
the supreme head under God and that no "earthly name . . . / Can
taste the free breath of a sacred king" (147–48). Blanche, kin to John
and betrothed to the Dauphin, is a voice of anguished ambivalence:

> Which is the side that I must go withal?
> I am with both, each army hath a hand,
> And in their rage, I having hold of both,
> They whirl asunder and dismember me.
>   (327–30)

So again the spectators view the issue in a context rendered ambiguous
by a human mixture of self-interest and selfless faith. Shakespeare, of
course, could count on the anti-Catholic sentiment of his audience to
lend support to the English king's position. Even so, since the audience
is given no forewarning whatever of the impasse, John's attitude seems
blatantly recalcitrant and politically unrealistic considering the political conditions of the moment; certainly the spectators can have no
assurance that he acts from moral conviction. John's decision to assassinate Arthur is clearly his vilest act, one that he can broach only with
considerable hesitation; he "would into [Hubert's] bosom pour [his]
thoughts. / But, ah, I will not! . . . Yon young boy . . . is a very ser-

pent in my way. . . . Dost thou understand me?" (III, ii, 53–54, 60, 61, 63).[16] His halting insinuations pale, however, in comparison with the attitude of Cardinal Pandulph, whose calculating determination to prompt the murder by the Dauphin's invasion of England and then to reap the political profit resulting from the subsequent disaffection of the English nobles is all the more chilling from the mouth of a priest:

> That John may stand, then Arthur needs must fall. . . .
> John lays you plots; the times conspire with you. . . .
> O sir, when he shall hear of your approach, . . .
> Even at that news [Arthur] dies; and then the hearts
> Of all his people shall revolt from him.
> . . . 'Tis wonderful
> . . . I will whet on the King.
> (139, 146, 162, 164–65, 178, 181)[17]

John's third decision is to be crowned a second time and thus to enforce new oaths of allegiance to counteract the excommunication which released his subjects from their original vows. Again a second view is expressed by his supporters who consider it as "superfluous . . . double pomp . . . [which] makes sound opinion sick, and truth suspected" (IV, ii, 4, 9, 26).

John's final actions, precipitating the defection of his nobles, the spectators observe from several divergent angles. For one, they see his own devious satisfaction (his promises to place Arthur in their control followed by his report that the young lad has died tonight) turn to consternation and horror when the barons defect and, in turn, to frantic joy when he learns that Arthur is alive and thus can be used to placate them. Hubert cannot bring himself to slay Arthur, finally admitting as much to John; yet when Arthur's body is discovered, he is immediately suspected as the executioner. Salisbury and Pembroke flatly condemn John's actions, shocked that "greatness should so grossly offer it" (ii, 94). Arthur's death, they perceive, is "the bloodiest shame, / The wildest savagery, the vilest stroke," an "unmatchable" and "heinous spectacle" (iii, 47–48, 52, 56); and they formally proclaim their support of the invading French force. Faulconbridge, like Blanche in the earlier scene, is a figure of ambivalence. On the one hand, he continues to be fiercely patriotic, exhorting John to gather his

energies to confront the foreign foe; on the other hand, he denounces
Arthur's murder as "a damned and a bloody work" (57), and he proclaims that Hubert, if guilty of this act, is "more deep damn'd than
Prince Lucifer" (122). Even when he is finally convinced of Hubert's
innocence, the Bastard pointedly reflects the confusion and terror rampant in the land—in short, the complete collapse of John's reign:

> England now is left
> To tug and scramble, and to part by th' teeth
> The unowed interest of proud swelling state.
> . . . .
> A thousand businesses are brief in hand,
> And heaven itself doth frown upon the land.
> (145–47, 158–59)

These comments, which conclude act 4, best capture the spirit of the
spectators, who alone have had an omniscient view of the flurry of
events confusing in various degrees to each of the characters. While no
one would condone John's attempt to murder his nephew, the spectators must also observe the ironic turn of events which first saves him
from being a murderer in fact, then prevents his utilizing Arthur as a
galvanizing influence to mobilize his forces against France and preserve his independent role.

The fifth act, as well, literally involving the survival of English
government, presents multiple angles of perception. John as a last re-
sort abjectly offers his crown to Cardinal Pandulph in order to receive
it back again with the blessings—and to no small extent the control—
of the Church. The papal legate readily supports him, of course, the
minute he indicates the proper submission to Rome. Lewis, the Dauphin, ostensibly invading in the name of the Church, nonetheless refuses to obey Pandulph by withdrawing his forces:

> What is that peace to me?
> I, by the honor of my marriage-bed,
> After young Arthur, claim this land for mine.
> . . . .
> Am I Rome's slave? (V, ii, 92–94, 97)

The Bastard overtly denounces John's submission to Rome as an "inglorious League," and he urges the King "to arms" against the "beardless boy, / [The] cock'red silken wanton [who] brave[s] our fields" (i, 65, 73, 69–70). The defecting English noblemen, warned that execution awaits them in the French army, scramble back toward the English forces, now vowing to "run on in obedience / Even to our ocean, to our great King John" (iv, 56–57). Obviously commodity and policy motivate the characters at the play's conclusion just as firmly as ever, and the spectators continue to view the actions from a variety of positions at once precluding a simplistic response and generating their involvement in a manner which, while not unlike that resulting from an intense focus on dynamic characterization, retains the broad perspective vital to the design of the history play as Shakespeare apparently has come to envision it.

The careful design of the play obviously suggests a need for reappraising earlier comments that it is "incoherent patchwork," "little more than a succession of episodes."[18] Virtually every scene provides a different angle of vision, and consequently a complex ambiguity emerges for each of the principal issues. Closely allied to this structural technique is the pattern, so successfully employed in *Richard II,* by which despite the pervasive ambivalence of each scene the audience's sympathy is made to fluctuate from character to character. Unlike the intense focus on two figures in the earlier play, the pattern here involves six figures, and structurally the broad perspective is again reinforced. Throughout the first two acts, for instance, the spectators' basic sympathies lie with King Philip of France. Announced as protector of Arthur's legitimate right to the English throne, he pursues the cause to Angiers and to open battle with the English. Meanwhile, John's cause is seriously undermined by his mother's admission of usurpation and by his inability convincingly to articulate his right to the throne in his speech to the officials of the city. Following the arranged betrothal between Blanche and Lewis, which Philip admits he has "turned to [his own] vantage" (II, i, 549), the sympathy shifts briefly to Constance and Arthur, now without a champion. Lamenting that "Fortune . . . is corrupted, chang'd, and won from [Arthur]" (III, i, 54–55), she sits weeping on the ground, bidding kings to come bow before her throne of sorrow.[19] Here the sheer suffering of the mother and the relative helplessness of young Arthur are the points of chief dramatic concern. John gains a degree of sympathy in act 3 when Pandulph so heavy-handedly issues his mandates in the name of the Church, but it veers sharply from him when he orders Arthur's execution. Again briefly the sympathy shifts to Constance, inconsolable in her grief, and in act 4 to Arthur, who falls from the castle wall during his attempt to escape, and to the English noblemen who desert John with a vow to revenge the death of the innocent lad. In the final act, even though there is no sense of development in John's character and no attempt either to justify or to refute his mistakes or crimes of the past, Shakespeare does demonstrably increase sympathy for the British king in order through heightening the ambiguities to achieve maximum dramatic effect. For one thing his submission to Rome in scene 1 is a crushing admission of failure, and his emotional trauma tends to dilute the spectators' critical response. Sympathy grows firmer in scene 2 as the invading French, ordered by the Church to abandon the campaign, show their true colors by refusing for purposes of national glory and the spoils of war to withdraw from their advantageous military position. In the third scene physical suffering renders John an even more pitiable figure; a "tyrant fever burns [him] up," and he is sick of heart (14, 4). The stark horror becomes apparent three scenes later with the revelation that the King has been poisoned by a monk, a fact which at once compounds sympathy for his physical agony and by association blackens the role of the Church. John never experiences an anagnorisis, to be sure, but it is the rare spectator who can withhold a strong measure of sympathy from the human form groveling in pain on the stage:

> Poison'd—ill fare! dead, forsook, cast off,
> And none of you will bid the winter come
> To thrust his icy fingers in my maw,
> Nor let my kingdom's rivers take their course
> Through my burn'd bosom, nor entreat the north
> To make his bleak winds kiss my parched lips
> And comfort me with cold.   (vii, 35–41)[20]

Finally, sympathy for the dead English king is reinforced through the intensely patriotic words of Faulconbridge as Henry III assumes the throne: "This England never did, nor never shall, / Lie at the proud foot of a conqueror, / But when it first did help to wound itself" (112–14). Ironically more than a small touch of realpolitik may influence the events of the final scenes—Rome, not England, is the major victor, for example—but Shakespeare has so ordered the action that France emerges as the visible foe, and the resolution clearly smacks of a military victory on which hinges the survival of the English nation.

Despite the degree of interest afforded John in act 5, Shakespeare throughout the play has demonstrably modified his primary source to achieve a breadth of vision and a degree of ambiguity appropriate to his dramatic intentions. In the case of the title figure himself, the portrayal is far less sympathetic as time and again his motives are pointedly dishonest. *The Troublesome Raigne*, moreover, focuses more directly on the English king. The prologue announces the story of a "warlike Christian" Englishman who endured peril and pain "For Christs true faith" (5, 6),[21] and true to character he describes his ultimate submission to Pandulph as an act of dissembling (II, 283). Praised even by Arthur for his stamina and mettle (I, 451), he nonetheless possesses a modesty and sensitivity not present in Shakespeare, a quality evident in his initial comments that he is unworthy of so high a place as the kingship (I, 10); he is also a man capable of moral retrospection bordering on anagnorisis in his dying moments:

> The world hath wearied me, and I have wearied it.
> . . . .
> Me thinks I see a cattalogue of sinne,
> Wrote by a friend in Marble characters,
> The least enough to loose my part in heaven.
> . . . .
> Dishonor did attaynt me in my life,
> And shame attendeth *John* unto his death.
> (II, 798, 1046–48, 1066–67)

Shakespeare's aim is to present the character in starker and more ambiguous detail, with equally persuasive views of the usurper, the would-be murderer, the terror-stricken capitulator, the sufferer, the patriot, and the kingly defender of his nation against the avarice of France and the superstition of Rome. For the same reason Shakespeare apparently rejects those scenes in which anti-Catholic sentiment is so flagrantly exploited that sympathy would automatically accrue to John —for instance the scene of venery between Friar Lawrence and Nun Alice and the scene in which a monk proclaims without remorse that he has committed a righteous murder against a king who dared to challenge the true Church. Similarly Shakespeare depicts Arthur as simple and innocent, deleting all traces of an impetuosity which helps to explain and to ameliorate, if not to justify, John's villainy (I, 1095–98).

All things considered, the structure of *King John* occupies a crucially significant position in the development of Shakespeare's historical perspective. Apparently representing a recommitment to breadth of focus, the play like the earlier *Henry VI* plays employs multiple plot lines, a diversity of settings, and a scattering of asides and soliloquies among several principal figures. Like *Richard II*, the play includes a pattern of shifting sympathies; but instead of an intense focus upon two characters, the pattern involves a full spectrum of figures. Most importantly, Shakespeare moves toward the *Henry IV* plays and a more complex concept of character. While not altering the static quality, the wide variety of angles from which the several principal characters are observed creates an ambivalence with genuine dramatic tension provocative of effective involvement on the part of the audience. In several important respects *King John* is frankly experimental; if it is not one of the perennial favorites in the canon, it nevertheless possesses powerful individual moments, and it points in structure to Shakespeare's most successful histories.

In *1, 2 Henry IV* and *Henry V* the ambivalence which in *King John* is built into each of the dominant issues is transferred to the principal figures themselves. This level of characterization in combination with the breadth of vision provoked by other components of the stage world results in Shakespeare's achievement of a powerfully complex historical perspective which effectively accommodates both the narrative thrust of history and the characterological focus of drama.

The structural devices by which Shakespeare consciously shapes the broad perspective in *1 Henry IV* evolve directly from the technique developed in the *Henry VI* plays and *King John*. Unlike the situation in *Richard II* and *Richard III,* no single figure dominates the action.[22] The title character speaks only 10 percent of the lines (340 of 3,049); three individuals in fact deliver a large number though none is as predominant as the central figures of the *Richard* plays (Hotspur: 18.6 percent, 566 lines; Hal: 18.7 percent, 569 lines; Falstaff: 20.4 percent, 623 lines). In terms of developing a close emotional rapport between the character and the spectator, the devices of internalization are relatively insignificant in the play (5 percent, 160 lines); the eight soliloquies are scattered among three characters, no one of whom speaks in private more than 3 percent of the total lines. Then too the stage is swarming with people representing all social classes; thirty characters have speaking parts, and diverse travellers, attendants, drawers, lords, and officers swell the scenes to overflowing.

For another thing, Shakespeare simultaneously develops three individually significant plot strands: Henry IV's apprehensions concerning both his kingship and his relations with his son, the activities of the rebellious feudal lords which center on the impetuous Hotspur, and Hal's escapades at Eastcheap involving the world of Falstaff and his debauched associates. Totally unlike either the single dramatic focus on Richard III's Machiavellian ascent to the throne or the intersecting personal and political fortunes of Richard II and Bolingbroke—and equally unlike the thematically related experience of the two family units in *Hamlet* or *King Lear* which intensifies the dramatic focus—the plot strands of the play expand the spectators' vision. While extensive and important parallels do exist between the comic and the serious scenes, the more notable fact is that each strand depicts a vision of a different sociopolitical stratum, and consequently the dramatic perspective tends to become broad and diffuse rather than narrow and intensely personal. The emerging theme focuses not on the experiences of a single individual but on the evolving condition of a nation as reflected in the fortunes and misfortunes of several significant personalities. The comic scenes function significantly in enlarging the perspective of these mature histories. Both the chronicles themselves and the older plays based on them tend to ignore the day-to-day lives of ordinary citizens. Only in the Jack Cade scenes of *2 Henry VI* does Shakespeare provide more than a glimpse of life below the aristocracy. In these later Henry plays such a world becomes important in its own right, and in part the broad appeal results from the dramatic realization that everyday life goes on despite the fulminations of a Hotspur, the cheatings of a Falstaff, the machinations of a John of Lancaster, or the patriotic drum-beating of a foreign war.

Both the action and the setting of the play are committed to this broad sweep of events as the spectators' concern extends to the crowded interplay of personalities and issues that characterize public history. The scenes, for example, take place in such diverse points as Windsor, Rochester, Gad's Hill, Northumberland, Wales, Shrewsbury, Coventry, and London; even the London scenes move from the polarities of the palace to the tavern at Eastcheap.[23] And the disparate plot strands are carefully interwoven within the eighteen scenes as established in F_1: the King's private concerns in three (I, i; III, ii; V, i: 426 lines); the rebels' perspective in seven (I, iii; II, iii; III i; IV, i; IV, iii; IV, iv; V, ii: 1,136 lines); the Falstaffian world in six (I, ii; II, i; II, ii; II, iv; III, iii; IV, ii: 1,279 lines). The strands coalesce, of course, in the final two scenes with principals from each strand in combat on Shrewsbury field. Prior to that point, however, the spectators view English society from several angles and from various geographical points, and the activities of both the Lancastrian lower classes and the aristocracy reflect the political and social instability which will culminate in open rebellion.

This theme of national instability Shakespeare accentuates by the juxtaposition of Henry and Hal as political foils in both *1* and *2 Henry IV*. Certain modifications which he imposed upon his sources, first described as such by A. R. Humphreys, underscore the dramatist's concern for such a conflict.[24] The historical events of the two plays are roughly in the chronological sequence found in the source, but the domestic events in Hal's relationship with his father are essentially Shakespeare's own creation. Daniel makes no mention whatever of discord between father and son, while Holinshed notes only that the old King in the final year of his life had suspicions about the Prince; though there is much ado in *The Famous Victories* concerning the Prince's debauchery, it is again late in Henry's life that he laments the curse of a son who will destroy him.

While establishing this human element so vital to effective drama, Shakespeare also maintains the focus upon the larger situation—the limited capacity of Henry IV as a ruler and its implications for the body politic of England—by measuring Henry and Hal against the concepts of monarchy shared by those in his contemporary audience. These late-sixteenth-century views, in very general terms, rest on two criteria: proper exercise of power and equitable dispensation of justice. Concerning the former, the king, who should receive the scepter as a direct lineal descendant of the royal family, is God's vicar or lieutenant on earth; "The king, yes, though he be an infidel, representeth the image of God upon earth."[25] The duty, both religious and social, of the populace is obedience. As a homily published in 1571 states, "Such subjects as are disobedient or rebellious against their princes, disobey God and procure their own damnation." In the body politic, obedience to the prince is essential; even a tyrant is preferable to anarchy, which would come with rebellion. It is argued that monarchy in form arose from nature as an extended concept of the family unit.[26] The prince's duty is analogous to a father's duty; he exercises rule from the awareness of the need for order, for the welfare of the total community and nation. Hence the king must be powerful, and he must be capable of using his authority to protect himself and his people.

Such essentially is Henry IV's concept of kingship, a concept, as Derek Traversi observes, predicated entirely on the ground of "political effectiveness."[27] Troubled by a realization that he has achieved the throne at the expense of the rightful King and by a sense of guilt for Richard's murder, he knows full well that his success as a ruler will be determined by his public virtue, specifically his ability to maintain civil order in the land. Regardless of whether Bolingbroke coldly and calculatingly planned to manipulate Northumberland as a stepping stone to political office, the fact is clear at the beginning of the play that Northumberland believes Henry to have broken his pledged word that he sought only the Dukedom of Lancaster. Moreover, established on the throne, the new King seems to shun the alliance from the north as readily as he had earlier embraced it. Dismissed from council, Worcester asserts, "Our house, my sovereign liege, little deserves / The scourge of greatness to be us'd on it, / And that same greatness which our own hands / Have holp to make so portly" (I, iii, 10–13). The king with royal dispatch evaluates the rebels' strength and moves to confront them. There is no hesitation before Shrewsbury; the armies of the King are well directed and deployed to fight for protection of order in the land.

Certainly the spectators of the play would admire a king who, so unlike Richard II or Henry VI, exercises without hesitation his royal authority with a positive determination to uphold the law of the kingdom against the hydra-head of rebellion.[28] Yet the spectator would perceive with equal clarity that this same king attempts in practice— as Machiavelli did in theory—to separate public and private virtue. Certainly the clearest key to this emphasis on appearance occurs in part 2 in his deathbed speech to the king-elect:

> God knows, my son,
> By what by-paths and indirect crook'd ways
> I met this crown, and I myself know well
> How troublesome it sate upon my head.
> To thee it shall descend with better quiet.
> . . . .
> And all [my] friends, which thou must make thy friends,
> Have but their stings and teeth newly ta'en out;
> By whose fell working I was first advanc'd,
> And by whose power I well might lodge a fear
> To be again displac'd; which to avoid,
> I cut them off.   (IV, v, 183–87, 204–9)

He is quick to counsel his son to "busy giddy minds / With foreign quarrels" (213–14) so that his own disjunction with his former allies might be put from the minds of the people. But in part 1, as well, Henry explains the method by which he won the public opinion "that

did help him to the crown" (III, ii, 42). By "being seldom seen"
(46) and on such occasions dressing himself "in such humility" (51),
Henry developed in reputation "like a robe pontifical" (52), which
"seldom but sumptuous, show'd like a feast" (58).

It is dramatically appropriate that this king, whose rule is vitally
dependent upon decisive and powerful action in the face of danger
and whose public reputation must appear inviolate even though his
private actions smack so strongly of blatant practicality, should draw
a specific analogy between Hotspur's valorous search for public glory
and Hal's debauchery and apparent lack of concern for his public
image. Indeed Hotspur, "the theme of honor's tongue" (I, i, 81),
"sweet Fortune's minion and her pride" (83), is a man of Henry's
own heart; the King can understand, in a way in which he is never able
to comprehend Hal, the political riser who is overtly conscious of public opinion. Kingly praise, it should be noted, comes even in the face
of Henry's knowledge of Hotspur's rebellious action of denying prisoners to the throne. Furthermore the King later praises Hotspur for
his public display of virtue (III, ii, 115ff.) in a scene immediately following Hotspur's compliance in a projected tripartite division of England. When the full effect of these scenes is considered, there can be
little doubt that Shakespeare is utilizing Henry's praise of the "politic
virtue" of Hotspur as yet another reflection of Bolingbroke's limited
concept of rule. For certainly Henry praises, as one having "more
worthy interest to the state / Than [Hal]" (98–99), a man who is
specifically exposed as lacking qualities inherent in the ideal ruler.

In any event, Henry IV meets the sixteenth-century demands of a
ruler who can and will exercise his power for the maintenance of unity
in the kingdom. Beyond that, however, the king, in whom public and
private virtue must agree in the equitable dispensation of justice,
should rule for the welfare of the subject. Gascoigne in *The Steel
Glass* (lines 114–34) strikes particularly at the ruler who would strive
"to maintain pomp and high, triumphant sights" and "never care . . .
to yield relief where needy lack appears." Castiglione lists among the
attributes of the ideal prince wisdom, justice, courtesy, and liberality
in this treatment and knowledge of his subjects. Similarly, Starkey

raises the specific issue that there is nothing more repugnant to nature than a whole nation governed by the will of a prince who neither understands the nature of his subjects nor knows their needs. Above all, it is Elyot who most clearly describes this concept of a king in his discussion of the training of a prince. Like the "principal bee" the prince moves through society; not with "prick or sting" but with "more knowledge than is in the residue"; though to understand his subjects he might move temporarily among "herbs that be venomous and stinking," he gathers "nothing but that shall be sweet and profitable." Though a prince study the classics diligently, his theoretical knowledge must be tempered by his experiences in society itself. As the prince moves in society, "What incredible delight is taken in beholding the diversities of people, . . . to know the sundry manners and conditions of people, and the variety of their natures."[29]

It would be difficult to escape the obvious contrast between Henry's constant concern to hold himself aloof from the people, and his son's ability to move with affable ease throughout the London populace. That the Prince is gaining useful knowledge of his future subjects through his associations is explicitly stated by Warwick in part 2.

> The Prince but studies his companions,
> Like a strange tongue, wherein, to gain the language,
> 'Tis needful. . . .
> The Prince will in the perfectness of time
> Cast off his followers, and their memory
> Shall as a pattern or a measure live,
> By which his Grace must mete the lives of others,
> Turning past evils to advantages.
>
> (IV, iv, 68–70, 75–79)

In part 1 the Prince suggests a similar advantage in a conversation with Poins: "They [the commoners of London] take it already upon their salvation, that though I be but Prince of Wales, yet I am the king of courtesy, and tell me . . . when I am the King of England I shall command all the good lads of Eastcheap" (II, iv, 9–15). In *Henry V* the new King notes to the French ambassador the use he made of his wilder days (I, ii, 268–69). Even Falstaff in his blustering manner implies that the Prince has tempered the cold-blooded valor which he inherited from his father by his association with and knowledge of his subjects (part 2, IV, iii, 118–23).

Although Prince Hal inherits kingly valor and courage from his father—as is witnessed in his exploits at Shrewsbury and in his victories over the French armies at Harfleur and Agincourt—he possesses an attitude toward the monarchy which his father never achieves. Instead of a usurped throne, he inherits an established one; instead of striking internecine blows to protect an unsettled position of authority, he will use the power of a unified England for the positive advantage of expanding his realm; instead of concentration upon the power to punish, he exercises a justice tempered with mercy. Henry IV's cruel treatment of Richard II and his sentencing of Worcester and Vernon to immediate execution might have been politically expedient, but the comparison with Prince Hal's mercy is striking. Immediately after Worcester and Vernon are sentenced, the Prince requests and receives permission "to dispose" of Douglas. In signal contrast to Henry IV's death sentences, Hal delivers Douglas "up to his pleasure, ransomless and free" (V, v, 28): "His valors shown upon our crests to-day / Have taught us how to cherish such high deeds / Even in the bosom of our adversaries" (29–31). This action is even more significant when one considers that the Prince is showing mercy to one who was at the very center of the rebellion. For Worcester had earlier utilized the capture of Douglas's son (I, iii, 261ff.) as the sole motivation for Hotspur's rallying troops against the King in Scotland, and it was Douglas who very nearly carried the day for the rebels in his personal combat with the King. The Prince also tempers justice with mercy in the much-discussed rejection of Falstaff and his associates; for although they are "banish'd till their conversations / Appear more wise and modest," the new King "hath intent his wonted followers / Shall all be very well provided for" (part 2, V, v, 98–99, 97). In Hal's later action as King he is overtly merciful in his unwarranted freeing, just before the army's departure to France, of one "That rail'd against our person. We consider / It was excess of wine that set him on, / And on his more advice we pardon him" (*Henry V*, II, ii, 41–43). Even to Cambridge, Exeter, and Grey, the traitors who have accepted bribery from the French, Henry states that, concerning his person, he seeks no revenge but that their execution is mandatory for the safety of the kingdom (II, ii, 174–75). Moreover Shakespeare consciously emphasizes the king's mercy in his actions against the citizens of Harfleur, though historically no such mercy was shown.[30]

A further distinction in *1 Henry IV* between Henry and Hal emerges from the dialectical tension created by their perceptions of the other principal figures in the play. Henry's estimation of both Hotspur and Falstaff, for example, is simplistic at best. The one he condones for his valor, merit, and ambition; the other he condemns for his morally reprehensible conduct and his parasitic attachment to the heir apparent. Hal's appraisals are sharply different; he sees both for what they are—individuals who, not devoid of charm, indeed possessing certain admirable qualities vital both to personal fulfillment and popular acclaim, are ultimately unbalanced, intemperate, and self-destructive. The dichotomy is established in the opening lines. Henry IV in his admiration of Hotspur would gladly believe the two Harrys to have been secretly exchanged at birth. Even facing a blatantly traitorous Hotspur at Shrewsbury in act 5, he for "considerations infinite" will not sanction a single combat between his son and the adversary of "great name and estimation" (i, 102, 98). Hal, while obviously recognizing Hotspur's courage and battlefield skills, also perceives the bravado and the unrestrained Herculean ambitions of the man. The one he parodies in conversation with Poins at the Eastcheap tavern:

> I am not yet of Percy's mind, the Hotspur of the north: he that kills me some six or seven dozen of Scots at a breakfast, washes his hands, and says to his wife, "Fie upon this quiet life! I want work." "O my sweet Harry," says she, "how many hast thou kill'd to-day?" "Give my roan horse a drench," says he, and answers, "Some fourteen," and hour after; "a trifle, a trifle." (II, iv, 101–8)

The other he addresses in soliloquy over Hotspur's body as an "ill-weav'd ambition" which, by provoking and feeding the conviction that a kingdom itself is too small, has resulted only in "two paces of the vilest earth" (V, iv, 88, 91).[31]

Their views of Falstaff and the society of commoners are equally divergent. Henry IV characterizes his son's relationship with them as one of "riot and dishonor" (I, i, 85), of "barren pleasures, rude society" (III, ii, 14); like Richard II Hal "amble[s] up and down, / With shallow jesters" and grows "a companion to the common streets" (60–61, 68). Hal, to the contrary, is never even partially blind to Falstaff's dissolute qualities. From first to last, he addresses his fat companion bluntly and honestly, if good-naturedly. Falstaff is a time waster courting trouble with the law (I, ii, 5, 42–43, 66–68); he is a "fat-guts" (II, ii, 31), a liar ("gross as a mountain, open, palpable," iv, 226), a villainous thief (314), a devil in the shape of a fat man (447–48), an impudent rascal in whose bosom "there's no room for faith, truth, nor honesty" (III, iii, 153–54). Over his presumably dead body Hal declares that Falstaff would be sorely missed "If I were much in love with vanity!" (V, iv, 106). Illustrations could continue at considerable length, but surely we must assume that Hal from the opening scenes of the play has no illusions whatsoever about his companion. Indeed, he specifically tells us as much in soliloquy. But he also sees beyond the present moment, suggesting that his present associations and actions will make him later shine more brightly when he throws off his "loose behavior" (I, ii, 208), just as the sun seems more brilliant when emerging from dark clouds. This tone of conscious analysis runs, in fact, like a thread through the entire play. Hal asserts that he is "of all humors" (II, iv, 92). He reports, in a statement which slices through the context of levity, that he eventually will banish "plump Jack" from his presence (479). And, on the battlefield he makes good the promise of his opening soliloquy; by openly referring to his truant youth and to an ostensibly instantaneous transformation, he dazzles those around him—even his enemy Vernon, who reports that he seems possessed of "such a grace / As if he mast'red there a double spirit / Of teaching and of learning instantly" (V, ii, 62–64).

The major advancement in the play is in Shakespeare's handling of characterization. While the principals are static, held at arm's length so as not to provoke the close rapport and intensity of attention which would tend to blur the larger vision of the scene, they also are possessed of a fundamental ambiguity that provokes a mixed response and belies such a simplistic conception. The movement of the drama, in other words, like that of the *Henry VI* plays in some respects, is created by the interplay of fixed types rather than by the developing nature of dynamic figures, but worlds removed is the technique which lends a degree of depth and dramatic vitality to the characterization. While Henry, Hal, Hotspur, and Falstaff do not develop in the course of the action, the spectators are forced to view them in widely divergent situations. The angles from which the character is observed, public and private, cumulatively produce an ambivalence that, for the spectators, moves far beyond the stylization of static characterization.

Prince Hal is perhaps the best case in point. A good many critics have labored at some length to describe his development or his education in one or both parts of the Henry IV plays. One can maintain, for example, that Hal progressively deepens in his perspective and in his understanding—that in part 1 he perceives and subdues his own boastful nature while proving his heroic capabilities through the slaying of Hotspur, and that in part 2 he rejects Falstaff (who shrinks in comic stature because he is unable to move with the change in the Prince) because he has come to see the destructive potential of his fat companion and is fully prepared to accept the responsibilities of kingship. This kind of argument, while it perhaps does no real damage to one's enjoyment of the play or of his general appreciation for Shakespeare's dramatic skills, is convincing only so long as he is caught up in it and the specific passages of the text that are cited in its support. Other passages, totally ignored in this argument, render the entire matter academic. Most important, Hal announces his intentions with absolute clarity in his soliloquy during his first appearance on stage, and he fulfills them in part at the conclusion of part 1 and in full at the conclusion of part 2. Along the way there is not the slightest doubt in the spectator's mind that he will do so. In fact, he reiterates his aims in his dialogue with Falstaff in part 1, II, iv, 481, and in his dialogue with Poins in part 2, II, ii, 176. The difficulty Shakespeare has with the character, as Peter Alexander has written, is that "while he had to talk about the Prince's becoming a different man he also had to make it clear from the beginning that there is no change whatever."[32] To compare Hal's experience with that of the prodigal son, one must "so rewrite the parable that the prodigal may say as he departs for the far country, 'I'll so offend, to make offense a skill' " (p. 112). Similarly, to argue the morality tradition as the shaping force, one must accept an Everyman character who knows how to manipulate both sides to best advantage. Ultimately the argument that Hal matures and develops is based entirely upon inference. At no point either in soliloquy or in dialogue does he give any indication of an internal struggle between the sense of duty and responsibility on the one hand and the temptation to waste himself in irresponsible actions with base companions on the other. In contrast, the power and the credibility of the characterization of the principals in both the major tragedies and the mature comedies lie precisely in the dramatization of these significant moments of struggle, from which emerges a new stage of self-realization and a sense of dynamic self-determination. Such characters as Antonio and Bassanio, Beatrice and Benedick, Hamlet, and Othello seem to grow and change in the course of the action; figures like Richard II and Brutus at the very least display a sensitivity of spirit and an introspection which strongly attract the spectators' interest. In the tragedies especially Shakespeare intensifies this focus through extensive use of the devices of internalization, and the spectators' consuming interest is in the developing figure whose critical moments they share.

If Hal does not develop, however, he is far from a simplistic figure of stylized ideality. Even placing the best interpretation on Hal's use of Falstaff's world to become better acquainted with all elements of his future kingdom, one is hard pressed to sanction certain acts: his passive participation in a robbery involving physical violence and outright defiance of civil law, whatever the rationalization and the mitigating circumstances (II, ii); his refusal to consult with Sir John Bracy, an emissary from his father, at a time of political disruption, indeed permitting Falstaff to speak for him as the rogue sees fit (II, iv, 297ff.); his arrant lie to the sheriff that Falstaff is not with him at the tavern, that instead he is employed on a special mission (513ff.); his sudden determination, without explanation, to procure Falstaff an honorable position in the wars, this in the face of his full knowledge of Falstaff's character (545ff.); and his willingness to grace the lie of Falstaff's slaying Hotspur in battle, an action which by implication at least condones Jack's earlier irresponsibility in substituting wine for his pistol[33] and his "discretionary" cowardice in feigning death—let alone his earlier gross abuse of funds for impressment of troops (V, v, 157ff.). One can place little credence in the claim that Hal, the ideal king in waiting, is presented without flaw or that any early indiscretions can be excused by his progressive development in spiritual and physical fortitude. He is indeed guilty of occasional lapses in moral judgment—as much at the end of the play as at the beginning—and certainly from the outset he knows his companions for what they are and calculatingly weighs the political advantages of his actions. Either to whitewash his character or to view him as subject to a kind of repentance which obviates a canny sense of political pragmatism is to enforce a reductionism which the full text will not support. Nor should he be viewed, with equal distortion, as a cunning schemer whose lust for power dictates his every move. If John Palmer begs the question with his assertion that Shakespeare "leaves us to decide for ourselves how far Henry really conducts himself according to plan, or how far he is merely creating an alibi for his misdemeanours,"[34] it is nonetheless true that the full context will support neither the view that Hal, morally beyond reproach, practices the golden mean of virtue[35] nor the view that he is a "self-complacent and self-centered" individual whose "incapacity for true feeling" leads him to discover a genuine Machiavellian energy.[36] Hal is, as it were, "his own foil."[37]

Neither saint nor sinner then, Hal is an intriguingly human combination of virtues and vices with a taste for the wild life and the thrill of defiance, a tendency to rationalize and mitigate his actions, a remarkable capacity for good humor and a toleration for the boon companion who epitomizes it, a crafty perception of political strategy and of human psychology, a splendid courage and magnanimity on the battlefield, and a genuine dedication to the Lancastrian throne. Certain characteristics may be dominant at times (suggesting perhaps a sense of development) but never to the exclusion of other features—hence the significance of the soliloquy declaring his self-knowledge in the midst of his antic moments with Falstaff and the law at the beginning of the play, and of his permitting Falstaff's lie in the context of his greatest military encounter at the end of the play. Hal anticipates the throne and the responsibilities which it entails from his first moment on stage. As a static figure moving inexorably toward the throne which will bring fame and glory both to him and to England, he does not, like Richard III and Richard II, emotionally engage the spectators in a restrictingly personal manner which would diminish the breadth of their perspective. At the same time he is a complex figure, far from the stylized qualities of heroism in Talbot, of virtue in Humphrey Duke of Gloucester, of villainy in Margaret of Anjou or Richard Duke of York.

The title figure the spectators know less intimately—an indication perhaps of the playwright's concern for a broad focus, especially when one considers the significance of the title roles in the earlier *Richard III* and *Richard II*.[38] Henry IV speaks not one private line in part 1, and he appears in fewer scenes than any of the other principals. There is no fundamental development in his character. Like Hal, however, he is a complex individual who commands the spectators' interest as they observe his personality from various angles. In I, i, for instance, we view the public Lancastrian face which seems carefully to calculate the political ramifications of every word. Henry is concerned for the kingdom so "shaken" with the "intestine shock . . . of civil butchery" (i, 12–13); were the sporadic insurrections to cease, he would as an act of national expiation lead an English force against the pagans in Jerusalem. Another aspect of the public face, admirably firm and decisive, is revealed in I, iii, in which Henry dismisses Worcester from the Council and sternly refuses Hotspur's condition for delivering prisoners of war; in III, ii, he moves with confident dispatch to align the three components of his battle force; similarly, the play concludes with his stacatto orders to pursue the rebels still at large. Yet another dimension, combining political acumen and magnanimity, is evidenced in the early moments of act 5. Prior to battle he extends "grace" and honorable reconciliation to the rebels (i, 106ff.), an offer which even Worcester describes as "liberal and kind" (ii, 2). Distinctly different, however, is the remorseful father who senses that his son's profligacy is "the hot vengeance, and the rod of heaven" sent to "punish [his] mistreadings" (III, ii, 10, 11). Sensing in Hal's seeming disregard for the throne a repudiation of all he has achieved, Henry laments that his son is his "nearest and dearest enemy," likely to fight in Percy's pay for "base inclination, and the start of spleen" (123, 125). The moment of reconciliation is charged with emotion, and a similar humanly vulnerable side is exposed later on the battlefield in words of gratitude to Hal for saving his life.

While there is no significant growth or alteration in personality, Henry IV is not one dimensional; and the same is true of both Hotspur and Falstaff. Certainly Hotspur in one sense fulfills Henry IV's simplistic description.[39] Vis-a-vis an effeminate lord from the court in I, iii, he is a veritable Mars on the battlefield, and he boldly asserts his position against the King himself. This same heroic stance the audience observes in Hotspur's disdain for those who shirk the battle from fear, yet claim political or domestic excuses: "He shows in this, he loves his own barn better than he loves our house. . . . What a frosty-spirited rogue is this!" (II, iii, 5–6, 20). And Hotspur bravely encounters Hal at Shrewsbury, lamenting in defeat that his sacrifice of "proud titles" is a far sharper pain than the loss of "brittle life" (V, iv, 78, 77). At the same time the spectators also see, far more plainly than Hal, the heir apparent's justification for mocking Hotspur's blustering and immoderate mien. Not only, following the King's order that all prisoners be delivered, does Hotspur develop such a passionate attack of logorrhea that his uncle declines further speech and his father brands him a "wasp-stung and impatient fool" (I, iii, 236); he also risks alienating his ally Glendower by bluntly calling him a liar (III, i, 58) and in a high dudgeon insists that the river Trent be turned so that his division of the kingdom will be larger; in both cases only the cooler head of the Welsh leader preserves the fragile rebel alliance (an odious comparison indeed, since Glendower himself is given to such hyperbolic rant). Similarly he later disregards the defections from his ranks, vowing that since "doomsday is near" all will "die merrily" (IV, i, 134) and insisting, against the advice of all of his counsellors, that the charge take place that very night (iii, 1–29). But the spectator, unlike the royal father and son, perceives yet another side. When Lady Percy expresses concern for her husband's sleeplessness and loss of appetite and berates him for not sharing his innermost problems, not the heroism or the bravado but the humanity surfaces. Like Portia, Kate fears for her husband's safety; and if Hotspur's response in II, iv, seems somewhat peremptory, his bantering tone hardly conceals his affection in III, i. In the presence of the amorous pair

Mortimer and his wife, for whom language is a barrier, Hotspur bluntly proclaims Kate "perfect in lying down" (226). She wittily threatens to break his head unless he keeps silence, but he insists that she swear a "good mouth-filling oath" (254). The two are obviously well matched, and the impression conveyed by the scene is one of genuine intimacy. Whatever Henry's or Hal's single-dimensional perception of Hotspur, the spectators see him in a far more complex light. Not only must they balance the opposing views of the royal family (and the manner in which these views functionally develop the conflict of father and son); they must also accommodate the more intimate vision of the man with wife, friends, and political allies.

The spectator's perception of Falstaff is no less complex. On the one hand, the character is indeed a fat parasite who, by inference at least, is a "grey Iniquity," a "villainous abominable misleader of youth" (II, iv, 453–54, 462–63).[40] On the other hand he is also a welcome participant in present mirth. Both views are readily illustrated. As a creature of malign influence, Falstaff is a "thief" (I, ii, 138; II, ii, 93) and a robber of the King's exchequer (55), a whoremonger and debtor to the hostess to the tavern (III, iii, 66), a traitor in his misuse of funds for assembling troops in a period of national emergency (IV, ii, 12), and an arrant coward on the field of battle (V, iii, 58–59; iv, 75ff.). At the same time the Prince without question pays Falstaff's tavern debts (I, ii, 51) and time and again delights in his resourceful excuses and rationalizations, whether involving the counterrobbery at Gad's Hill (II, iv, 267–68), the pocket-picking at Eastcheap (III, iii, 164–66), or the parodic role-changing (II, iv, 376–481);[41] Hal will even tolerate dishonesty at Shrewsbury for the sake of such friendship:

> Come bring your luggage nobly on your back.
> For my part, if a lie may do thee grace,
> I'll gild it with the happiest terms I have.
> (V, iv, 156–58)

But there is yet another side to Falstaff which only the spectators perceive, and it is this quality which in large part accounts for the universal popularity of the character. Not only is this "huge hill of flesh" a voice of merry abandon; he also epitomizes that part of human nature which places a paramount value on life and survival and which disdains a commitment to violence and destruction for such pompous abstractions as national power and honor. Moments before the battle begins, he privately shares with the spectators his catechism of honor —it may spur one to fight but it has never been able to set a leg or an arm or to mitigate the "grief of a wound" (V, i, 132). This concept of honor as a mere word for glorifying militaristic actions which result in death is a recurrent theme through several of his soliloquies in the final act.[42] Standing over the slain Sir Walter Blount, Falstaff sardonically observes the vanity of honor's prompting the nobleman to fight in the King's disguise (iii, 30–39); later he is more grotesquely pointed: "I like not such grinning honor as Sir Walter hath. Give me life, which if I can save, so; if not, honor comes unlook'd for, and there's an end" (58–61). When compelled to feign death to save life, he proclaims that he is "no counterfeit. To die is to be a counterfeit, for he is but the counterfeit of a man who hath not the life of a man; but to counterfeit dying, when a man thereby liveth, is to be no counterfeit, but the true and perfect image of life indeed. The better part of valor is discretion" (iv, 115–20).[43] He may at one moment be ashamed of the ragamuffins who follow him, but such embarrassment fails to dampen his enthusiasm for squandering the money he has appropriated (IV, ii, 11ff.). And he may at another moment vow to "purge and leave sack, and live cleanly," but he admits that he follows, "as they say, for reward" (V, iv, 164–65, 162). Falstaff is worlds removed from the equally extreme battlefield heroics of Hotspur; but like Percy's son he is human in his habitude, and the interweaving of such powerfully ambivalent figures provides a rich and controlled perspective for dramatizing chronicle material.

Shakespeare's structural technique in *2 Henry IV* is a direct continuation of that of part 1. Debate over the nature of the play and its place in the canon has raged as long as the critics have addressed the play: whether, for example, it is a separate dramatic creation written to capitalize on the success of a play first published in 1598 and reprinted four times prior to the Folio or whether it is an integral portion of a drama originally conceived in ten acts or at least envisioned before the completion of part 1.[44] Whatever the case, *2 Henry IV* stands or falls on its own merits. It may, like the Henry VI plays, assume certain larger significances when viewed as a part of a two-part play or even of double tetralogies, but it is also a separate dramatic entity for an afternoon's performance, and its success depends not on narrative and character continuities but on the effective presentation of the immediate theme.

The perspective of *2 Henry IV* is again broad and diffuse, accommodating a historical rather than a personal focus and creating, as Gareth Lloyd Evans observes, an interplay of dimensions which "makes of history much more than a chronicle tapestry."[45] The multiple plot strands, in fact, are even more diverse than those of the earlier play. For one thing, the use of Rumor as a prologue figure and of the epilogue speaker's reference to forthcoming French campaigns serves to frame a theme of national political and personal disorientation. At the outset civil war is rampant, families are divided, and lapses in communication only reinforce the suffering and apprehension which grip the kingdom.[46] If there is talk of peace, Rumor assures the spectators that "covert enmity / Under the smile of safety wounds the world" (9–10). Rumor, moreover, keeps the "still-discordant wav'-ring multitude" in constant turmoil (19). Only in the last few lines does the figure of the induction address himself to a particular character, and here the purpose of noting that Northumberland will receive false information of Hotspur's victory is to establish the detachment of dramatic irony through which the spectators will view the initial scenes. For another thing, in the fourteen remaining scenes as marked in the Folio, Shakespeare not only provides a continuation of the three plot strands of part 1, he also subdivides two of them for yet further narrative multiplicity. One group of scenes continues to depict the activities of those rebellious to King Henry. All that is left of the earlier alliance of Northumberland-Worcester-Glendower-Mortimer-Douglas, however, is the "crafty-sick" Northumberland (I, ii; II, iii).[47] The more significant facet of rebellion arises from a new alliance (I, iii; IV, i) made up of Archbishop Scroop, who appears quite briefly in part 1, with Mowbray, Hastings, and Bardolph, none of whom has previously appeared.[48] The plot strand concerning Hal's escapades with the Falstaffian world is similarly bifurcated. In only one scene prior to Hal's banishment of his fat companion do the two actually meet (II, iv); yet seven additional scenes feature characters from the world of the London streets. In two scenes Falstaff encounters a new verbal combatant in the Lord Chief Justice, three scenes describe his activities with his acquaintance of younger years Justice Shallow, and another involves his battlefield encounter with Sir John Coleville. Poins appears with Hal in II, ii, while V, iv, depicts the unhappy plight of Nell and Doll. The third plot strand involves Henry IV, grievously troubled by a guilt-ridden conscience, defending his kingdom by proxy as a consequence of his own declining health (III, i; IV, iv; IV, v; V, ii). This title figure does not appear until the third act, but both his personal soul-searching and his confrontation with Hal are vital to the total design. The broad diversity of action in the play is well illustrated by the fact that material dealing with the rebels constitutes 19 percent of the total lineation, that dealing with the Falstaffian world 50 percent, and that dealing with the king himself 19 percent. The remaining scenes involve interaction of the various strands: the rebels' fateful parley at Gaultree Forest with Henry's deputy, Prince John of Lancaster; Falstaff's encounter with Prince John (IV, iii); and Falstaff's final meeting with Hal, now Henry V (V, v).

No single individual figures in all three plot lines, and not surprisingly no dominant character emerges in the play. For one thing, an amazingly large number of named characters, forty-one, appear on stage. *1 Henry IV*, by comparison, utilizes twenty-three named characters; *Henry V*, thirty-eight; *Richard III*, thirty-seven; the *Henry VI* plays, twenty-nine, thirty-five, and thirty. Indeed, while the large cast is characteristic of Shakespeare's history plays in general, this play represents the largest *dramatis personae* in the canon. Equally striking— and surely also another record—nineteen named characters appear in only one scene. Of those who figure more prominently in the action, none is on stage in as many as half of the scenes, and ten individuals speak 3 percent or more of the lines; by actual count of lines, the principal figures are Falstaff (20.7 percent), Hal (9.6 percent), King Henry IV (8.7 percent), Shallow (6.2 percent), and Mistress Quickly (5.5 percent). As in *1 Henry IV* the scenes establish both a geographical and a social cross-section of the kingdom, with settings ranging from Warkworth, York, Gaultree Forest, and Gloucestershire to the palace at Westminster and to the London streets and the Boar's Head Tavern at Eastcheap. Plot, setting, and character contribute to a broad focus, and the spectator unobtrusively is encouraged to develop an interest in a panoramic scene depicting the fortunes of a wide variety of individuals caught in the political uncertainties and the economic and social instabilities which characterize Henry IV's reign.

Whatever the relationship of the composition, the two Henry IV plays are structurally akin revealing, as Robert Ornstein notes, parallelism of scenes, echoings of motif and theme, and juxtapositions and contrasts of character and attitude.[40] Both introduce a budding rebellion in act 1 which takes more definite shape in the third scene of act 2; in part 1 the struggle between rebel and king, Hotspur and Hal, constitutes the culminating action, whereas in part 2 the battle at Gaultree Forest between Archbishop Scroop and John of Lancaster is resolved in act 4. Both also introduce the figure of comic misrule in the second scene of act 1, with Falstaff crossing wits with Hal in part 1 and with the Lord Chief Justice in part 2. This material in both plays occupies scenes 1, 2, and 4 of act 2; indeed scene 4 is the comic high point as Hal through trickery exposes Falstaff for a coward and buffoon—in the one play by perpetrating a counterrobbery at Gad's Hill, in the other by disguising himself as a drawer at the tavern in Eastcheap. In both instances Falstaff, caught in palpable lies, amuses Hal and the spectators through his incredible efforts to extricate himself. In both plays Falstaff receives for the impressment of soldiers a sum of money which he abominably misuses (part 1, IV, ii; part 2, III, ii); and in both Falstaff figures prominently in the final scene, his claim over Hotspur's body condoned by Prince Hal in the one, his claim to fast friendship and influence condemned by Henry V in the other. Both plays present in the initial appearance of the title figure a king plagued by doubts of his son's loyalty as well as a later scene involving apparent reconciliation and mutual understanding; while in part 1

Henry's apprehension appears at the outset of the action (I, i) and in part 2 not until the middle (III, i), the reconciliation scenes occur prior to the major resolution in both instances (part 1, III, ii; part 2, IV, v). Such similarities can hardly be coincidental, and one must logically infer that Shakespeare consciously constructed part 2 at least loosely on the structural lines utilized successfully to achieve a broad dramatic focus in part 1.

Another key to the effectiveness of the perspective of *2 Henry IV* is again the quality of the characterization. As in part 1 a suggestive ambivalence in the central figures, while not altering the fundamental nature of the character and not creating a singular intensity of focus, does result in a semblance of lifelikeness and a sense of drama based on character interaction. The characters admittedly have a certain symbolic quality within the design of the play, a quality possible because they are fixed; they also, however, become interesting as human figures. Revealing the "personal and private side of his public men," Shakespeare produces "enharmonic changes" to yield what A. P. Rossiter describes as "a precise evocation of the paradox of human experience."[50] In other words the characters function, in a way not required of the central characters in comedy or tragedy, both as fixed historical ideas and as human and individual personalities. Henry, for example, typifies the able usurper who has restored a sense of control and personal stability to the land but who has done so at the expense of the doctrinal right to rule and must engage in combat time and again to consolidate his kingdom and defend the strong-man principle to which he is perforce dedicated. Hal to the popular Elizabethan mind represents the ideal of kingship, a concept which to Shakespeare presumes a certain manipulative capability involving both one's actions and his acquaintances. Both Falstaff and Northumberland from the outset typify in their own ways the spirit of disorder, Northumberland in his political opposition to the concept of control and Falstaff in his moral opposition to all that such order at least abstractly implies. One could easily describe the remaining host who populate this stage world—the senile Shallow living in the memory of his youth, the blustering Pistol, the dependable and unwavering Lord Chief Justice, the amiable but undesigning Poins, the sternly Machiavellian Prince John. But with the four principals, as in part 1, Shakespeare moves beyond stylization. If the characters are basically unchanging in nature, the spectator is nonetheless permitted to view them from different angles; here the soliloquy becomes the means for seeing beyond the sense of self-sufficiency which the character type suggests, and the spectator alone enjoys the perspective for appreciating fully the emotions inherent in the dramatic confrontations.

Henry IV does not provoke a dispassionate response from the spectators. There is no qualitative change; he never offers to renounce his throne—indeed he never fails through his military organization ably to defend his throne and his possessions. He will meet his "inward wars" "like necessities" (III, i, 107, 93). While he would prefer to lead the youth of the land "on to higher fields" (IV, iv, 3), he moves with practicality and expediency against the rebel threat: "Our navy is address'd, our power collected, / Our substitutes in absence well invested, / And everything lies level to our wish" (5–7). He also, however, is a man beset with doubts about his son and plagued with a sense of guilt concerning all which he has accomplished; "the responsibilities of rule," as A. R. Humphreys writes, "rendered harsh by his own axe, and his capacity for melancholy analysis, ally him with the flawed heroes of the tragedies."[51] Speaking in a soliloquy at his initial appearance, Henry laments his inability to rest:

> O sleep! O gentle sleep!
> Nature's soft nurse, how have I frighted thee,
> That thou no more wilt weigh my eyelids down
> And steep my senses in forgetfulness?
> . . . .
> Canst thou, O partial sleep
> . . . .
> Deny [thy repose] to a king? Then [happy] low, lie down!
> Uneasy lies the head that wears a crown.
> (III, i, 5–8, 26, 30–31)

He is concerned with the "rank diseases" that continue to grow in "the body of [his] kingdom" (39, 38), and he mournfully recalls that those who now oppose him were the mainstay of his rebellion against Richard. Concerning the complexity of Henry's character, certainly the most revealing single moment is his admission on his death bed that he achieved the crown, "God knows," by "by-paths and indirect crook'd ways" (IV, v, 183–84) and that his Jerusalem campaign was in large part a psychological ploy (208–10), juxtaposed with his chilling political advice to Hal: "Be it thy course to busy giddy minds / With foreign quarrels, that action, hence borne out, / May waste the memory of the former days" (213–15). From another angle his sense of frustration is perhaps most keen in his comments about the "headstrong riot" and the "rage and hot blood" of his son: "The blood weeps from my heart when I do shape, / In forms imaginary, th' unguided days / And rotten times" which await the nation (IV, iv, 58ff.). He fears that the fifth Henry will seek for new ways to commit the oldest sins, that with all restraints lifted "the wild dog / Shall flesh his tooth on every innocent" (IV, v, 131–32), that in a word all shall be lost in a moment by a son lacking respect for both father and kingdom. Such a conflict of generations is a universal theme, and while a reconciliation of words does indeed occur, he surely goes to his death harboring more than fleeting moments of doubt concerning the grand achievements for which he has sacrificed integrity and peace of mind.

Henry then is pervasively ambivalent, and the spectator cannot help perceiving the genuinely human side of political power successfully usurped. Precisely the opposite—the human side of unsuccessful political maneuvering—is visible in Northumberland. A relatively minor figure, to be sure, appearing in only two scenes and speaking barely over one hundred lines, Northumberland is nonetheless another illustration of the method by which Shakespeare develops a compelling and effective historical perspective. The other principal rebel, Archbishop Scroop, appears in a greater number of scenes and delivers half again as many lines; he is moreover a dominant presence during the actual confrontation at Gaultree Forest. By comparison, however, he is a shallow, stylized figure who monolithically states his reasons for opposing Lancastrian rule; without personal malice, he is also without deceit, and thus he becomes ready prey for Prince John's tactics.[52] The important point here, however, is that he is also lacking significant human credibility. As an individual with awesome religious responsibilities, he never suggests the personal difficulties in his decision to rebel, and his sole response to John's treachery at Gaultree Forest is the amazingly dispassionate and fleshless query, "Will you thus break your faith?" (IV, ii, 112). As such a stylized figure, the Archbishop does of course conveniently serve the design of the piece—the "virtuous" rebel as a foil to John, the "villainous" loyalist, or an emblematic depiction of the necessities of emerging political realities. A character like Northumberland, on the other hand, serves both the purposes of historical design and of effective stage craft. He also is a static figure, but he provokes an emotional response from the spectator which moves beyond that of intellectual abstraction. The prologue figure reports that Northumberland lies at home "crafty-sick" (37), a point established in part 1. Now he must experience the agony of that earlier decision which cost his son his life through, first, the rumor of Hotspur's victory, then the reality of the son's defeat and death. When he responds with a determination to fight, he must endure Morton's observation that the time is not now so ripe as when he sent Hotspur forth alone to battle (I, i, 168ff.). Even more poignant is his daughter-in-law's later assertion that he has already lost his honor in failing to support Hotspur:

> The time was, father, that you broke your word,
> When you were more [endear'd] to it than now,
> When your own Percy, when my heart's dear Harry,
> Threw many a northward look to see his father
> Bring up his powers; but he did long in vain.
>   (II, iii, 10–14)

Now she would have him remain at home, again failing to support the rebel cause in which he has played a dominant role. Few lines convey such despondence as his final comment: "Fain would I go to meet the Archbishop, / But many thousand reasons hold me back" (65–66). That Earl Northumberland is captured by the sheriff of York, as Harcourt later reports (IV, iv, 97–99), is the crowning irony in the life of a rebel who, however reluctant, could not escape his role and whose ending is by no means dissimilar to that of the king whose forces are victorious.

Prince Hal, as in part 1, announces his goals and his methods to the spectators during his first appearance on stage. If his choice of friends and his casual behavior seem inappropriate for an heir apparent, he observes that the "end" must "try the man" (II, ii, 47; cf. part 1, I, ii, 195ff.).[53] A man destined for "transformation," he makes use of present company to prepare himself for his future task. As he informs Ned Poins, "in everything the purpose must weigh with the folly" (175–76; cf. part 1, II, iv, 6ff.), a point later explicitly reiterated in Westmoreland's comments to Henry IV that the "Prince but studies his companions" (IV, iv, 68). In due time ostensible reconciliation with his father does indeed occur, with Hal's reassuring Henry IV that the king but misinterprets his "present wildness," that he intends to "show th' incredulous world / [A] noble change" (IV, v, 153–54; cf. part 1, III, ii, 18ff.).[54] And just as he testifies to his prophecy in part 1 by saving his father's life at Shrewsbury and slaying the arch-rebel Hotspur, so in part 2 he publicly banishes his former companion in fun:

> I know thee not, old man, fall to thy prayers.
> . . . .
> I have long dreamt of such a kind of man,
> So surfeit-swell'd, so old, and so profane;
> But being awak'd, I do despise my dream.
> . . . .
> Presume not that I am the thing I was,
> For God doth know, so shall the world perceive,
> That I have turn'd away my former self.
>
> (V, v, 47, 49–51, 56–58)

In an open display of such a transformation, he embraces his brothers as both father and brother and proclaims the Lord Chief Justice, who earlier had imprisoned him for his behavior, an honored official in the new reign.

There is never any question that Hal is a man of necessity who perceives his early actions as a part of the design for his future; time and again the spectators are informed that any fundamental transformation in character will be far more apparent than real. In this sense the Prince, as in part 1, is a firm and symbolic figure of the self-conscious heir apparent who systematically prepares himself for effective leadership. Indeed, Shakespeare's intentions become even clearer when one considers the delineation of Hal in the earlier *Famous Victories of Henry V,* a play which the Arden editor describes as like "going through the *Henry IV–Henry V* sequence in a bad dream, so close to Shakespeare is it in fragments, so worlds removed in skill."[55] Specifically, note that Hal in the old chronicle play is a robber in fact, a crass joker about his father's illness, a schemer who enters the chamber of his ill father with dagger drawn to hasten his day of rule. A consistent figure in Shakespeare's stage world, Hal is never disrespectful of either father or crown.

Prince Hal's consistency of purpose, however, once again belies the dramatic ambivalence created by the manipulation of the spectator's angle of vision. At times his conscious sense of self-manipulation, with its inevitable moment of truth, lends him what some critics have labeled a Machiavellian touch.[56] At other moments the spectators glimpse other sides of Hal's personality: the continued pleasure he gains, for example, from his verbal sparring with Falstaff and his companionship with Poins or the affection he feels for his father and his apprehensions concerning the weight of responsibility which the crown involves. He reveals to Poins that his "heart bleeds inwardly that [his] father is so sick" (II, ii, 48), and he admits to his cronies that he feels "much to blame / So idly to profane the precious time" (iv, 361–62). In his only soliloquy he reflects at length on the "tears and heavy sorrows of the blood" provoked by his father's condition, and he muses on the "polish'd perturbation," the "golden care" which brings sleepless nights, the "imperial crown" with the burden of protecting the honor and safety of the kingdom (IV, v, 38, 22, 23, 40, 41). Absent are the introspective soliloquies in which Hal might articulate his choice among these values, moments which—as with Brutus, Hamlet, and Othello—would draw the spectators to an intensely personal relationship with the character. Even so, such glimpses of the various aspects of Hal's personality are sufficient to provide a sense of depth and human credibility without sacrificing breadth of perspective.

Falstaff is without question the most complex figure in the play.[57] At first glance he appears to have several redeeming traits. He is still able, for example, to turn a scene to jests, as in his pretending not to hear the call of the Lord Chief Justice (I, ii); or in his response to the

135

THE MATURITY OF PERSPECTIVE

same official, in the face of the hostess' suit for his arrest, that she "is a poor [mad] soul [who] . . . says up and down the town that her eldest son is like [the Lord Chief Justice]" (II, i, 104–5); or in his response to Hal when he is caught in the act of slandering the heir apparent to Nell and Doll, that he "disprais'd [Hal] before the wicked, that the wicked might not fall in love with him" (II, iv, 319–21). There are also moments when Falstaff gives superficial evidence of a degree of courage, as in his forcibly driving Pistol from the tavern in order to calm the hostess (II, iv, 203) or his firm stand (albeit merely vocal) in arresting Sir John Coleville. Perhaps most telling is the fact that he seems to provoke not only other people's wit but their affection as well; the hostess, for example, is all too easily reconciled (II, i, 158–60), and Doll's interest surpasses that of the professional prostitute (II, iv, 278–80, 389–91). Justice Shallow recalls with unmitigated fondness his past escapades with the fat knight.

These touches, however, while suggesting an ambivalence effective for the drama, do not alter the fundamental nature of the character. His irresponsible promise to "double charge" Shallow "with dignities" and to provide him with his choice of offices in the land (V, iii, 122ff.) is not a sudden degeneration of character. Such lines are merely the culmination and the clearest statement of Falstaff's basic motivations throughout the drama (and throughout part 1 as well): "Be what thou wilt, I am fortune's steward. . . . Let us take any man's horses, the laws of England are at my commandment. Blessed are they that have been my friends, and woe to my Lord Chief Justice!" (130–31, 135–38). Falstaff, in brief, is a totally self-centered individual whose fall from Hal's favor is a fact of both political and moral necessity hidden to no one since the opening scenes. He is a parasite whose word is without value. Both the tailor in I, ii, and hostess in II, i, question his credit; indeed Mistress Quickly claims that, were Falstaff an honest man, he would owe her both purse and person. Her subsequent willingness to delay payment is juxtaposed with his seamy private command to Bardolph to "hook on, hook on" (II, i, 162). Falstaff is, moreover, a cheat with an itchy palm, willing for a price to release the ablest villagers from military impressment (III, ii, 252–53, 259–62). In part 1 at least he took his soldiers to Shrewsbury; in part 2, as James

Black has noted, "his fraudulent recruiting has been refined to where he simply fills the muster books with names without bothering to produce the men themselves."[58] He is a skilled liar; his epistle to Hal in II, ii, warns against Ned Poins's intentions to wed the heir apparent to "his sister Nell" (129), and in II, iv, he berates the prince as a shallow fellow who would have made a good pantry worker, a prankster with "a weak mind and an able body" (251–52). He is a glutton (34ff.), a coward whose "tardy tricks" keep him from the heat of battle (IV, iii, 28), an abuser of friends ready to fleece a senile companion: "I have him already temp'ring between my fingers and my thumb, and shortly will I seal with him" (IV, iii, 130–32; see also III, ii, 328–30; V, i, 78–81). Falstaff runs the full gamut of vices. As the Lord Chief Justice observes, this "whoreson candle-mine" lives "in great infamy" (II, iv, 300; I, ii, 136–37); he has "misled the youthful prince," following him "up and down, like his ill angel" (144, 163–64). By far the most convincing evidence comes through the soliloquy, here used not to express the anguished introspection arising from moments of decision but rather to proclaim the true nature of the man. In his first stage appearance, Falstaff admits in an aside that it is impossible to separate age and covetousness, and in a soliloquy a few lines later he proclaims that he can and will make use of anything, even a war, for his own advantage (I, ii, 228–30; 247–48). Later he uses the private comment on two occasions to inform the spectators that he sees "the bottom of Justice Shallow" and will shortly return to "make him a philosopher's two stones" for self-benefit (III, ii, 302, 329–30; V, i, 62–85).

Falstaff then is of a piece throughout *2 Henry IV,* but the spectators observe him, like the other principals, from a variety of angles which lend ambivalence to the characterization. Moreover, Shakespeare in the course of the two plays arranges the scenes in such a way as to reveal progressively the dissipation concealed for a time by his high degree of wit. While there is no alteration in Falstaff himself, the manipulation of the spectator's vision does produce an increasing realization of Falstaff's ability through the quick retort to make the worse appear the better. In a word, he is simply less funny in *2 Henry IV* than in the earlier play. In wit combat with the Lord Chief Justice, the very symbol of law and morality in the land, rather than with a young prince of antic disposition, Falstaff is less persuasive and his humor less redeeming; as the possibility draws closer of his being a direct influence on the king himself, he seems increasingly to be involved in dialogue concerning matters which directly would affect the order and security of the kingdom. Moreover Falstaff in part 2 is more openly abusive. The literal depiction of his misuse of the king's funds provokes a more sharply critical response than does the report of such action in part 1. And his flagrant manipulation of both Shallow and Mistress Quickly creates an image which one can hardly erase with laughter.

If Shakespeare through an increasingly consistent focus on the sordid qualities consciously prepares the spectators for Falstaff's downfall, he also seems intent upon maintaining the vivacious quality of the low-life scenes which contribute significantly to the broad focus of the play. The array of husbandmen and craftsmen who stand for impressment creates a humorous glimpse of the war's effect upon the common citizens. More overtly comic are the two elderly country justices, the bumbling sergeants Fang and Snare, and the blustering Pistol, whose bombast can reduce any scene to laughter. Doll Tearsheet is an important addition to the London scene, and a major transformation has occurred in the voluble hostess of the tavern. "History," as Mark Van Doren has observed, "is enlarged to make room for taverns and trollops and potations of sack, and the heroic drama is modified by gigantic mockery, by the roared voice of truth" (p. 97). If one must be duly cautioned about leaping to "the truth" at any single point, it does seem possible, especially in the growth of the hostess in importance, to observe a striking illustration of Shakespeare's solution to the problem of maintaining the vitality of his comic crew even while Falstaff must be darkened and ultimately banished.

The barest of sketches can reveal the extent of expansion in the characterization of the hostess. She appears in *1 Henry IV* simply as the "hostess" of the tavern in Eastcheap. In III, iii, there are numerous references to her honest husband and the respectability of their inn. In *2 Henry IV,* now "Mistress Quickly" (II, i, 45), she claims to be a "poor widow of Eastcheap" (70) and asserts that Falstaff, whom she has known for twenty-nine years, has promised to marry her. Here her circle of acquaintances has widened to include the prostitute Doll Tearsheet, and together they entertain Falstaff before he sets out for Gloucestershire. In V, iv, she is carried off to prison with Doll, vaguely on the charge that the brothels are being torn down with the advent of the reign of the new Henry, specifically on the charge that "the man is dead that you and Pistol beat amongst you" (16–17). In *Henry V* "Nell" Quickly will be married to Pistol, although Nym was troth-plight to her, a union in itself curious since Dame Quickly in *2 Henry IV* cannot abide the sight of Pistol and implores Falstaff to drive him from her inn.

Such development is the more striking when one considers that the hostess, sketchily drafted in *1 Henry IV* as a comic character in the Falstaff circle, is essentially a composite portrait created from suggestions in *The Famous Victories of Henry V*. Three women in the comic scenes (two by description, one by appearance) must have furnished Shakespeare's inspiration for the garrulous proprietress. First to mind when Hal and Ned are considering where they will celebrate following their successful robbery of the king's receivers is the ale house and "our old hostes at Feversham" (lines 112–13), but Henry suggests the tavern in Eastcheap, where there is "a pretie wench that can talke well" (120).[59] Later the shrewish wife of John Cobler engages in a wit combat with Dericke, a fat rover who parasitically attaches himself to Cobler's household. Dericke, in many ways similar to Falstaff,[60] brands her "a stinking whore" (814), "a verie knave" (831) for serving him a dish of roots, though she implies he has offered no payment to merit being otherwise served. When called with Cobler to the wars against France, Dericke struts out with her potlid for a shield, but she over-takes him and, in the best of the tradition of dramatic termagants, raps him about the pate. Flustered, the braggadocio cries, "And I had my dagger here I wold worie you al to peeces, that I would!" (1240–41).[61] With his threats to "clap the law on [her] backe" (1246), Dericke reminds one of the hostess in her vain attempts in *Henry IV* to have the law on Falstaff for refusal to pay his tavern reckonings.

There is then no single character from the old play which provides a clear prototype for Nell, but admitting the critics' case that Shakespeare is indebted in matters of comic incident and specific characteristics of Falstaff, Ned Poins, and Hal, one must conclude the composite female personality which emerges to be more than sheer coincidence.[62] Shakespeare draws freely for Dame Quickly, the "old hostes," not at Feversham but at "the olde taverne in Eastcheape," certainly a "wench that can talke well." And along with her loquacity there is a constant bantering and contentiousness with Falstaff, who like Dericke plays the parasite and makes no proffer of payment for services rendered.

In *1 Henry IV* the hostess's role is primarily to illumine certain humorous aspects of Falstaff. Before she appears, Hal tells us that she is "a sweet wench of the tavern" at which he has often paid Falstaff's reckonings (I, ii, 45ff.). As the robbery and counterrobbery at Gad's Hill are planned, Falstaff, Hal, and Poins, just as in *The Famous Victories,* plan to reconvene at the Eastcheap tavern. The hostess actually appears in only two scenes. In II, iv, she twice announces the arrival at the inn of persons from the serious world of history outside: first of Sir John Bracy with news of the rebellion against Henry IV, and later of the sheriff and the watch who are come "to search the house" (490) concerning the Gad's Hill robbery. Evidently a fluttering and excitable soul (hence the pertinence of Falstaff's later calling her "Dame Partlet, the hen," III, iii, 52), she rushes in, distractedly wailing "O, Jesu, my Lord, my Lord!" (II, iv, 486). Part of the comic effect is gained by the agitated flurry and the way in which she breaks in upon moments of high comedy. Throughout the scene in which Hal and Falstaff parodically exchange the role of father and prodigal son, she augments Falstaff's wit by her actions more than by her conversation. As Falstaff assumes the chair ("my state," 378) and speaks with passion "in King Cambyses' vein" (387), the hostess is unable to restrain her laughter and tears of merriment: "O Jesu, this is excellent sport, i' faith! . . . O, the father, how he holds his countenance! . . . O Jesu, he doth it as like one of these harlotry players as ever I see!" (390, 392, 395–96). Falstaff, equal to the occasion, incorporates her tears into his parody of Henry IV's parental grief by elevating her to the queenship: "Weep not, sweet queen, for trickling tears are vain. . . . / For God's sake, lords, convey my [tristful] queen, / For tears do stop the floodgates of her eyes" (391ff.). As the only character in the tavern crowd to interrupt the lengthy dialogue between Falstaff and Hal, her role is a small one, but the scene on the boards is definitely funnier for her presence.

The manner in which she plays the straight man to Falstaff is more obvious in III, iii, where, incidentally, Hal first calls her Mistress Quickly and twice alludes to her husband. On numerous occasions she furnishes a line which triggers Falstaff's witty retort. For example, called to account for his tavern reckonings, Falstaff claims his pockets have been picked, a charge to which the hostess reacts with indignation. "Why, Sir John, what do you think, Sir John? Do you think I keep thieves in my house? I have search'd, I have inquir'd, so has my husband. . . . The [tithe] of a hair was never lost in my house before" (54–56, 57–58). Falstaff's ready wit immediately turns upon the last line: "ye lie, hostess, Bardolph was shav'd, and lost many a hair" (59–60). To her later comment that, unless she has reported correctly his slanderous remarks concerning the prince, "there's neither faith, truth, nor womanhood in me" (110–11), Falstaff retorts: "There's no more faith in thee than in a stew'd prune, nor no more truth in thee than in a drawn fox, and for womanhood, Maid Marian may be the deputy's wife of the ward to thee" (112–15). Such parrying, with Mistress Quickly inevitably on the short end, is perhaps most effectively illustrated in Falstaff's charge that she is an otter—neither fish nor flesh—and that a man knows not where to have her. Her feeble reply that indeed "thou or any man knows where to have me" (129–30) only adds to the revelry.

In *1 Henry IV* then Mistress Quickly is little more than the amorphous sketch suggested in *The Famous Victories*. As either the butt or the recounter of his badgering, she draws her vitality from Falstaff, who is at the height of his comic fortunes. As Falstaff's fortunes decline in part 2, however, his contentious squabbling with Hostess Quickly most clearly reflects the basic change in the nature of the comic matter. Whereas in *1 Henry IV* Falstaff is, practical jokes to the contrary, a harmonious part of the bawdy comic crew which is pitted against the respectable characters, here Falstaff clearly reveals the potential threat to Hal and to the crown through his willingness to manipulate friend and cohort to his own avaricious schemes. While

Falstaff's gaiety wanes, that of Mistress Quickly increases. To be sure, she is still humorous in relation to Sir John, as the garrulous gossip and the butt of his clever and evasive retorts. But more important, she is independently comic—a dizzard of high merriment apart from Falstaff. Her growth in comic importance is effected through her new status as a widow with aspirations both for Falstaff and social prestige and through her newfound linguistic dexterity as a bungler of language who commits malapropisms and doubles entendres with equal aplomb.

The first mention of Mistress Quickly in part 2 signals the important comic alteration in her relationship with Falstaff. As Falstaff prepares to depart for the wars to fight under Prince John, he commands his page to bear a letter to the hostess, here fondly referred to as Ursula (little she-bear), "whom I have weekly sworn to marry since I perceiv'd the first white hair of my chin" (I, ii, 240–42). Later, stressing that she is "a poor widow of Eastcheap" arresting Falstaff not for "sum" ("some") but for "all," she avers that her due is, "if thou wert an honest man, thyself and the money too" (II, i, 70, 72, 73, 85–86). With a wonderful flow of chatter which gushes out in a continuous and illogical torrent, she vacillates between infatuation and exasperation with the "huge bombard of sack" who continually abuses her.

> Thou didst swear to me upon a parcel-gilt goblet, sitting in my Dolphin chamber, at the round table by a sea-coal fire, upon Wednesday in Wheeson week, when the Prince broke thy head for liking his father to a singing-man of Windsor, thou didst swear to make me then, as I was washing thy wound, to marry me and make me my lady thy wife. Canst thou deny it? Did not goodwife Keech, the butcher's wife, come in then and call me gossip Quickly? coming in to borrow a mess of vinegar, telling us she had a good dish of prawns, whereby thou didst desire to eat some, whereby I told thee they were ill for a green wound? And didst thou not, when she was gone down stairs, desire me to be no more so familiarity with such poor people, saying that ere long they should call me madam? (86–101)

Indeed her social sights are set high—the wife of a knight, the title of a madam—though obviously the social gain to be realized as the wife of Sir John is humorously suspect. Nonetheless, she is vociferous in her denunciation of the swaggering Pistol, who seeks entrance at her inn: "I must live among my neighbors; I'll no swaggerers, I am in good name and fame with the very best. . . . I'll foreswear keeping house afore I'll be in these tirrits and frights" (II, iv, 74–76, 204–5). Yet at the very moment she defends her decency and integrity so ada-mantly, she is playing the common procuress in encouraging, arrang-ing, and overseeing the assignation in her tavern between Falstaff and Doll Tearsheet. And her own virtue is far from spotless; in another scene the Lord Chief Justice berates Falstaff because he has "practic'd upon the easy-yielding spirit of this woman, and made her serve your uses both in purse and in person" (II, i, 114–16). While there is nothing funny in the desire for a good name and a social position per se, the comic gap between appearance and reality—culpable venality and hypocritical pretension—has always been potential material for comedy.

Mistress Quickly's numerous doubles entendres effectively illustrate this comic gap. When Snare warns Fang to beware of Falstaff's stab, the hostess retorts: "Alas the day, take heed of him! He stabb'd me in mine own house, most beastly, in good faith. 'A cares not what mis-chief he does, if his weapon be out. He will foin like any devil, he will spare neither man, woman, nor child" (II, i, 13–17). In describing the extent of Falstaff's indebtedness to her, she blurts: "A hundred mark is a long one for a poor lone woman to bear, and I have borne, and borne, and borne, and have been fubb'd off, and fubb'd off, and fubb'd off, from this day to that day, that it is a shame to be thought on. There is no honesty in such dealing, unless a woman should be made an ass and a beast, to bear every knave's wrong" (32–38). She swears, un-less Falstaff pay her, to "ride thee a'nights like the mare" (76–77), to which Falstaff's reply determines the context: "I think I am as like to ride the mare, if I have any vantage of ground to get up" (78–79). In a later scene, to Falstaff's charge that Pistol discharge himself, Mis-tress Quickly naively exclaims: "No, good Captain Pistol, not here, sweet captain" (II, iv, 138–39). Nor has the laughter subsided before she addresses Pistol as "Good Captain Peesel" ("pizzle") and fears for Falstaff that he is "hurt i' th' groin. Methought a' made a shrewd thrust at your belly" (161, 210–11).

143

Undoubtedly her leading comic quality is her linguistic ineptness resulting in flagrant and continual malapropisms, several of which occur in passages cited above (*familiarity—familiar, debuty—deputy, tirrists—terrors, Peesel—Pistol*). No one, not even Dogberry and Verges, is in this respect the equal of Mistress Quickly. There occur the following in II, i: *infinitive—infinite; continuantly—continuously; indited—invited; Lubber's Head—Leopard's Head; Lumbert—Lombard; exion—action; honeysuckle—homicidal; honeyseed—homicide; man-queller—man killer*. And there are others in II, iv: *temperality—temper; pulsidge—pulse; calm—qualm; confirmities—infirmities; beseek—beseech; aggravate—moderate*. While a bare listing can do little to suggest the humor of such blunders in context, it at least serves to illustrate a significant comic development in the hostess of *2 Henry IV*.

In the final act Mistress Quickly, with Doll, is dragged off to jail as an accomplice of Pistol in a case of manslaughter. At this point Shakespeare meaningfully relates Nell's action to the serious matter; for the laws of England which Falstaff thought to be at his command are seen in active operation against his old associates. His later boast, "I will deliver her" (V, v, 39), immediately precedes his own arrest and dispatch to prison. Surely there is humor in Nell's reliance on Falstaff for rescue and Doll's unsuccessful attempts to escape imprisonment by claiming pregnancy with the help of "a dozen of cushions" (V, iv, 14–15). But there is thematic aptness in the hostess's flustered quip, "O God, that right should thus overcome might" (24–25).

Nell, then, along with such figures as Shallow and Pistol, keeps the Falstaffian world alive with humor even as the "cause that is wit in other men" (I, ii, 10) arrives at the nadir of his fortunes. That his fall is not without sympathy is testimony to Shakespeare's structural skill in manipulating the spectator's view of a totally decadent individual to suggest a credible ambivalence. Similarly provocative characterizations of Hal, Henry IV, and Northumberland are set against a sizeable number of stylized figures reflecting, on the one hand, a boisterous and frequently comic low-life and, on the other, the cancer of rebellion among the lords which continues to plague the Lancastrian ruler. The result is a complexity of perspective which combines a compelling interest in character with a focus as broad as the kingdom itself.

In summary, Shakespeare's historical perspective reaches a new level of maturation in the two Henry IV plays, a level which would seem flatly to refute the recent assertion by James Calderwood that the spectator "cannot simultaneously be involved in the immediate experience of the play and yet be detached from it." [63] On the one hand, no longer as in the Henry VI plays is character abstractly fitted to idea. For the most part flat and one-dimensional, the characters of those earlier stage worlds merely serve the purposes of the narrative. Consequently the plot builds upon a series of scenes in which stylized character types are set in confrontation, and the perspective takes in the full range of action rather than focusing on the complexity of a single individual. On the other hand, Shakespeare—for the purposes of history at least— seems almost consciously to depart from the technique which, in his contemporary romantic comedies, directs attention to characters who grow in the knowledge of love and, in his contemporary tragedies, draws the spectators to the private level of the protagonist through a concentration of soliloquies and asides. Whatever the nature of the external action in the tragic works, for example, and of the characters who move in opposition to the protagonist, the spectators' consuming interest is in the developing central figure whose critical moments they share. Perforce the perspective is both narrow and intense; the tragic impact arises from the spectators' personal identification with the protagonist and the quality of the insights gleaned from the suffering his error has provoked. The perspectives of both *Richard III* and *Richard II,* although remarkably different in quality, share this intensity of focus. *Richard III* celebrates his villainy with the spectators through a continuing run of soliloquies and asides forming a private level of perception. In *Richard II,* instead of the brittle relationship built on shared confidences about the gullibility of others, the perspective assumes a more emotionally empathetic quality as, in the final acts of the play, emphasis is more sharply upon the suffering of the man than the abuses of his royal office.

In *1, 2 Henry IV* Shakespeare has developed a middle ground between these two polarities of dramatic technique. Several principal characters, each of whom reflects a significant aspect of the national culture, command relatively equal attention, thus projecting the focus beyond a single individual. These characters, by sharing private thoughts or critical moments with the spectators, exhibit an ambivalent human dimension which moves beyond the comprehension of the other characters on stage; the spectators alone realize the full dimensions of the several major figures and thus possess the perspective for responding to the human consequences of the historical events of the narrative. While ambivalent, however, these characters are essentially fixed and consequently serve the purpose of a broader design reflecting divergent philosophies of life and attitudes toward the kingship. Ultimately this design reveals an England emerging precariously from medieval feudalism, characterized in turn by guilt, decadence, fanatical heroism, and sagacious practicality. Neither individual tragedies with historic settings nor plays which, for want of sufficient characterization, fail to engage the spectators dramatically, *1, 2 Henry IV* present a broad scene in which interaction becomes history unfolding the narrative of a nation struggling for unity at the expense of individual ambition in the lords, of unchecked hedonistic abandon among the common citizens, and of the loss of integrity in the royal household.

Henry V, never a favorite among Shakespeare's plays, strikes most critics and theatergoers as distinctly inferior to the Henry IV plays. Certainly there have been periods of approval during crests of intense nationalism. And on occasion there have been positive appraisals of the pageantry and of the epic qualities of the piece.[64] Critics have even appreciatively, if diversely, acknowledged the design of the title figure: the ideal King of England, on the one hand, the steely and calculating Machiavellian, the ultimate Lancastrian, on the other.[65] Productions generally illustrate this same kind of reductionism. The Olivier film version in 1944 made savage cuts in the text, removing virtually every doubt from the hero's mind in order to create a splendidly patriotic pageant; the Old Vic production in 1951, directed by Glen B. Shaw, likewise eliminated all negative aspects of Henry's character and magnified the unattractiveness of his opponents. On the other hand, the Royal Shakespeare Company's antiwar production in 1964, like that of Michael Kahn for the American Shakespeare Theater in 1969, deemphasized the traditional heroics. "The martial events leading up to and including the battle of Agincourt [were] presented as bloody, clobbering and unpleasant";[66] the ragged army and desperately fatigued leader epitomized not the heroics but the horrors of war.

Whatever the case, critics and directors alike more often than not have spoken without the enthusiasm which results when drama commands genuine emotional involvement, when the fortunes and misfortunes of the characters of the stage world become the consuming interest as a paradigm of human experience. Admittedly a knowledgeable spectator can take pleasure in recognizing the structural features which contribute to the total design of a play and the manner in which each scene functions within the general theme, just as some individuals can perceptively respond to the harmonic design and the structural components of a sonata or a symphony. So also one can be cognizant of the technical virtuosity of performance either of an actor's role or a musical composition. In the final analysis, though, art involves more than a cerebral response; indeed drama encompasses not merely an emotional response but an emotional interaction—hence the actor's passion for a live audience. The spectator is never oblivious of the mimetic abstraction of the stage, to be sure, but in the most powerful drama he also becomes an emotional part of the human conflict unfolding before him. For many, *Henry V* simply fails to achieve this quality of simultaneous engagement and detachment.

Other voices are beginning to be heard, however. Terry Hands's goal in his 1975 Stratford production was to stress from the opening moments the duality and tension in a play that "runs hot and cold. . . . Its ambiguity is constant." And Norman Rabkin quite recently has argued that it is "too good a play for criticism to go on calling it a failure"; like Shakespeare's great tragedies it requires "that we hold in balance incompatible and radically opposed views each of which seems exclusively true."[67] At the very least one must admit that the relative unpopularity of *Henry V* is highly ironic since in many ways

147

it represents the culmination of Shakespeare's efforts in the English history play.[68] Demonstrably in *1, 2 Henry IV* a combination of structural devices establishes a perspective of adequately broad scope for the historical theme which yet features a sufficiently detailed quality of characterization to provoke and sustain at least limited emotional involvement. Similar devices are utilized in *Henry V*. Shakespeare develops a stylized and highly patriotic theme throughout the three movements of the plot: the preparation for war, the combat itself, and the concluding of the peace. With the multiple plots, the diverse settings, the use of the chorus as a persistent pointing device, and the essentially fixed characterization, he establishes and maintains a broad perspective by blocking a close emotional rapport between the spectators and any individual character. At the same time, he labors carefully to make Henry a dramatically compelling figure. This quality he accomplishes through a brief but significantly placed soliloquy, through a constant focus upon Henry resulting from the diverse manners in which the surrounding characters view him, and through the consistent interweaving of thematically related episodes which suspend the spectators between the level of allegorical abstraction on the one hand and of absorption in character analysis on the other.

Breadth of perspective is once more achieved through the interweaving of several significant plot strands, in this instance drawn both from opposing nations and from different sociopolitical English strata. The struggle between England and France is depicted alternately from the view of English theologians, English aristocracy, King Henry, citizens of Eastcheap, English common soldiers, French aristocracy, and Princess Katherine of France. Five separate plot lines are involved. Henry V's pursuit of the war—both the preparation in England and the execution on the French battlefields—comprises approximately 40 percent of the total lines (1,264 of 3,146); the action of his French counterpart and the scene of their capitulation account for 21 percent (656);[69] the dialogue of Nell Quickly and her cohorts makes up 6 percent (193); the scenes with Katherine, 8 percent (256). The fifth plot strand, 26 percent of the total lines (819), is a virtual microcosm of the nation—the English Gower, Welsh Fluellen, Irish MacMorris, and Scots Jamy; in these figures Shakespeare conspicuously reflects the diverse national components (the busied giddy minds) united against the common foe. Enhancing the broad angle of vision resulting from these multiple plot strands, no fewer than forty-two characters have speaking parts, a total in Shakespeare's canon second only to that of *2 Henry IV*. And the location of the action shifts abruptly from England to France. The act division established in the Folio (no scenes are marked) involves an English setting in act 1—Henry's palace, the London streets, and Southampton—and a French setting for the remainder of the play—King Charles' palace, Harfleur, Rouen, Picardy, and Agincourt.[70] The eight settings (actually a greater number if one considers the multiple locations within the two palaces and the opposing camps at Agincourt) create an almost kaleidoscopic effect, even for the eclectic Elizabethan stage.

The chorus, another feature not utilized extensively in Shakespeare's previous histories, establishes a tone of unmitigated patriotism, which in turn enhances the stylization of the play.[71] The stage will be a kingdom, the actors princes and monarchs. "Warlike Harry [will] / Assume the port of Mars" (prologue, 5–6); he is the "mirror of all Christian kings" (II, 6) who will lead the honor-seeking and expectant "youth of England" (1) against the trembling French who seek to avoid war through "pale policy" (14): "O England! model to thy inward greatness, / Like little body with a mighty heart" (16–17). We are told in act 3 of England's brave and majestical fleet (5, 16) filled with "cull'd and choice-drawn cavaliers" (24) who travel toward Harfleur and destiny. And in act 4 the chorus describes the "hum" of the two camps the evening before battle, the "confident and overlusty French" (18) and the "poor condemned English" (22) cheered by "a little touch of Harry in the night" (47):

> And so our scene must to the battle fly;
> Where—O for pity!—We shall much disgrace,
> With four or five most vile and ragged foils
> (Right ill disposed, in brawl ridiculous)
> The name of Agincourt.   (48–52)

In the final act King Henry, "free from vainness and self-glorious pride" (20), returns to London and is welcomed by his subjects as a conquering hero, after which he returns to France to conclude negotiations for a treaty with the French king.[72] The epilogue strikes the patriotic chord once more, referring to Agincourt as an event in which "most greatly lived / This star of England" (5–6). Indeed the lone qualifying moment to the consistently hyperbolic and monolithic tone established by the choric figure is the closing reference to the infant Henry VI and to those around him lusting for power who will subsequently lose France and make England bleed (12).

Still another structural feature designed to maintain the broad historical scene, through attention to multiple character interaction rather than individual character analysis, is the virtual absence of soliloquies and asides. While, with the exception of Richard III, no single individual in Shakespeare's previous history plays engages in such private moments to a major extent, the soliloquy does function significantly in those earlier stage worlds. Among the three Henry VI plays and the two Henry IV plays, for example, soliloquies and asides comprise more than 5 percent of the total lines in every instance; the percentage is over 6.5 percent in three and as high as 8.5 percent in one. In signal contrast *Henry V* features no asides and only six soliloquies for 2.5 percent. Only three of twenty-three scenes (as marked in modern editions) are involved, and Henry's soliloquies occur in a single scene preceding Agincourt. While that scene is critically important, the fact is that Henry is essentially an external characterization. The spectators are not for the most part permitted to share either his private responses or those of the surrounding figures to the decisions (moral and otherwise) which dictate the actions of the play; and considering the relatively extensive use of soliloquies in the preceding stage worlds, one must logically infer that the move is a deliberate one on Shakespeare's part.

The spectators, more specifically, are not permitted a glimpse of Henry's private reaction to the irony of the Church's offer, toward the wars in France, of "a greater sum / Than ever at one time the clergy yet / Did to his predecessors part withal" (I, i, 79–81) at the same time a bill is under consideration which would strip the Church of "the better half of our possession" (8). Henry could hardly be blind to the ploy, and the perceptive spectators must inevitably wonder whose giddy mind is being busied with foreign quarrels. In any case the resulting ambiguity is complex; Henry is either almost incredibly naive, or he is caught up in the emotional frenzy of national patriotism, or he is the master calculator able to conceal his own devious thirst for expansion and martial glory in the seeming tolerance of the vested interests of those around him. Similarly, the spectators do not share Henry's private thoughts concerning the Dauphin's presentation of tennis balls, a gift which brings to mind Hal's wilder days. Likewise they see only the furious courage of the King at Harfleur and only his official proclamation of victory following the battle at Agincourt. When Henry in Picardy hears the report that "one Bardolph, if your majesty know the man" (III, vi, 101–2), is likely to be executed for plundering a church, he is permitted not the least semblance of recognition of their former friendly acquaintance in the peremptory retort: "We would have all such offenders so cut off" (107–8). Least of all does the audience comprehend Henry's true feelings for Katherine of France. The offer of the princess is rejected prior to the siege of Harfleur (chorus, III, 30–32), yet in act 5 he argues that he loves her cruelly (ii, 202–3). As in act 1 there is never a private word to guide us between the two extremes of the spectrum. While Henry, then, delivers fully 31 percent of the lines in the play (1,054), over 750 more than those of the next highest figure (Fluellen, 298), he speaks virtually without soliloquy. With the exception of an eleven-line passage by the boy who guards the luggage at the English camp (IV, iv, 67–77) and a ten-line passage by Pistol (V, i, 80–89), no other character in the play addresses the spectators privately. Neither of these moments, moreover, is of psychological significance: in the one the boy merely pronounces Pistol a greater coward than Bardolph and Nym, both of whom have been hanged for pillaging, and in the other Pistol admits that "Honor is cudgell'd" from his limbs and that upon his return to England he will turn bawd and cutpurse.

Henry V utilizes the soliloquy and the aside to a smaller degree than any other work in Shakespeare's canon; in many respects a remarkably public play, it focuses upon the numerous interactions and confrontations of characters rather than the subtle complexities of an individual figure. With Henry appearing in such a predominant number of scenes

the structure is somewhat akin to that of *Richard III* without the soliloquies. Rather than a persistent juxtaposition of the King's private
and public face, the spectators observe only the King's public actions
in a stage world crowded with virtual supernumeraries—thirty-three
characters who appear in three scenes or fewer (nineteen in a single
scene). Certainly not surprisingly the characterization is static. Henry
may face progressively more difficult decisions in the kingship, but he
does not develop in the course of the play; whatever his unrevealed
motivations he is from first to last the firm but just English monarch
for whom the good of the nation is inseparable from his personal fortunes.[73] The Henry who seeks a satisfactory public rationalization for
moving against the French in act 1 is the same Henry who carefully
negotiates the political-romantic arrangement with Katherine in act 5.
The retributively destructive anger which flashes at the arrival of the
Dauphin's gift of tennis balls recurs when the French attack the English camp and murder the young boys who guard it. And the same
mercy exercised for the common English soldier at Southampton is
visited upon the French at Harfleur, just as the military discipline
which leads him unhesitatingly to order the execution of the English
traitors at Southampton is evidenced again in his firm leadership at
Agincourt. The chronology of the events in the play obviously is vital
to the historical narrative, but so monolithic is Henry's character that
the sequence of his appearances is of no significance whatever. The
most important of the secondary figures, though functioning at times
to undercut the dominant pattern of Henry's heroic posture, are themselves no less uniform in quality: for example, the arrogant and
somewhat dimwitted Dauphin, who at the very least is furiously nationalistic; the rather pallid and acquiescent Katherine, whose primary
dramatic value is her difficulty in pronouncing the King's English; the
English traitors who, properly chastened, praise the justice of their
fate; the four Englishmen who reflect the various nationalities yoked
in the struggle with a common enemy; the incorrigible Pistol whose
expediential courage keeps him from the French sword if not from
Fluellen's leek and whose return to England bodes no promise of a
fortune clear of the law.[74]

The broad historical perspective of *Henry V,* in summary, is a direct consequence of Shakespeare's methodic combination of structural devices developed in his previous plays—the multiple plot lines, the diverse settings, the static characterizations—with structural features unique to this stage world—the chorus as a pointing voice which unilaterally directs attention to the theme of national patriotism and the virtual absence of internalization in either the central or the surrounding figures. With such principles so firmly established, it is perhaps understandable that more than one critic has considered the drama so rigidly externalized as to preclude profound dramatic conflict. The genuine complexity of the perspective, however, results from the fact that another structural pattern works in subtle opposition to the first and ultimately tends to render such a monolithic view untenable. For one thing, the lone scene in which Henry speaks in soliloquies prior to the Battle of Agincourt reveals a genuine moral sensitivity not otherwise visible in the man. Intimating what Peter Phialas describes as a tragic element in his character, the soliloquy suggests the "loneliness of supreme office."[75] His private remarks may have no direct bearing upon his decisions or his military actions; one could hardly imagine, for example, Henry's refusing to lead his troops into battle even if he were not convinced of the King's innocence concerning their deaths. The soliloquies, moreover, admittedly lead to no moral resolution on Henry's part; if he is convinced that "great greatness" (IV, i, 251) is sick and that "idol Ceremony" (240) alone sets the ruler apart from the wretched slave, he later gives no hint of it; in fact his enigmatic wooing of Katherine gives every indication of his determination to expand and strengthen his royal role. Even so, Henry on that one occasion privately voices the same moral questions which the perceptive spectators tend to raise, and although his actions may not be dictated by such contemplation, the soliloquies (IV, i, 34; 83–84; 230–84; 289–305) do lend a human credibility to the figure. He questions, for example, whether the King's position, his "proud dream" (257), is worth the price of his inability to cloak himself in anonymity and shed the responsibilities of rule:

> Art thou ought else but place, degree, and form,
> Creating awe and fear in other men?
> Wherein thou art less happy, being fear'd,

153

Than they in fearing.
What drink'st thou oft, in stead of homage sweet,
But poison'd flattery?   (246–51)

Moments later he seeks God's blessings upon himself and his troops, "imploring pardon" (305) for the guilt of his father's usurpation with a specific reference to the "contrite tears" (296), the gifts to the poor and lame, and the construction of new chantries where masses are sung daily for Richard's soul.

These insights through soliloquy comprise only a brief moment, of course, and they occur relatively late in the play. Nonetheless they complement a pattern of divergent angles of vision provided by those who surround Henry. While it is not unusual for minor characters to express varying attitudes toward the central figure, the remarkable persistency of focus in this play results in a complexity of character which belies the monolithic quality of Henry's stage presence. In the opening scene, for instance, the Archbishop of Canterbury and the Bishop of Ely discuss the King's wild days of past years, the "courses of his youth" which, like "th' offending Adam," promised not his present state of "grace and fair regard" (I, i, 24, 29, 22):

> His addiction was to courses vain,
> His companies unletter'd, rude, and shallow,
> His hours fill'd up with riots, banquets, sports;
> And never noted in him any study,
> And retirement, any sequestration
> From open haunts and popularity.   (54–59)

The Prince, Bishop Ely observes, no doubt "obscur'd his contemplation / Under the veil of wildness" (63–64). The Dauphin's gift of tennis balls, "meeter for [Henry's] spirit" than warfare (ii, 254), obviously reinforces the point: "there's naught in France / That can be with a nimble galliard won; / You cannot revel into dukedoms there" (251–53). While the account of Hal's apparently untutored days forms an important motif in *1, 2 Henry IV,* King Henry V is an altogether more decorous figure; and this angle of vision provides an imaginative dimension of personality not literally visible to the spectators.

A similarly provocative perception is provided by Henry's erstwhile Eastcheap companions in act 2. With word that Falstaff is grievously ill and Nell Quickly's comment that the "King has kill'd his heart" (i, 88), the spectators confront the full range of ambivalent emotions concomitant to Hal's banishment of his former companion in fun in the preceding play.[76] According to Nym, the King "hath run bad humors on the knight; that's the even of it. . . . The King is a good king, but it must be as it may; he passes some humors and careers" (121–22, 125–26). Falstaff's heart, adds Pistol, is "fracted and corroborate" (124). The description of his death two scenes later makes no direct reference to the King, but the intimation of blame still rings in the spectators' ears. And Fluellen, in act 4, equates Henry's action with a telling classical analogy: "As Alexander kill'd his friend Clytus, being in his ales and his cups, so also Harry Monmouth, being in his right wits and his good judgments, turn'd away the fat knight with the great belly doublet" (vii, 44–48); the extreme remorse experienced by Alexander notably has no visible parallel in Henry.[77]

Yet another multifaceted view of the King is provided by the participants in the opposing armies. At one point the Dauphin's assumption that England is "idly king'd," her scepter "fantastically borne, / By a vain, giddy, shallow, humorous youth" (II, iv, 26, 27–28), is countered by the Constable's opinion that Henry is "modest in exception" and "terrible in constant resolution" (34, 35); "his vanities forespent / Were but the outside of the Roman Brutus, / Covering discretion with a coat of folly" (36–38). Similarly Charles VI reminds his son that Henry is a "stem / Of that victorious stock" of Edward, the Black Prince, who moved so powerfully against the nation (62–63). Later, as the Battle of Agincourt draws near, the French mock the English leader and imagine the fear which grips his heart; "Poor Harry" no doubt would hold back the fateful dawn rather than issue into battle both outmanned and outwitted: "What a wretched and peevish fellow is this King of England, to mope with his fat-brain'd followers so far out of his knowledge!" (vii, 132–34). Disguised as Harry le Roy, Henry receives an equally wide variety of opinions from his own troops. Pistol may describe him as "most valiant" with "a heart of gold" (IV, i, 46, 44), but Bates believes that he secretly fears the approaching combat (113–15). And Williams rather testily adds that, however much the King may deny it, Henry is not above the coward's way out; "when our throats are cut, he may be ransom'd, and we ne'er the wiser" (193–94).

Throughout the play, in brief, Shakespeare provides added dimensions to the King's characterization through the words of surrounding characters. On stage, with the exception of his brief lines of soliloquy, Henry may be virtually one-dimensional, an intensely patriotic stylization of ideal kingship; the pattern of commentary about him, however, woven consistently throughout the action, focuses directly upon his vulnerable side: the dissipation of his earlier days, the human consequences of his turning away a boon companion, the universal emotions of fear and of despair in the face of woefully uneven odds.

One further structural device helps Shakespeare to achieve most subtly (and potentially most effectively) the ambivalence which has progressively characterized the history plays. Just as the figure of Henry is given the semblance of a full and vital personality despite the stylization, so the play as a whole is afforded dramatic credibility despite the simplistic patriotic fervor which characterizes its surface. Shakespeare has methodically incorporated into each phase of the action a human dimension which qualifies the abstract design. This material may be included in the main action or it may be presented in separate juxtaposed passages. Its relationship to the main action may be parodic or ironic, or it may simply be an extension of the action to a more intimate and personal level. The point is that Shakespeare, for all the surface brilliance of Henry V's reign and of England's military victories over France, is demonstrably attempting to establish the interest in character and human interaction on which drama depends.

The opening scene, concerned essentially with England's psychological and physical preparation for the military invasion of France, provides a ready illustration. Amid the praise of the King's marvelous faculties for theology and politics, his own determination openly to establish the legal justification for war, and the fierce patriotism of his response to the Dauphin's gift, the characters perform purely public stylized roles; Henry's triple references to God in the last twenty-two lines of the act have the brazen ring of religion twisted to the service of public policy. The scenes are not without the appeal of both pageantry and patriotism, to be sure, but the characters give the impression of being created for the lines they speak; there is little hint of the flesh and blood beneath the civic role. Such a glimpse is provided though in the private dialogue of Canterbury and Ely which renders highly ironic the Church's unmitigated support of Henry's military cause. Canterbury asserts that there is no barrier to Henry's claim to the French throne, urging him to "stand for your own, unwind your bloody flag" (ii, 101) even as Ely challenges him with his "puissant arm [to] renew" the feats of his ancestors (116). What only the spectators know is that both men are more concerned with the financial state of the Church than with Henry's foreign policy. The opening words of the drama find Canterbury insisting that a plan must be devised to resist a law which, if passed, would cost "the better half of our possession" (i, 8). The King at the moment is impartial, but "for mitigation of this bill" Canterbury has offered the remarkably large gift of money as a military incentive. It is no doubt an overstatement to claim that Shakespeare through the clergymen totally vitiates the heroic or patriotic view of war or even that this "bribery" is the first in a long line of incidents which renders Henry V a Machiavel and the stage world a sordid and decadent satiric attack upon militarism and nationalism; in actuality there is no such continuity of either tone or incident. What is vitally important to the spectators is the human view of a topic too broad to comprehend emotionally, a dimension, in this particular instance in the form of action to protect vested interests, which provides psychological insight into the less grandiloquent causes of the war and saves the scene from abstraction.

Altogether different types of incidents serve a similar function in act 2. The chorus firmly pronounces that "all the youth of England are on fire" (1); unified for the nation's great military adventure, the people have forgotten individual grievances as "honors thought / Reigns solely in the breast of every man" (3–4). And indeed in II, i, Bardolph, Nym, and Pistol are described as "three sworn brothers to

France" (12–13). Human nature again rather abruptly intrudes upon the stylized design, however. Both Nym and Pistol lay claim to Nell Quickly's affections; the hostess has married Pistol despite her betrothal to Nym and her avowed distaste for the swaggerer in *2 Henry IV*, and insults and threats fly freely over the drawn swords. Nym is an "egregious dog," a "braggard vile and damned furious wight" whose "grave doth gape, and doting death is near" (46, 60–61); his colloquial style, as John Draper observes, is "purposefully calculated as an adjunct to his apparent martial prowess."[78] Pistol will be scoured with Nym's rapier; "I would prick your guts a little in good terms. . . . I will cut thy throat one time or other in fair terms" (58, 69–70). Only Bardolph maintains the peace with his threat to run to the hilt who strikes first and his timely reminder that they "must to France together; why the devil should we keep knives to cut one another's throats?" (91–92). In an entirely opposite manner the human dimension surfaces in Henry's denunciation of the traitors at Southampton. Despite the symbolically ceremonial significance of this exposure, a public testimony to the necessity of unity of national purpose and the elimination of those who would prevent it, Scroop's defection seems to give Henry genuine grief, and for a moment the man, not the King, speaks. Henry may well be invoking "the second office of charity . . . to uphold the order and obedience necessary to state and army,"[79] but the incident is also personally painful. Lord Scroop bore "the key of all [Henry's] counsels"; he knew "the very bottom of [his] soul" (II, ii, 96–97): "I will weep for thee; / For this revolt of thine, methinks, is like / Another fall of man" (140–42). The moment is brief. Henry quickly resumes his public posture in the formal proclamation of the charges and the arrests, and any private sensitivity is totally subsumed in his assertion that God's bringing such treason to light bodes "a fair and lucky war. . . . No king of England, if not king of France" (184, 193). Even so, the scene provides another illustration of the manner in which Shakespeare subtly interweaves through the public pageantry of national heroism and kingly ideality the human element vital to effective drama.

The middle phase of the action (acts 3–4) utilizes precisely the same structural principle. Overtly the action involves the actual con-

duct of the war in France: the courageous charge at Harfleur; the siege
and final offer of mercy to the inhabitants of the city; the apprehension
of the English army, outmanned and riddled with sickness, at Agincourt; and, probably the single most glorious moment in England's
military past, the magnificently heroic victory achieved in the face of
overwhelming adversity. As in acts 1 and 2 this national theme is delineated with a stylized fervor which, while tending toward abstraction, nonetheless does maintain a broad historical perspective. Again,
however, the human dimension is interspersed throughout the action.
Juxtaposed to Henry's fiercely brilliant oration at Harfleur, in which he
charges his troops to stiffen the sinews, set the teeth, and bend the
spirit, is Nym's observation that he has no desire to move to the
breach: "The knocks are too hot; and for mine own part, I have not a
case of lives" (III, ii, 3–5). And Pistol, with the boy, would prefer to
be in an alehouse in London. As the boy summarizes the situation,
Bardolph is white-liver'd and red-fac'd," Pistol "hath a killing tongue
and a quiet sword," and Nym's "few bad words are match'd with a
few good deeds" (32, 34, 39). Such comments do not denigrate Henry's courageous posture in the scene preceding; what they do is to remind the spectators that, whatever the magnitude of the events, they
are still performed by human beings plagued in many instances by
doubt, fear, and the overriding instinct to survive. Similarly human is
the touch provided in the scene juxtaposed to the siege of Harfleur.
Seemingly oblivious of the harsh realities of war, Katherine engages
in an English lesson with her maid Alice; if homonymic puns resulting
from her halting pronunciation create a bit of pit play, she nonetheless
is looking beyond the present moment to a time when she will confront an English Harry devoid of armor. Yet another human touch
surfaces in the French camp the evening before Agincourt. The Dauphin, a youthfully headstrong and recklessly optimistic braggart, proclaims that he will pave his way with English faces and at midnight
takes leave of his companions to arm himself for battle. Wiser and
older heads comment sarcastically after his departure that he is "simply
the most active gentleman of France," but one who, in doing, has
never done harm; "nor will do none tomorrow"; "he will eat all he
kills" (III, vii, 97, 191, 92).

The spectators also perceive several human moments during the heat of battle. At Picardy, Pistol, fresh from impressing Fluellen with his "brave words" at the bridge, pleads for Bardolph, who for stealing a pax is condemned to be hanged. When good words transform to insults, Gower brands him "a gull, a fool, a rogue, that now and then goes to the wars, to grace himself at his return into London under the form of a soldier" (III, vi, 67–69). Again such action defies the monolithic delineation of the heroic English army which the chorus articulates; so also does Pistol's subsequent avaricious insistence on money for the life of a prisoner: "Peasant, unless thou give me crowns, brave crowns; / Or mangled shalt thou be by this my sword. . . . As I such blood, I will some mercy show" (IV, iv, 38–39, 64). Quite different is the emotional touch in the final conversation among the English leaders before the battle. Chances of success are minimal, but there is no shrinking from the task; they speak of a joyful parting, even if it must last "till we meet in heaven. . . . If we are mark'd to die, we are enow / To do our country loss" (IV, iii, 7, 20–21). Similar affection is reflected later in Henry's "mistful eyes" when he learns of the death of York and Suffolk (IV, vi, 34). Certainly the most compelling single scene is that in which Henry speaks briefly in soliloquy; indeed his private reference to "poison'd flattery" and to the human vulnerability of "great greatness" (IV, i, 251) encompasses the heart of the ambiguity so pervasive throughout the drama. His comment to Bates while he himself is disguised as a fellow common soldier has the similar effect of a soliloquy:[80] "I think the King is but a man, as I am: the violet smells to him as it does to me; the element shows to him as it doth to me; all his senses have but human conditions. His ceremonies laid by, in his nakedness he appears but a man; and though his affections are higher mounted than ours, yet when they stoop, they stoop with the like wing. Therefore, when he sees reason of fears, as we do, his fears, out of doubt, be of the same relish as ours are" (101–9). Such a moment, albeit brief, graphically reveals the human spirit concealed for the most part beneath the symbol of the "star of England" (epilogue, 6).

The final phase of the play (act 5) again combines dramatically interesting detail with abstract stylization. Certainly the major thrust of the action sets forth the conditions of settlement between the opposing nations, conditions which epitomize the glory of Henry's kingship and of France's capitulation to the English military demands. Both the chorus to act 5 and the epilogue predictably stress the theme of national greatness. So too the action itself celebrates, on the one hand, the Welsh heritage of Fluellen and by extension of the King and, on the other hand, the totality of the English victory. The peace is bought with "full accord to all our just demands" (V, ii, 71); Henry "love[s] France so well" that he will not be deprived of even the smallest village (173); and, as Westmoreland reports, Charles VI agrees to every article set down by the victorious Henry. Amid the pageantry and the patriotic splendor, however, the human dimension emerges in each of the final scenes. In the first, Pistol, like a kind of anti-Henry, finds only shame and ignominy in France. Beaten by Fluellen for his insulting swaggering and forced to eat the leek which he has mocked, the braggadocio is dismissed by Gower as "a counterfeit cowardly knave. . . . Henceforth let a Welsh correction teach you a good English condition" (i, 69–70, 81–82). There is a touch of nostalgia in his private remark that his Doll (perhaps Doll Tearsheet, more likely Nell Quickly) is dead from venereal disease. And his parting quip, if it provokes no sympathy, leaves little doubt that common and flawed humanity has played a very present role in England's idealized victory:

> Old I do wax, and from my weary limbs
> Honor is cudgell'd. Well, bawd I'll turn,
> And something lean to cutpurse of quick hand.
> To England will I steal, and there I'll steal;
> And patches will I get unto these cudgell'd scars,
> And [swear] I got them in the Gallia wars.
> (84–89)

In the second scene an altogether different kind of human credibility surfaces in Henry's exchange with Katherine. The "richly human" scene, as Bertrand Evans describes it,[81] is replete with the almost ritualistic discussion of the terms of peace, even to the point of continued veiled threats from the English ruler should France not accede to his demands, but there are private moments between the couple when Henry speaks not as a confident and demanding King but as a tentative and self-abasing young man. He describes himself as so plain "that thou wouldst think I had sold my farm to buy my crown" (126–27); he claims no "cunning in protestation" (144), and his "face is not worth sunburning" (147). He explains that his looks are fierce because his father was thinking of civil wars when he begot him. "But in faith, Kate, the elder I wax, the better I shall appear. My comfort is, that old age, that ill layer-up of beauty, can do no more spoil upon my face" (228–31). The emergent picture is not one of a tender supplicant, to be sure, but the comments do qualify the rigidly one-dimensional figure which would otherwise appear.

In *1, 2 Henry IV* Shakespeare learned to combine structural devices of breadth with devices of depth. *Henry V* involves a greater concentration of the action upon the King himself, a characteristic posing two distinct structural problems. On the one hand, with the greater focus upon a single figure the playwright is forced to sharpen the devices of stylization in order to prevent the undue concentration of attention which would limit the scope of the spectators' vision. On the other hand, since the absence of an appreciable presence for the key surrounding figures removes the possibility of balancing the spectators' interest on three or four characters as in the Henry IV plays, there is no way to utilize the narrative continuity of subplots or multiple plots to develop (as with Hal, Falstaff, and Henry IV) contrasting views of a character in the significantly differing contexts which produce the semblance of dynamic human dimensions. Shakespeare's solution to the latter problem is the sporadic insertion throughout the action of brief moments of human insight among a wide variety of characters whose roles are otherwise almost rigidly stylized. That this structural feature is unique to *Henry V* further attests to his continuing experimentation to achieve the most effective dramatic perspective for the historical theme. "The treatment of characters," as Arthur Sewall notes, remains "subordinate to the comprehensive vision of the play."[82]

The question obviously persists: if *Henry V* represents the culmination of Shakespeare's efforts in the English history play and if in important respects it contains the most sophisticated utilization of structural techniques which he developed for this particular dramatic form, why should the play strike many a critic and many a playgoer as something less dramatically profound than his other works in the final years of the sixteenth century? Even if one agrees that his artistic intentions in the history play—and hence the structural principles which determine the dramatic perspective—are altogether distinct from those which lead to his romantic comedies and to his major tragic achievements, there is still the problem of why, to many, *Henry V* is a lesser creation than the Henry IV plays. The problem may well lie quite literally in the eye of the beholder—in this instance in the complex synthesis demanded of the spectators if the play is to maintain a properly balanced perspective. It is entirely possible that Shakespeare's contemporary audiences were more receptive to this synthesis than his post-Restoration spectators. Accustomed to the complete plasticity of the Elizabethan stage and the symbolism at the heart of the play, they perhaps could respond more readily to a "plane of emotional truth but factual impossibility."[83] Certainly Shakespeare is acutely aware of the need for the spectators' "imaginary forces" to be at work (prologue, 18). The cockpit will hold "the vasty fields of France" (12), and the "Wooden O" (13) must contain the image of Agincourt itself. The scene flies to Harfleur "with imagin'd wing" (chorus, III, 1); the stage is all too small to capture the "full course of the glory" achieved by England's "mighty men" in conquering the "world's best garden" (epilogue, 4, 3, 7).

The audience is admittedly an active participant in every Shakespearean stage world. In the most powerful tragedies, the spectators through their omniscient perspective are forced to sit in judgment on the protagonist even as they emotionally respond to his spiritual struggle. In these stage worlds, however, various structural devices such as the soliloquy, the pointing commentary of other figures, and thematically related subplot material combine to guide the spectator coherently to the point of simultaneous engagement and detachment. Similarly, the spectators in the preceding Henry IV plays, privy to the private thoughts or critical moments of the several major figures, alone possess the perspective for responding most fully to the human consequences of the historical events of the narrative. Even so, the ambivalence of Henry IV, Hal, Hotspur, Northumberland, and Falstaff, so vital to the complexity of the spectators' response to them both individually and collectively, is in each case the point of specific discussion and interrelationship by the surrounding characters. In *Henry V,* as well, Shakespeare's intention is both the broad perspective necessary for the historical theme and the ambivalence which lends a human dimension and thus a dramatic viability to the characters and to the events. Here, however, the playwright utilizes what Richard Levin has called a spatial integration of plots to create, through ambivalencies and ironical tensions, a foil to Henry's glorious exploits. The effect, as Levin observes, is that of "a musical chord, contingent upon the absolute emotional 'pitch' of each action as well as the relative emotional 'distance' between them."[84] The task of interrelating the components of the plot to achieve this response, however, is left in large part to the spectators. They alone are privy to Canterbury's and Ely's desire to protect a large portion of the Church's wealth; they alone must relate the nature of Nym's, Bardolph's, and Pistol's military activities to the stylized heroism of the English army and its idealized leader. The references to Falstaff's reaction to his repudiation by Hal and the momentary pathos during Nell Quickly's description of his death are never explored in relation to himself; the applicability is left entirely to the imagination of the spectators. The soul-searching evidenced in the King's soliloquy in the middle of the play is, except in the mind of the viewer, ostensibly forgotten in the Henry of act 5. The chorus, instead of providing an integrating and analytic commentary, delivers a veritable encomium on the magnificent and heroic English military accomplishments.

In one sense then Shakespeare's historical perspective has reached a new level of sophistication in the rich ambiguities involved in the spectators' manner of relating the various components of the play. The spectators, like those of Jonson's *Sejanus* and *Catiline,* inevitably respond to some degree in terms of their own moral and emotional nature; that is, they are forced to provide, and to test the limitations of, their own personal scale of values as a gauge by which to respond to decisions and actions which precipitate Henry's mounting political successes. In another sense, the perspective has grown so subtle in the active role which it forces upon the audience that the human dimensions might be lost entirely to many a modern viewer, for whom the play becomes stylized either as a crass display of Machiavellian politics or a brittle dramatization of patriotic glory. The spectator's perception, in a word, determines whether *Henry V* is the most complex or among the most simplistic of the histories. Of Shakespeare's intentions there can be little room for reasonable doubt.

CHAPTER V

A Celebration of History:
Henry VIII

To some degree each of the plays discussed in the earlier chapters was of political and social relevance to its original audiences. The interest in large part stemmed from the Elizabethans' fascination with their past. On occasion particular contemporary political issues and problems were mirrored in an earlier historical context, but in more general terms the dramatization of the preceding years of political turbulence became a means of glorifying present unity and national power. No play, however, so directly celebrates the contemporary age as does *The Famous History of the Life of King Henry the Eighth*. What provoked Shakespeare's return to the theme of British history well over a decade after the composition of *Henry V* and precisely how much he contributed to the writing of the play are points of continuing debate.[1] To be sure, the popularity of the chronicle play had long since waned; whereas seventy plays based directly on British history were written between 1590 and 1604, only nineteen appeared between 1605 and the closing of the theaters in 1642 (seven between 1605 and Shakespeare's death).[2] In many respects *Henry VIII* is decidedly inferior to the best of Shakespeare's earlier histories; even the repetitive pattern of action in *1 Henry VI* and the dominance of particular characters (Humphrey, Duke of Gloucester, and Richard Plantagenet, Duke of York) in *2 Henry VI* provide more effective dramatic cohesion than one perceives, at least initially, in this stage world. On the other hand, no one questioned Shakespeare's authorship in the seventeenth century; Heminge and Condell apparently did not cavil at including the piece in the first folio, and there is no mention of the play in the collected works of Beaumont and Fletcher (F$_1$ 1647). Even more significantly, whatever the degree of its dramatic merits, *Henry VIII* does seem to grow directly out of the techniques of structure and of characterization developed in Shakespeare's histories in the 1590s.

The various structural devices utilized with increasing sophistication in the earlier histories assure a broad historical perspective for this play as well. While the scenes are confined to London and the palace, thirty-eight actors representing the full social spectrum crowd the stage, in addition to an undetermined number of mute scribes, officers, guards, attendants upon the Queen, and figures in various dumb shows. Sixteen individuals have substantial speaking parts, none delivering more than 16.5 percent (Henry) and five others speaking over 5 percent of the total lines (Wolsey, 15.8 percent; Katherine, 13.5 percent; Norfolk, 7.6 percent; Buckingham, 7 percent; and Chamberlain, 5.5 percent). The total number of soliloquies and asides—101 lines, 3.6 percent of the total lineation—is remarkably low in comparison with those of Shakespeare's highly internalized tragedies; indeed, excepting *Henry V,* it is the smallest number to be found in the history plays themselves. Hence there is little tendency to involve the spectators emotionally at a personal level. Even these internal lines are divided among nine figures. Most of these passages, moreover, merely transmit information to the spectator rather than invite emotional involvement at a moment of critical decision; and with the exception of King Henry, who speaks six lines in act 2 and two lines in act 5, no individual delivers private lines in more than one act. In a word, since there is no dominant figure throughout the play, the spectators' interest perforce focuses upon that nexus of events which precipitates, on the one hand, Henry's break with Rome and the establishment of Protestantism and, on the other, the divorce from Katherine, the ascension of Anne, and the birth of Elizabeth.

The breadth of focus is reinforced through the use of choric figures in eight separate scenes, fully half of those in the play as divided in F_1. At one moment various characters deplore the foreign fashions that are all the rage shortly after Wolsey concludes his treaty with the French: "they keep state so"; "they have all new legs"; "their clothes" have a "pagan cut"; "a French song and a fiddle has no fellow" (I, iii, 10, 11, 13, 41). At another, they point to the color and excitement of events of state, whether it be a gala dinner party hosted by the Lord Chancellor, Cardinal Wolsey, and graced by the presence of Henry himself as one of a party of "maskers, habited like shepherds" (I, iv) or the report of the splendor of the Field of the Cloth of Gold where "Those sons of glory, those two lights of men, / Met in the vale of Andren" (I, i, 6–7); in this incomparable "view of earthly glory, . . . The two kings, / Equal in lustre, were now best, now worst / As presence did present them" (14, 28–30). Similarly the description of the coronation of Anne comes exclusively through the conversation among these gentlemen: this period of "general joy" is filled with "shows, / Pageants, and sights of honor" (IV, i, 7, 10–11); the royal procession features in Anne the "sweetest face I ever look'd on, . . . an angel" (43, 44):

> I am stifled
> With the mere rankness of their [the crowd's] joy.
> . . . .
> The rich stream
> Of lords and ladies, having brought the Queen
> To a prepar'd place in the choir, fell off.
> . . . .
> At length her Grace rose, and with modest paces
> Came to the altar, where she kneel'd, and saint-like
> . . . pray'd devoutly;
> . . . the choir,
> With all the choicest music of the kingdom,
> Together sung *Te Deum*.
> (58–59, 62–64, 82–84, 90–92)

So too the altercation between the Porter, his man, and the Lord Chamberlain reflects the national excitement surrounding the christening of the infant Elizabeth. The mob "take[s] the court for Parish Garden. . . . We may as well push against Powle's as stir 'em" (V, iii, 2, 16); "Mercy o' me, what a multitude are here! / They grow still too; from all parts they are coming, / As if we kept a fair here!" (67–69). On three occasions the choric figures discuss political matters, in particular the fortunes and misfortunes of Cardinal Wolsey: "All the commons / Hate him perniciously" (II, i, 49–50); they perceive Katherine's fall as his manipulation to gain revenge on Charles V, the Holy Roman Emperor, for not bestowing the archbishopric of Toledo upon him (161–64); this "imperious man" dives into "the King's soul, and there scatters / Dangers, doubts, wringing of the conscience" (II, ii, 46, 26–27). And with obvious delight they report the imminent fall of the Lord Chancellor; the Cardinal's letter to the Pope concerning the divorce and an inventory of his own material possessions, both of which strangely miscarried to the King, constitute "Matter against him that forever mars / The honey of his language" (III, ii, 21–22). As for Buckingham's arrest and subsequent execution, the events will bring, "I fear, too many curses on their heads / That were the authors" (II, i, 138–39).

More so than in any previous history then, Shakespeare has utilized the choric figures to provide a detached perspective for the spectators. It may well be true that in practical terms the playwright through such a structure is able to narrate particular scenes and situations that would be extremely difficult to dramatize directly. The multiple pointers may also represent the continuation of a device utilized extensively in the final tragedies to create a profound sense of ambivalence concerning both the protagonist and the ethical values operable in his society.[3] However, relating numerous events through minor and relatively impersonal characters certainly has the direct result of blocking the spectators from the development of a significant emotional rapport with the principal figures and hence of maintaining a broad historical perspective. Given the cumulative weight of the various structural devices which contribute to the broad focus in this particular work and, as well, the progressive development of such a perspective in the earlier histories, it would be naive to assume that Shakespeare was oblivious of the effect upon the audience's relationship to the action.

Two additional features reinforce the detachment: scenes which directly dramatize the pomp and ceremony of the kingship and a prologue-epilogue figure who specifically emphasizes the theatricality of the occasion. Eight different scenes visually address the audience in such a manner; though all of the romances include mask or mask-like elements and though earlier histories depict momentous battles and various events of significance for the monarch and the nobility, no previous play is so pervasively given to spectacular visual effects.[4] In act 1, following the description of the Field of the Cloth of Gold, the spectators directly view the state entrance of the Lord Chancellor. Detailed stage directions specify that Wolsey is to be preceded by one bearing the great seal of his office and accompanied by several members of the guard and two secretaries. This lavishly dressed group has barely departed from the stage when Henry himself enters. Again Shakespeare specifically notes the cornets and the grandiloquent royal train in a scene rendered emblematic as well by Henry's leaning upon the shoulder of Wolsey, who, once Henry is seated on a raised and canopied area, "places himself under the King's feet on his right side" (I, ii). Two scenes later Wolsey stages an elaborate dinner dance at York Place. Guests, including Anne Bullen, are sumptuously attired for the occasion, which reaches new heights of splendor with hautboys announcing the arrival of the shepherd maskers, Henry himself among them. Altogether different in tone, though equally appealing to the eye, is Katherine's state trial in act 2. Again Shakespeare carefully arranges the scene through a long blocking direction, and the stage is literally crowded with officials of varying degrees of importance. Vergers with silver wands, scribes capped and gowned as doctors of law, the Bishops of Lincoln, Ely, Rochester, and Saint Asaph, a gentleman bearing the great seal and a cardinal's hat, priests carrying silver crosses, a Sergeant at Arms with a silver mace, gentlemen bearing Wolsey's silver insignia, cardinals, noblemen with a sword and mace —in all at least twenty mute figures creating a remarkable backdrop for Wolsey, Henry, and Katherine. Whatever the nature of the trial itself, the spectators can only be dazzled by the pageantlike display of lavish costumes and the impressive physical props of royalty and aristocracy. Similar visual brilliance is evidenced in act 4 where, prior to a choric description of Anne's coronation at Westminster Abbey, Shakespeare elaborately stages the royal procession in ten individually itemized progressions. Elizabeth's christening in the final act (scene 4) is accompanied by an impressive ritual involving at least nineteen "richly habited" nobles, only three of whom have speaking roles. Cranmer's trial in the council chamber (V, iii) and Katherine's masklike vision of paradisiac bliss shortly before her death are further illustrations of the lavish display. Shakespeare's directions in the first folio text of *Henry VIII* for such staging effects, quite exclusive of the customary directions of characters on and off stage, run to more than three times those of *The Tempest* and *Hamlet,* plays with the next highest count; and they quadruple those of *1 Henry IV,* the history with the next highest count. Again, as in the case of the multiple choric figures, it would be naive to assume that Shakespeare was oblivious of the impact of this dramaturgical feature. There can be no argument whatever that history can be captured in color, ritual, and pageantry; clearly these are methods of strengthening the historical perspective, of maintaining the spectators' interest in the broad pattern of events rather than the fortunes or misfortunes of particular characters central to the dramatic design.

While Shakespeare through such effects continues to experiment as a chronicle playwright, he repeats in his prologue and epilogue a device utilized in *Henry V.* Again the intention is self-consciously to call attention to the play qua play: if not to the inadequacies of the playhouse in staging particular historical events, then to the goal of staging a "weighty and serious" theme and to the responsibility of the spectator who by willfully misperceiving can destroy all dramatic integrity. The prologue figure proclaims that these "noble themes" are "high, and working, full of state" (4, 3); they may well provoke a tear in delineating "how soon this mightiness meets misery" (30), but they will not please the spectator anticipating merry bawdry, the "noise of targets," and the fool dressed in "a long motley coat guarded with yellow" (15, 16). The epilogue deplores the spectators who come only to "take their ease, / And sleep an act or two" (2–3) and those who expect to "hear the city / Abused extremely" in the name of wit (5– 6). These "first and happier hearers of the town" (prologue, 24) are encouraged instead to use the mind's eye to imagine

> the very persons of our noble story
> As they were living. Think you see them great,

> And follow'd with the general throng and sweat
> Of thousand friends.   (26–29)

The play both opens and closes with a call for the discriminating spectator who is willing to use drama as a means of exploring present values and traditions in the context of the earlier, more turbulent years in which they were formulated.

In any number of dramaturgical ways, then, Shakespeare in *Henry VIII* creates for the spectators an inclusive angle of vision. Not so easily addressed is his manner of achieving their emotional involvement in the play. One of my abiding concerns in this study has been Shakespeare's consistent effort throughout his histories to combine the detachment inherent in a broad perspective with the engagement arising from characters possessed of sufficient emotional credibility to be dramatically interesting. In earlier chapters I have traced the increasing sophistication with which he accomplishes this latter quality. *Henry VIII,* on first reading and (unless the visual pageantry numbs the normal dramatic expectations) on first viewing, seems to lack narrative coherence. And certainly the critics have been quick to condemn. The structure is "cynically arbitrary,"[5] "conspicuously lacking in unity";[6] the play is "a stream of declamation,"[7] "not only episodic but also repetitious."[8] The King himself is the sole figure who participates in the action throughout all five acts, but unlike Henry V in a similar structure, he is central neither to the narrative nor to the emotional concerns of the spectators. The action seems to ramble from character to character with little cohesive forward movement; if, for example, Cardinal Wolsey's machinations appear initially to provide narrative continuity, he last appears in III, ii, and his death is reported in IV, ii.

If the play lacks visible architectonic unity, however, it does on hindsight hold together reasonably well. For it becomes obvious in the final act that the central thrust of the play is the birth of Elizabeth and the prophecy of the culmination of Tudor greatness and that the early acts depict the particular decisions and events of Henry's reign which produce Elizabeth's Protestant rule, more particularly the divorce of Katherine, the fall of Wolsey, and the break with Rome. In her reign and that of her successor James I, England shall prosper as a nation:

172

She shall be, to the happiness of England,
An aged princess. . . .
His honor and the greatness of his name
Shall be, and make new nations.

(V, iv, 56–57, 51–52)

The play envisions then a unified Protestant England beyond the turbulent years of the power struggle between Somerset and Northumberland during Edward's reign and the bloody Catholic persecutions of Mary, an idealized England on which God showers blessings as the frame of colonial power begins to take shape. The view undeniably is extreme that it "binds and clasps [Shakespeare's] massive life-work into a single whole," that no other play "has a more decided character of unity."[9] The point is well taken, however, that the drama effectively reflects the cyclic process of history.[10] It depicts the "human context of political crashes,"[11] and the "importance of each character depends —as usual in the histories—on the relation between that character and the king."[12]

Shakespeare is obviously concerned that the spectators fundamentally approve of the fates of these characters. At the same time, if the play is to be dramatically compelling, they must command at least a limited emotional rapport. As in his most successful earlier histories, he attempts to achieve this quality in *Henry VIII* through characters (in this instance Buckingham, Katherine, Wolsey, and Cranmer) who, though essentially static, are depicted in ambivalent situations.

Katherine is destined to marital misery, and no positive response could normally be anticipated from the largely anti-Catholic English audiences of the early seventeenth century.[13] To offset this bias, however, Shakespeare depicts the Spanish princess as an innocent creature victimized by the Machiavellian English cardinal; and though she appears in only four scenes, she is strongly sympathetic in each instance.[14] In I, ii, she warns the King of the grievous taxations that have been imposed upon each citizen, and she expresses sorrow for the King's incarceration of Buckingham, warning that his accusers charge a noble and innocent person; in both cases the spectators, fully aware of Wolsey's villainous role, perceive Katherine as the voice of right reason.

173

She is on trial in her next appearance, asserting that she has been a "true and humble wife" (II, iv, 23); and she flatly refuses to have Wolsey as a judge: "You are mine enemy. . . . [Y]our heart / Is cramm'd with arrogancy, spleen, and pride. . . . / You tender more your person's honor than / Your high profession spiritual" (77, 109–10, 116–17). In the following scene, she bravely faces the Cardinal in her apartment, refusing to withdraw with him into her private chamber ("Speak it here; / There's nothing I have done yet, o' my conscience, / Deserves a corner" [III, i, 29–31]) and, like Webster's Vittoria, disdaining the use of Latin for legal charges brought against her:

> O, good my lord, no Latin;
> . . . .
>
> A strange tongue makes my cause more strange, suspicious;
> Pray speak in English. . . .
> The willing'st sin I ever yet committed
> May be absolv'd in English
> (41, 45–46, 49–50)

A dying woman in her final scene, she has outlived Wolsey, yet there is not bitterness. She knew him as "a man / Of an unbounded stomach" who made "His own opinion . . . his law" (IV, ii, 33–34, 37). But in his death she pities him and bids him peace (75); similarly with her final words she wishes the King continued good health and implores him to love and protect their daughter Mary:

> Remember me
> In all humility unto his Highness.
> . . . .
>
> Tell him in death I bless him;
> . . . .
>
> I was a chaste wife to my grave.
> (160–61, 163, 170)

Thus in her brief time on stage Katherine is more than a stylized figure who acts out her role allotted by history. She is firmly and unswervingly Catholic and as such arouses the immediate animosities of an audience that considers the Pope a veritable Antichrist. But she is also a dramatic human figure through whom Shakespeare commands an ambivalent response and consequently through whom he moves history beyond abstract design.

Similar victims who gain a sympathetic rapport with the spectators are the Duke of Buckingham and Thomas Cranmer, Archbishop of Canterbury, the one destroyed and the other saved by Henry's intervention. If Henry seems crassly indifferent to the Duke, we must remember, as Peter Saccio has observed, that Buckingham was "a dynastic threat to the Tudors" (p. 217), a direct descent of Thomas of Woodstock and an English lord in the old style. Early in the play he is the dominant figure of concern, a vocal obstacle to Wolsey's greed for political power. He is quick to denounce the Cardinal's "ambitious finger" in the pageantry of the Field of the Cloth of Gold, an extravagance which issued in nothing of productive and permanent political value (I, i, 23ff.). Aware of Wolsey's personal hatred and of his inordinate influence over the king, Buckingham threatens to "quite cry down / This Ipswich fellow's insolence" (137–38). His ultimate charge is treason, that the Cardinal "Does buy and sell his honor as he pleases / And for his own advantage" (192–93). Specifically he claims that Wolsey has accepted a bribe from Charles, the Holy Roman Emperor, in return for drawing up an agreement between the French and the English kings that will not result in unity since neither will be able to honor it for long. Despite the apparent accuracy of his perceptions, however, Buckingham is possessed of a passionate nature which lends color to the otherwise static characterization. A minor alteration in history provides the opportunity for Shakespeare to establish this dominant trait at the outset of the play. Buckingham, historically present at the events of the Field of the Cloth of Gold, in *Henry VIII* remains in England indisposed and consequently must question Norfolk later concerning the ceremonious meeting between Henry and Francis. The moment he is informed that Wolsey staged the affair, his entire manner is altered as he hurls verbal abuses at the ambitious "butcher's cur" (I, i, 120). Norfolk, while affirming Wolsey's villainy, bluntly warns Buckingham to "let your reason with your choler question" (130), to quench the "fire of passion" with the "sap of reason" (149, 148):

> Ask God for temp'rance, that's th' appliance only
> Which your disease requires. . . .
> > Be advis'd.
> Heat not a furnace for your foe so hot
> That it do singe yourself. (124–25, 139–41)

Buckingham admits his "flow of gall" (152) but insists nonetheless that he will assert his charges before the King himself. Moments later, even though the question of Buckingham's guilt or innocence is never definitely answered, Shakespeare establishes strong bonds of sympathy with the spectators as he is arrested through Wolsey's manipulation on the charge of conspiring against the life of the monarch. Buckingham claims that his surveyor, the chief witness against him, has been bribed with the Cardinal's gold, and Queen Katherine asserts the Duke's innocence before both the king (I, ii, 109–10) and the accuser (171–76); similarly, as we noted earlier, a choric figure implicates the Cardinal, acknowledging that "the commons / Hate him perniciously" and "love and dote on" the Duke (II, i, 39, 49–50, 52). At the trial itself, according to reports, Buckingham initially "spoke in choler, ill, and hasty" (34) but quickly regained his composure and "show'd a most noble patience" (36). In his final remarks to those gathered on the street before Westminster as he makes his way toward his execution, he speaks with the calm assurance and conviction of a martyr. Again he proclaims his innocence, yet in the same breath he forgives his enemies; he implores his friends to go with him "like good angels" and to pray that his soul be lifted to heaven even "as the long divorce of steel falls" upon him (75, 76).

> My vows and prayers
> Yet are the King's; and, till my soul forsake,
> Shall cry for blessings on him.   (88–90)

His parting words ominously caution those in earshot to be liberal, but not careless, of their "loves and counsels," lest they be felled by those they love most (126ff.).

So while both Katherine and Buckingham are static, they are given dramatic interest through their genuinely human traits, in Katherine a fierce if short-lived determination to protect her marriage and her dignity and sense of compassion in a masculine world of conniving intrigue, in Buckingham a passionate nature which bursts out almost uncontrollably on several occasions. Thomas Cranmer is an altogether more passive character. Totally innocent as the play projects him, he too is indirectly Wolsey's victim. Not only does the Cardinal denounce Cranmer as "An heretic, an arch-one . . . [who] / Hath crawl'd into the favor of the King" (III, ii, 102–3); he also is directly responsible for the appointment of Gardiner, Cranmer's later adversary, as Henry's secretary. The relationship between the churchman and his sycophant is ominously clear in Gardiner's aside that he is "to be commanded / For ever by your Grace, whose hand has rais'd me" (II, ii, 118–19); even more bluntly, Wolsey remarks of Doctor Pace, the secretary's predecessor:

> He was a fool—
> For he would needs be virtuous. That good fellow [Gardiner],
> If I command him, follows my appointment;
> I will have none so near else.   (131–34)

Not surprisingly, then, in act 5 Gardiner (now Bishop of Winchester) strongly opposes Cranmer, who has replaced William Warham as Archbishop of Canterbury. He asserts that conditions in England "will ne'er be well" until Cranmer, along with both Queen Anne and Cromwell, is dead (i, 29ff.), and he openly accuses him in the King's council of being an "arch-heretic, a pestilence / That does infect the land" (45–46). At the hearing itself Gardiner proclaims that the Archbishop's heretical teachings must be stopped forcefully and suddenly; he would have him divested of office and committed to the Tower as a "sectary" (ii, 105).

Cranmer admittedly lacks the passion which humanizes both Katherine and Buckingham; even so, the consternation registered in his asides does lend dramatic coloration. Called to the palace to confront the council, he is fearful of the King's frown: " 'Tis his aspect of terror" (V, i, 88); awaiting the council's pleasure outside the door and aware of the disrespectful and insulting treatment he is receiving, he is terrified of the plots laid by his enemies to "quench mine honor," and he prays that God will "turn their hearts! I never sought their malice" (ii, 16, 15). The trump card in this affair is Henry's assumption of Cranmer's innocence and his personal intervention into the council's proceedings at the critical moment; nonetheless, yet another moment of history has been transformed into engaging drama through the brief human interactions between the spectators and the historical character.

Certainly the most compelling figure in this stage world is Cardinal Wolsey. A religious adaptation of the steely self-determination of Richard III, his villainy literally pervades and motivates the action of the first three acts. Like his Machiavellian forebears on the Shakespearean stage, he commands an awesome fascination through his ability to subordinate everything to his ambitious design. Methodically he eliminates Buckingham when the latter too overtly voices opposition to his foreign policy, and only reluctantly does he agree at Henry's insistence to abrogate a tax claiming one-sixth of the substance from each of the citizens; the clear implications are that the Archbishop is handsomely lining his own coffers. Interestingly, when Henry orders the tax removed, Wolsey whispers to his secretary to noise it about that "through our intercession this revokement / And pardon comes" (I, ii, 106–7); the use of the royal pronoun is surely an indication of his unbounded ambition rather than a slip of his tongue or Shakespeare's pen. A similar arrogance is observed in II, ii, when the Lord Chamberlain receives a letter informing him that his horses "by commission and main power" have been claimed by the Lord Cardinal, who will "be serv'd before a subject, if not before the King" (6, 7–8). Norfolk mockingly proclaims him a "king-cardinal," an "imperious man [who] will work us all / From princes into pages" (19, 46–47); and Suffolk acknowledges the slavery of the court, wishing the Cardinal would go to the devil—"him that made him proud, the Pope" (43, 55). To be sure, he operates not only "holily" (23) but also socially. His dinner-dance at York Place for the lords and ladies of the court is a grand and noble affair. It also, of course, provides him the opportunity to ingratiate himself among those whose support is vital. At the height of his power he moves directly against the Queen herself, not to accommodate Henry's desire to wed Anne Bullen but in order to achieve an even more secure place in the power structure of the English throne. After pressing the King to admit the possible sin in marrying his brother's widow, Wolsey introduces Campeius as the Pope's personal voice in the necessary trial. Katherine's refusal to sit through the hearing merely plays into his hands; and when she accuses him of "tender[ing] more your person's honor than / Your high profession spiritual" (II, iv, 116–17), he persuades Henry publicly to defend his character by proclaiming his innocence of any self-serving motive; moreover, presumably with Henry's knowledge and consent, Wolsey relentlessly pursues the attack upon Katherine during a visit to her private apartment.

Wolsey's fall from such a lofty perch is sudden and devastating when Henry discovers both a communication urging the Pope to postpone any action on the King's divorce and a paper listing the Cardinal's not inconsiderable material possessions; the divorce he would delay so that he can arrange a royal wedding with the Duchess of Alencon, and the wealth he has amassed to "fee [his] friends in Rome" in seeking the papacy (III, ii, 213). Acknowledging that he "shall fall / Like a bright exhalation in the evening" (225–26), he is nonetheless reluctant to render up the great seal to Henry's courtiers. Moments later, however, he utters a poignant soliloquy to which even his cautious critics among the spectators must respond. The mutability of his fortune typifies the very "state of man" (352), and he fully admits the "high-blown pride" which now, broken under him, has left him "weary and old with service" (361, 363):

> Vain pomp and glory of this world, I hate ye!
> I feel my heart new open'd. O, how wretched
> Is that poor man that hangs on princes' favors.
> (365–67)

His parting words with Cromwell are even more affecting. He asserts that he now possesses the peaceful comfort of "a still and quiet conscience" (380). Cromwell he urges to flee from him, "a poor fall'n man, unworthy now / To be thy lord and master" (413–14), and to use his ruin as a grim reminder of ambition's folly:

> Love thyself last, cherish those hearts that hate thee;
> . . . Be just, and fear not;

. . . O Cromwell, Cromwell.
Had I but serv'd my God with half the zeal
I serv'd my king, he would not in mine age
Have left me naked to mine enemies.
. . . my hopes in heaven do dwell.

(443, 446, 454–57, 459)

Wolsey is sharply depicted within the play as villain and regenerate. In both roles he commands the spectators' interest and concern; in both he assumes a dramatic credibility and a human dimension which move beyond that of a stylized, monolithic figure. Nonetheless, since the two roles are kept distinctly separate, he is fundamentally simplistic.[15] That is, in five scenes he is the conniving and ambitious Machiavel for whom conscience is a toy and for whom a heady sense of power and authority is an unquestioned summum bonum; in one he is a morose figure who privately acknowledges his present misery and the vanity of all earthly glory. What the spectators pointedly do not see is a scene of transformation from one face to another, a scene which would lend a genuinely dynamic quality to the characterization. The dramatic benefits are considerable, to be sure, because there are moments of an emotional rapport provoked by the spectators' reaction to Wolsey's suffering and his acute awareness of his misery. At the same time the emotional attachment is limited and carefully controlled; in the final analysis, as with Falstaff, Prince Hal, or Henry V, we are seeing two angles of vision so distinctly different that they seem to suggest a growth of development in character. But with no indication whatever of the least moral sensitivity during the period of the Cardinal's political success, the spectators simply cannot be convinced that his anguish represents more than a keen sensitivity toward his loss of power and possession.

Structurally then, *Henry VIII*, with its "complicated but symmetrical balance of themes and of modes of presentation,"[16] represents an extension of the dramaturgical techniques fully developed in *King John, 1, 2, Henry IV,* and *Henry V.* The absence of a dominant central figure, the minimal use of soliloquies and asides and the distribution of these few internalizing lines among several individuals, the extensive utilization of choric figures (including the prologue and epilogue), the frequency of pageantic scenes in which spectacle supplements narrative in depicting crucial moments of Henry's reign—all such devices distance the spectators from particular events and personalities and thereby encourage the broad view vital for the historical perspective. At the same time, certain characters are sketched in sufficient detail to command a limited emotional appeal and thus to provide the interest in character on which any drama this side of pageant is predicated. These characters, in other words, are essentially static, but they do possess a human dimension which extends beyond the intellectual interest in historical design. The play, of a piece if not of a quality with its predecessors, is one final example of the complex structural pattern Shakespeare evolved for the history plays, a dramatic perspective distinct from that of comedy or tragedy.

Overriding the focus on a series of individuals whose rises and falls provoke ambivalent responses from the spectators is a larger pattern which establishes the fundamental rhythm of the play. The action is arranged as a diptych, acts 1–3 characterized by tyranny, oppression, and misjudgment and acts 4–5 reflecting the celebration of justice and the joyous anticipation of a period of national prosperity and happiness.[17] This larger structural pattern, unique among the histories though basic to the design of *The Winter's Tale,* is the principal device by which the play becomes a festive glorification of the reigns of Elizabeth and James. In the first movement horror methodically follows horror: the political folly of the Field of the Cloth of Gold, the falls of Buckingham and Abergavenney, oppressive taxation, an all-too-obvious trial of convenience against Katherine, the rise of the political sycophant Gardiner, and the collapse of Cardinal Wolsey's world in lamentation and self-reproach. The England visualized through this pattern of action is a land of political corruption and personal insecurity. The last two acts provide a diametrically opposite experience. The new day is signaled by a reference to Queen Anne's coronation as a time of "general joy" (IV, i, 7); the citizens will spend the day "in celebration" (10); an observer is "stifled / With the mere rankness of their joy" (58–59); the later christening of the infant Elizabeth creates a "Holy-day" for all Englishmen (V, iii, 76). If the first three acts look backward to the incessant and turbulent political struggles of

Shakespeare's previous histories, the last two provide an idealized vision of England's golden age.

Aside from the events of state (the coronation and the christening), three specific events sharply distinguish the tone of the latter half of the play from that of the first: Henry's dramatic intervention on Cranmer's behalf at the council meeting, Katherine's beatific vision, and Cranmer's prophetic description of England's future years. Cranmer produces the King's ring in the face of Gardiner's peremptory order for the guards to imprison him in the Tower, after which Henry himself enters, taking his seat and "frowning on them." In stark contrast to Henry's inability or unwillingness to see through Wolsey's self-interested manipulations, here his judgment is perceptive and his leadership firm: "I come not / To hear such flattery now. . . . You play the spaniel, / And think with wagging of your tongue to win me" (V, iii, 123–24, 126–27):

> I had thought I had men of some understanding
> And wisdom of my Council; but I find none.
> . . . .
>
> my lord of Winchester [Gardiner], I charge you.
> Embrace and love this man.
>
> (170–71, 204–5)

Katherine's vision is visible only to her and to the spectators. Obviously Shakespeare cannot mitigate her tragedy on the public level; Katherine's fall, after all, is the path of Anne's ascension and Elizabeth's belated legitimacy. But on a private level he does produce a sense of peaceful resolution for her difficult life. Six figures dressed in white and "wearing on their heads garlands of bays," a symbol of triumph, move across the stage, bowing before her and two by two holding a garland over her head. It is probably futile to search for extensive allegory in the mask; Katherine herself describes it as merely "a blessed troop" promising her "eternal happiness" (IV, ii, 87, 90).[18] Her remaining words to the King, delivered through Capucius, an ambassador from Emperor Charles V, reflect no trace of continued agitation; now she would simply invoke God's blessings on Henry and commend to him their young daughter and her household staff. Altogether different in form, though functioning as a similar point of joyous resolution, is the public proclamation at Elizabeth's christening by the Archbishop of Canterbury. Led by heaven, Cranmer prophesies that Elizabeth "promises / Upon this land a thousand thousand blessings" (V, iv, 18–19); she is destined to be a glass of royal fashion, a "pattern to all princes" (22):

> Truth shall nurse her,
> Holy and heavenly thoughts still counsel her.
> She shall be lov'd and fear'd. . . .
> In her days every man shall eat in safety
> Under his own vine what he plants, and sing
> The merry songs of peace to all his neighbors.
> God shall be truly known.   (28–30, 33–36)

Like the phoenix she will "leave her blessedness to one" who shall rise "from the sacred ashes of her honor" (43, 45). His reign shall also be characterized by the qualities of prosperity, mercy, and control— "Peace, plenty, love, truth, terror"—and the "honor and the greatness of his name" shall "make new nations" and bless "our children's children" (47, 51, 54).

With the pattern of joy and hopeful anticipation totally reversing the earlier pattern of corruption and politically motivated trials and executions, it seems short-sighted indeed to argue that Shakespeare pointedly refuses to mythologize Henry as a means of glorifying Elizabethan and Jacobean England, that any references to future greatness are undercut by the recent death of Prince Henry and the loss forever of the royal namesake. To be sure, *Henry VIII* is not a stage encomium of Henry's reign like that of contemporary playwrights; indeed it is precisely Shakespeare's refusal to create such a monolithic view that apparently leads to the dramatic diptych. Henry is clearly not without fault, nor is his reign without blemish, and Shakespeare, as we have observed throughout his histories, is concerned not with eulogistic pageantry but with the manner in which the past can be effectively revealed through the human condition.[19] As we noted earlier, Shakespeare in *Henry VIII* is relating the past to the present more overtly than in any other play, and his view of Elizabethan-Jacobean England is positive, one fundamentally compatible with his societal perceptions in the romances. Even so, just as he utilizes two generations in those stage worlds to capture the tragedy as well as the joy of life and regeneration, so here he employs a two-part structure to capture both the reality and the romance of history. The final movement of the play may well depict an idealized view of the nation, but considered together the two movements capture the human agony and political conniving which ushered in the Reformation and a foreign policy based on maintaining a balance of power among the major European countries. It is left entirely to contemporary spectators to accept, qualify, or reject the edenic vision of Elizabethan-Jacobean England; the playwright on that point is silent.

My purpose has not been to proclaim *Henry VIII* the last and best of the histories. There is no disputing the fact either that the principals lack the degree of ambivalence found in such earlier characters as John, Prince Hal, and Falstaff or that the narrative itself suffers from diffuseness despite the firm tonal rhythm of the play. Critics will undoubtedly continue to explain it away as a work of the left hand, of old age, or of collaboration. It may well be all three. But, at the very least, the pattern of the diptych and the extensive utilization of visual pageantry suggest a playwright, rarely satisfied with repetition, who continues to probe for an artistically credible vision of history and the effective transformation of that vision into the medium of drama. That the play was selected for performance at the Old Vic in London in 1953 to celebrate the coronation of Elizabeth II is no small measure of his success.

CHAPTER VI

Summary

EXCEPT FOR *Henry VIII,* all of Shakespeare's history plays were composed within a ten-year period during which, whether the comparison is drawn within his own canon or with the work of others, both his artistic vision and his dramaturgical skills developed at a remarkable pace. The *Henry VI* plays are in quality a level above their contemporaries to be sure, but in form and technique they are fundamentally not unlike the work of Lodge, Greene, or Peele. The significant point is the manner in which they reveal Shakespeare's steady advance in technical mastery. In each of the plays he seems conscious of the necessity for a breadth of vision which, by forcing the spectators to observe the action from a multiplicity of angles, accommodates a focus larger than the fortunes and misfortunes of any single individual. At the same time he increasingly seeks the harmonious blend of those elements of detachment and breadth with those of emotional engagement through depth of characterization. In part 1 a pattern of four thematically related plot strands, each involving open hostility followed by an unstable reconciliation, calls attention to the action itself, and interest in individual characterization is perforce minimized; even so, there are effective emotional moments during the soliloquies spoken by Talbot, Gloucester, and Winchester. In part 2 the action centers on two stylized individuals, the saintly Gloucester and the devilish York, yet Henry's ambivalence not only prevents a melodramatic encounter but also directly involves the spectators in the value judgments central to the drama; the king's passivity, even though motivated by a moral sensibility, provokes both Gloucester's murder and York's ambition, and the spectators must sit in final judgment on both the characters and the ambiguous situations prompting their actions. Part 3 presents in Henry and Richard the first major accumulation of soliloquies and asides for internal focus as the playwright intersects the two patterns of internalization, the one character sensitive to his moral dilemma, the other devoted entirely to Machiavellian principles. Perhaps most important, Henry through his moral persistence comes very close to tragedy, seeming to achieve in his final moments a spiritual insight which transcends the physical destruction.

Shakespeare's Richard plays extend and amplify the patterns of characterization introduced in *3 Henry VI*, with the consequence that the breadth of the historical perspective is minimized. In the conceptualization of the character of Richard III, Shakespeare explores the full implications of the self-centered villain-hero; instead of focusing the action outward on a sweep of historical events, he narrows his dramatic vision to those particular events which pertain to Richard's gaining and losing of the crown. Similarly in *Richard II* he explores in depth the potentially tragic qualities of a character like Henry VI. Sensitive and imaginative, flawed by indecisiveness and the lust for self-gratification, woefully miscast in the role of king, Richard is delineated as abominable in his abuses of the royal prerogative and yet genuinely sympathetic in his sufferings as a man. While both of the Richard plays possess structural features which suggest a broad perspective, they nonetheless mark a distinct turn away from a historical perspective and toward a more intense focus upon the central figure.

In *King John* and the Henry IV plays, Shakespeare commits himself anew to the development of a powerfully ambivalent historical perspective combining the elements of depth and breadth. On the one hand, he simultaneously develops several plot lines or central issues, scatters the setting across two nations, and utilizes static characterization—structural devices designed to broaden the spectators' vision beyond any single figure or single chain of incidents. On the other hand, his design in *King John* forces the spectators to observe each of the major issues—for example, John's right to the throne and his actions leading to the failure of his rule—from a wide diversity of views with the result that these issues assume an ambivalence that provides a genuine human dimension for the play. In *1, 2 Henry IV* Shakespeare's ambivalence is directed to the characters themselves. While the central figures are static and hence do not command the close rapport that would distort the larger vision of the scene, the spectators experience a mixed response because they are forced to view each of the principals in both plays in widely divergent situations. Henry, Hal, Hotspur, and

Falstaff, for example, are observed in moments public and private, courageous and cowardly, melancholic and carefree, philosophic and pragmatic. The consequence is a cumulative ambiguity in the characters, a sense of vitality and spontaneity which belies their essentially static quality.

Henry V, if not the most successful, is in many ways structurally the most complex of Shakespeare's histories. The multiple plots, the diversity of setting, the use of the chorus as a pointing device, and the static characterization—these are Shakespeare's standard methods for establishing and maintaining the broad perspective vital to the historical theme. The innovative quality comes in his attempt to provide a dramatically engaging dimension for the play through Henry's brief but significantly placed soliloquy, through a constant focus upon the young king resulting from the diverse manners in which the surrounding characters view him, and through the consistent interweaving of thematically related episodes which suspend the spectators between allegorical abstraction and absorption in character analysis. Only the spectators are in a position to relate the various components of the play and to perceive the rich ambiguities and ironies both in the character of Henry and in the careful arrangement of the heroic and the comic scenes. For those who are successful, the play is a complex exploration of human character caught in the web of historical circumstance. For those who are not, the play is either a simplistic exposé of crass Machiavellianism or a pageantlike display of fervid patriotism.

Henry VIII, although in many respects a lesser play than its predecessors, reflects both Shakespeare's use of past techniques and his continuing experimentation. Aside from the devices which distance the spectators from particular events and personalities and thereby encourage the broad view, the various principal figures, though fundamentally static, are again depicted with an ambivalence that lends at least a degree of emotional credibility. Unique to the histories is the arrangement of this action as a diptych, acts 1–3 characterized by tyranny, oppression, and misjudgment; acts 4–5 reflecting the celebration of justice and the joyous anticipation of the period of national prosperity and happiness. The two-part structure captures, at least partially successfully, both the reality and the romance of history, the idealized

187

view of the nation alongside the human suffering and frustration and the crafty maneuvering dictated by the historical necessity of an absolutist monarchy in England within the context of the political structure of the European States.

With its prophetic concern for both Elizabeth and James, *Henry VIII* is Shakespeare's tenth and final history. As a group the plays project a dramatic vision which extends backward to the reign of John in the early years of the thirteenth century and forward to the time of the latest composition. This four-hundred-year period chronicles England's development from a small island kingdom to a major power involved in colonization and world trade, from a land continuously torn asunder by internecine strife to a nation which for more than a century was peacefully united under firm monarchical control. More important for our purposes, the plays afford the opportunity to observe Shakespeare's constant experimentation from one stage world to the next and, in particular, the importance of *King John* and *1 Henry IV* to the refinement for his most powerful histories of a dramatic technique distinct from that of the major tragedies, a structure combining the detachment of a documentary necessary for a broad intellectual view of history and the engagement between character and spectator without which no drama can be profoundly and emotionally engaging. While the history play in many respects was a creation of a particular age, like comedy and tragedy it assumes in Shakespeare's hands a universal relevance to the human condition.

Notes

CHAPTER I: INTRODUCTION

1. J. B. Henneman speaks of the "succession or stringing together of scenes or episodes" ("The Episodes in Shakespeare's *1 Henry VI*," *PMLA*, 15 [1900], 293), and Robert Y. Turner describes Shakespeare's repeated use of the Marlovian device of "a confrontation of groups to express a struggle for political power" ("Shakespeare and the Public Confrontation Scene in Early History Plays," *MP*, 62 [1964], 1). Contrarily, both John Arthos (*Shakespeare: The Early Writings* [Totowa, N.J.: Rowman and Littlefield, 1972], p. 189) and E. W. Talbert (*Elizabethan Drama and Shakespeare's Early Plays* [Chapel Hill: Univ. of North Carolina Press, 1963], p. 175) argue that the repetitive pattern is an effective means of "focus[ing] on many matters at once."

2. Wilson, *Shakespearian and Other Studies,* ed. Helen Gardner (Oxford: Clarendon, 1969), p. 14; Lawrence V. Ryan, ed., *Henry VI, Part One* (New York: New American Library, 1967), p. xxiv.

3. Wilson may be correct in his assertion that plays based on British history did not exist prior to the Armada (*Marlowe and the Early Shakespeare* [Oxford: Clarendon, 1953], pp. 105–6), but clearly the history play, loosely defined, was no novelty by 1592, the terminus ad quem for the composition of *1 Henry VI.*

4. Alfred Harbage, ed., *Annals of English Drama,* 2nd ed., rev. Samuel Schoenbaum (Philadelphia: Univ. of Pennsylvania Press, 1964).

5. *The Shakespeare Revolution: Criticism and Performance in the Twentieth Century* (Cambridge: Cambridge Univ. Press, 1977), p. 3. Norman Sanders aptly notes that recent productions in England have demonstrated "the extraordinary richness and variety that the histories have on the boards" ("American Criticism of Shakespeare's History Plays," *Shakespeare Studies,* 9 [1976], 22).

CHAPTER II: *HENRY VI*

1. Maurice Morgann, *On the Dramatic Character of Sir John Falstaff,* ed. W. A. Gill (1912; rpt. Freeport, N.Y.: Books for Libraries Press, 1970), p. 49.

2. H. B. Charlton, *Shakespeare, Politics, and Politicians* (Oxford: Oxford Univ. Press, 1929), p. 8. "A fairly shapeless piece of writing" (Clifford Leech, *Shakespeare: The Chronicles* [London: Longmans, Green, 1962], p. 14), it is "one of the worst plays in the canon" (J. Dover Wilson, ed., *1 Henry VI* [Cambridge: Cambridge Univ. Press, 1952], p. ix), "a fantasia on historical themes" (Geoffrey Bullough, ed., *Narrative and Dramatic Sources of Shakespeare,* 3 [New York: Columbia Univ. Press, 1960], 25).

3. Riggs, p. 16. Possessed of a genuine thematic unity (H. M. Richmond, *Shakespeare's Political Plays* [New York: Random House, 1967], p. 36), it has no parallel "since Aeschylus wrote the trilogy of which the *Persians* is the surviving fragment" (R. W. Chambers, *The Jacobean Shakespeare and Measure for Measure* [Oxford: Oxford Univ. Press, 1937], p. 6).

4. Tillyard, Ribner, Campbell, Reese, Sen Gupta.

5. See Nicholas Brooke's heroic view of Richard III ("Reflecting Gems and Dead Bones: Tragedy Versus History in *Richard III,*" *CQ,* 7 [1965], 123–34); also Robert Ornstein, *A Kingdom for a Stage: The Achievement of Shakespeare's History Plays* (Cambridge: Harvard Univ. Press, 1972).

6. Manheim; A. L. French, "*Henry VI* and the Ghost of Richard II," *English Studies,* 50, Anglo-American Supplement (1969), xxxvii–xliii.

7. Prior; Arthur Sewell, *Character and Society in Shakespeare* (Oxford: Oxford Univ. Press, 1951).

8. Riggs, pp. 9, 14; see also Robert B. Pierce, *Shakespeare's History Plays: The Family and the State* (Columbus: Ohio State Univ. Press, 1971).

9. Hereward T. Price in 1951 based his discussion of thematic unity on the concept of single authorship (*Construction in Shakespeare* [Ann Arbor: Univ. of Michigan, 1951]); Andrew S. Cairncross, editor of the New Arden volume, flatly assumes the Henry VI plays to "bear the stamp of a single mind" and to be written "in natural sequence" (London: Methuen, 1962), pp. xxxvii, liii.

10. Both Wolfgang H. Clemen ("Anticipation and Foreboding in Shakespeare's Early Histories," *Shakespeare Survey,* 6 [1953], 26) and Peter Bilton (*Commentary and Control in Shakespeare's Plays* [New York: Humanities Press, 1974], p. 25) take especial note of Exeter's choric function.

11. Line references to Shakespeare's plays throughout this study are to the edition of G. B. Evans, *The Riverside Shakespeare* (Boston: Houghton Mifflin, 1974).

12. Faye L. Kelly, "Oaths in Shakespeare's *Henry VI* Plays," *SQ,* 24 (1973), 359.

13. See David Scott Kastan, "The Shape of Time: Form and Value in the Shakespearean History Play," *Comparative Drama,* 7 (1973–74), 272.

14. P. 35. The scene reveals "play hardening into reality" (John W. Blanpied, " 'Art and Baleful Sorcery': The Counterconsciousness of *Henry VI, Part I,*" *SEL,* 15 [1975], 218).

15. Ronald Berman is certainly accurate in his observation that Henry lacks the necessary "combination of piety and power" ("Fathers and Sons in the Henry VI Plays," *SQ,* 13 [1962], 488); yet, as Mattie Swayne notes, the King is basically a sympathetic figure ("Shakespeare's King Henry VI as a Pacifist," *College English,* 3 [1941–42], 144).

16. Marco Mincoff, "The Composition of *Henry VI, Part I,*" *SQ,* 16 (1965), 279. Sigurd Burckhardt argues that the scene is a vital prefiguring of the new style which Shakespeare must teach his nation, a style "of grace, of easy self-confidence, of implicit courtesy and generosity, of function rather than ceremony" (*Shakespearean Meanings* [Princeton: Princeton Univ. Press, 1968], pp. 49, 74). F. W. Brownlow argues that the scene reflects the "baleful influence of women as a running motif in *Henry VI*" (*Two Shakespearean Sequences* [Pittsburgh: Univ. of Pittsburgh Press, 1977], p. 22).

17. See Allison Gaw, *The Origin and Development of One Henry VI* (New York, 1926; rpt. AMS Press, 1971), p. 35; and J. D. Wilson, p. x.

18. David Bevington brands her "claim of pregnancy to avoid execution . . . an outrageous travesty of the Virgin birth" ("The Domineering Female in *1 Henry VI,*" *Shakespeare Studies,* 2 [1966], 52). Treated ironically throughout (Leo Kirschbaum, "The Authorship of *1 Henry VI,*" *PMLA,* 67 [1952], 818ff.), she is a spokesman for anarchic revolt, a "virtual parody of the Marlovian prototype" (Riggs, pp. 22, 84).

19. J. P. Brockbank, in an excellent study, points to the symbolic importance of the "language of pageantry" ("The Frame of Disorder: *Henry VI*" in *Early Shakespeare,* ed. J. R. Brown and B. Harris [London: Arnold, 1961], pp. 73, 75).

20. A. P. Rossiter calls the "doubleness" between the triumph of human destiny and the frustration of the individual man a quality "just short of the tragic" (*Angel with Horns,* ed. Graham Storey [New York: Theatre Arts Books, 1961], p. 42). See also Michael Quinn, "Providence in Shakespeare's Yorkist Plays," *SQ,* 10 (1959), 51.

21. The emphasis is upon the infinite varieties of insatiable ambition (Arthos, p. 205) which vitiate the very concepts of justice and law (Edward I. Berry, *Patterns of Decay: Shakespeare's Early Histories* [Charlottesville: Univ. Press of Virginia, 1975], p. 29).

22. For an extensive discussion of the motif of the disobedient wife, see Pierce, pp. 58ff.

23. The animal imagery has recently been examined in some detail by Virginia M. Carr ("Animal Imagery in *2 Henry VI*," *ES*, 53 [1972], 408–12) and Carol M. Kay ("Traps, Slaughter, and Chaos: A Study of Shakespeare's *Henry VI* Plays," *Studies in the Literary Imagination*, 5 [1972], 1–26). James L. Calderwood extends his discussion to the function of the four dominant images: trapping, sight, elevation, and hands ("Shakespeare's Evolving Imagery in *2 Henry VI*," *ES*, 48 [1967], 481–93).

24. Samuel M. Pratt, "Shakespeare and Humphrey Duke of Gloucester: A Study of Myth," *SQ*, 16 (1965), 216.

25. The charges brought against Gloucester, as Bullough points out, are actually a combination of crimes ascribed to others (3:94).

26. Ornstein notes especially the double entendres involving "dying" (p. 44), and Pierce speaks of the principal characters' coming to have a "unique voice" in the play (p. 53); see also J. D. Wilson, ed., *II Henry VI*, New Cambridge Shakespeare (Cambridge: Cambridge Univ. Press, 1952), pp. l–liii.

27. However much Suffolk deserves his fate, Hardin Craig and Bevington correctly observe that the commoners' taking justice into their own hands is a further reflection of the growing cancer of anarchy (eds., *The Complete Works of Shakespeare*, 2nd ed., rev. [Glenview: Scott, Foresman, 1973], p. 209). They represent the "most lawless element in society, . . . [a] pirate band made up of military deserters" (Don M. Ricks, *Shakespeare's Emergent Form: A Study of the Structures of the Henry VI Plays* [Logan: Utah State Univ. Press, 1968], p. 73). To the contrary, Bilton argues that Walter Whitmore serves to vent the audience's disapproval of the villain Suffolk (p. 28).

28. Webster, *Shakespeare Without Tears* (New York: McGraw-Hill, 1942), p. 122; Jackson, "On Producing *Henry VI*," *Shakespeare Survey*, 6 (1953), 50; Brockbank, p. 73. See also Wayne L. Billings, "Ironic Lapses: Plotting in *Henry VI*," *Studies in the Literary Imagination*, 5 (1972), 27; and Kelly, p. 359.

29. Pp. 88, 107. See also H. C. Goddard, *The Meaning of Shakespeare* (Chicago: Univ. of Chicago Press, 1951), 1:30; and Swayne, p. 144.

30. *The Problem of Order* (Chapel Hill: Univ. of North Carolina Press, 1962), p. 197. C. T. Prouty notes that, whereas Margaret in Q_1 condemns Henry for bookishness, she in F_1 emphasizes his utter disregard for things temporal (*The Contention and Shakespeare's 2 Henry VI* [New Haven: Yale Univ. Press, 1954], p. 60).

31. Blanpied, "History as Play in *Henry VI, Part II*," *Susquehanna University Studies*, 9 (1972), 88.

32. Leech views this fight between "two simple men, one terrified, one drunk," as a parody of chivalric encounter implying "a critical attitude toward the warring nobles" (p. 17).

33. Reese, p. 123; Ribner, p. 108; Berman, p. 493. To Brents Stirling the scenes represent Shakespeare's reaction to the rioting Brownists and Anabaptists of his own day (*The Populace in Shakespeare* [New York: Columbia Univ. Press, 1949], p. 101).

34. C. L. Barber, *Shakespeare's Festive Comedy* (Princeton: Princeton Univ. Press, 1959), p. 13; Berry, p. 46; A. C. Hamilton, *The Early Shakespeare* (San Marino: Huntington Library, 1967), p. 45; Rossiter, p. 280.

35. Clemen, p. 26; see further his *Shakespeare's Dramatic Art* (London: Methuen, 1972), pp. 18ff.

36. If it is an overstatement to speak of "a strong current of unquestioning belief in the principle of divine vengeance" in *2 Henry VI* (Sister M. B. Mroz, *Divine Vengeance* [1941; rpt. New York: Haskell House, 1971], p. 121), it is less misleading than the assertion that "there are no gods in Shakespeare," that "history has no meaning and stands still" (Jan Kott, *Shakespeare Our Contemporary,* trans. Boleslaw Taborski [Garden City: Doubleday, 1964], pp. 19, 37). Whereas Halle stresses the inscrutable ways of providence, Shakespeare "presents in detail the human causes for Henry's failure" (Prior, p. 39).

37. Several decades ago the view was almost commonplace that the play was little more than a "naive stringing of episode upon episode" (E. K. Chambers, *Shakespeare: A Survey* [London: Sidgwick and Jackson, 1925], p. 1). While an occasional critic might still comment on the "structural flaccidity" (Norman Rabkin, *Shakespeare and the Common Understanding* [New York: Free Press, 1967], p. 43), current emphasis is on the complex manner in which Shakespeare organizes the plot—through open quarrel, allegorical pageant, and internal struggle (Hamilton, p. 35)—to force us to "confront our existence as 'time's subjects' released in a world of contingency and flux" (p. 275). The structure derives from the "confluence of the Senecal dramatic tradition, with its ruthless retributive morality, and the Christian (or Hebraic) cult of *Vindicta Dei*" (Brockbank, p. 107).

38. Arthur Freeman, ed., *Henry VI, Part 2* (New York: New American Library, 1967), p. xxiv.

39. Pratt, p. 216.

40. Shakespeare provides the king a "set of values above those of the victors and has produced sympathy or even admiration for him in defeat" (Swayne, p. 144).

41. While Richmond's charge that Henry is a "bore" riddled with "the defects of his character" may be extreme (p. 57), one must agree that Hen-

ry at this point is "too simple for a politician" and "too ready to trust to conciliation to be a soldier" (Una Ellis-Fermor, *The Frontiers of Drama* [London: Methuen, 1945], p. 38).

42. Billings describes Warwick's subsequent defection to the Lancastrian cause as thematically pivotal, reflecting "the noble or the great undermined by the mean, the ignoble, and unheroic" (p. 49).

43. He may indeed seem "a born leader from the first" (John Palmer, *Political Characters of Shakespeare* [London: Macmillan, 1948], p. 67), but he is also recognized as "the incomparable symbol of treachery and deceit" (Milton Crane, ed., *Henry VI, Part 3* [New York: Signet, 1968], p. xxx). To J. D. Wilson he is a puppet upon Fortune's wheel, "turned by the hand of Providence" (ed., *The Third Part of King Henry VI* [Cambridge: Cambridge Univ. Press, 1952], p. xxvii).

44. Kelly argues that the "complete disregard for the sanctity of an oath" characterizes the political chaos of the play (p. 359).

45. The very qualities which doom him as king permit him to retain his humanity (Prior, p. 37); the effectiveness of the characterization tempts Goddard to suspect the possibility of revision during Shakespeare's maturity (1:30).

46. Hamilton, p. 61; Berman, "Power and Humility in Shakespeare," *SAQ*, 60 (1961), 412.

47. Berry considers Henry as the divine polarity (p. 71), and Tillyard describes him as "the chief instrument of the expression of the working of providence and heavenly forces" (p. 217).

48. Whether described as "a Ciceronian *habitus*" (Talbert, p. 219) or as an "all but transcendent" moral force (Brockbank, p. 98), Henry in his conduct in the final act renders virtually irrelevant John Bromley's assertion that the murder of the king "is a needed purging of the state" (*The Shakespearean Kings* [Boulder: Colorado Associated Univ. Press, 1971], p. 24).

49. On the image patterns in the play, see G. Wilson Knight, *The Shakespearean Tempest* (Oxford: Oxford Univ. Press, 1932), chap. 2; Alvin B. Kernan, "A Comparison of the Imagery in *3 Henry VI* and *The True Tragedie of Richard Duke of York*," *SP*, 51 (1954), 431–42; and Kay, pp. 1–26.

50. From the "balanced pattern of confrontation" in the opening scenes (Turner, *Shakespeare's Apprenticeship* [Chicago: Univ. of Chicago Press, 1974], p. 44), Shakespeare sets forth a "play of battles, each more savage than the last" (Herschel Baker, "Introduction" to *Henry VI, Parts 1, 2, and 3* in *The Riverside Shakespeare*, p. 592), in which the opposing value judgments of the rival claimants "are subsumed" and "both are valid" (Rossiter, p. 51).

51. "Anticipation and Foreboding," p. 26.

52. Jackson notes of a recent production: the "static tableau . . . threw more light on the horror of civil war than all the scenes of wasteful bloodshed" (p. 51). The vision of Henry "fixed in a pose of Sorrow" (M. C. Bradbrook, *Shakespeare and Elizabethan Poetry* [New York: Oxford Univ. Press, 1952], p. 127) is "worth a thousand words" from choric figures (Bilton, p. 30). The ritual setting, according to Ornstein, "focuses attention on the moral perversity rather than the physical horror of the crimes" (p. 55).

53. Measured by what is to come the play, to some critics, is sprawling and formless (E. K. Chambers, p. 5), winding its way "through unmanageable and embarrassing matter" (Roman Dyboski, *The Rise and Fall of Shakespeare's Dramatic Art,* quoted in Cairncross, p. xlix); see also Charlton, p. 8.

54. Eds., *The Second and Third Parts of King Henry VI,* in *William Shakespeare: The Complete Works,* gen. ed. Alfred Harbage (Baltimore: Penguin, 1969), p. 475.

55. Derek A. Traversi, *An Approach to Shakespeare* (New York: Doubleday, 1956), p. 14. See also, Leech, p. 22; and Peter Alexander, *Introductions to Shakespeare* (London: Collins, 1964), p. 132.

CHAPTER III: *RICHARD III, RICHARD II*

1. Margaret's function is reminiscent of the furies of Senecan tragedy (O. J. Campbell, ed., *The Living Shakespeare* [New York: Macmillan, 1958], pp. 117–18); yet as Clemen points out ("Tradition and Originality in Shakespeare's *Richard III,*" *SQ,* 5 [1954], 25), in the older tradition curses "occur . . . as conventional gestures at moments of despair and wrath"; here they represent "the principle of historical continuity within which the play achieves its meaning" (Tom F. Driver, *The Sense of History in Greek and Shakespearean Drama* [New York: Columbia Univ. Press, 1960], p. 98). She is "the one voice [Richard] quails before" (Rossiter, p. 13), the spokesman for "inscrutable providence" (Craig, ed., *The Complete Works of Shakespeare* [Chicago: Scott, Foresman, 1951], p. 301).

2. Both this scene (Kristian Smidt, *Injurious Imposters and Richard III* [New York: Humanities Press, 1964], p. 168) and the earlier scene of Margaret's curse (E. K. Chambers, *William Shakespeare: Facts and Problems* [Oxford: Oxford Univ. Press, 1930], 1:301) may well be afterthoughts, but the effect in each instance is to heighten the architectonic structure of the piece.

3. Aerol Arnold quite correctly describes Shakespeare's foreshadowing and recapitulatory uses of dreams in the play, but the text simply will not support the assertion that Clarence achieves a full repentance in contrast to the remorseless Richard ("The Recapitulation Dream in *Richard III* and *Macbeth*," *SQ*, 6 [1955], 53).

4. The interpretation of Richard's final cry as an implication that "the ecstasy of the fight is worth a dozen kingdoms" (G. B. Shaw, *Shaw on Shakespeare*, ed. Edwin Wilson [New York: Dutton, 1961], p. 172) is not supported by the full context. More to the point is H. C. Goddard's observation that the final words are a desperate confession "that the worldly kingdom . . . is worth less than the few seconds by which another horse might postpone his doom" (1:39).

5. The symbolic significance which some critics attach to Richard limits his effective development as a tragic figure. Destroyed wholly by supernatural forces (R. Simpson, *Political Use of Historical Plays* [London, 1873], p. 423), Richard, in the operation of nemesis (R. G. Moulton, *Shakespeare as a Dramatic Artist* [Oxford, 1888], p. 110; Reese, p. 223), is transformed from "credibly motivated villain to a symbol . . . of diabolism" (Tillyard, p. 241). In his will to resist the mounting weight of historical retribution, Richard becomes "Mankind . . . resisting oppression and being destroyed" (Brooke, p. 134); see also Richard P. Wheeler, "History, Character, and Conscience in *Richard III*," *Comparative Drama*, 5 (1971–72), 319 and Michael Neill, "Shakespeare's Halle of Mirrors: Play, Politics, and Psychology in *Richard III*," *Shakespeare Studies*, 8 (1975), 126. For an analysis of Richard's terrifying dream, see Bettie Anne Doebler, " 'Despair and Dye': The Ultimate Temptation of *Richard III*," *Shakespeare Studies*, 7 (1974), 75–85.

6. Richard's "many-sidedness" humanizes him (C. Coe, *Shakespeare's Villains* [New York: Bookman Associates, 1957], p. 24); the "consummate actor" (E. K. Chambers, *Survey*, p. 16), Richard "has what no Senecan villain possesses: the power of self-ridicule, the habit of ironic detachment" (Sidney Thomas, *The Antic Hamlet and Richard III* [New York: King's Crown Press, 1943], p. 15). He "deceives the stupid and dares the wiser sort to challenge his integrity" (Alexander, p. 135).

7. "Tragic irony, found as a rare device here and there in pre-Shakespearean drama, becomes in *Richard III* a deliberately applied instrument of foreshadowing and cross-referencing" (Clemen, "Tradition and Originality," p. 251).

8. "At this moment, crucial both in the play and in Shakespeare's career, the play turns to tragedy" (Rabkin, p. 251). Shakespeare approaches "division and self-knowledge in Richard" (R. B. Heilman, *Tragedy and Melodrama* [Seattle: Univ. of Washington Press, 1968], p. 179); his in-

ternalization is explored extensively by William B. Toole in "The Motif of Psychic Division in *Richard III*," *Shakespeare Survey*, 27 (1974), 28. Shakespeare clearly does not intend for the final soliloquy to suggest either a "sudden and unprecedented change in Richard's character" (Rabkin, p. 251) or a "*drift*[ing]—into an unexpected deepening of [it]" (Heilman, "Satiety and Conscience: Aspects of Richard III," *The Antioch Review*, 24 [1964–65], 67).

9. *Shakespeare and the Mystery of God's Judgments* (Athens: Univ. of Georgia Press, 1976), p. 69.

10. H. Ulrici in 1876 criticized the "internal uniformity of the play" (*Shakespeare's Dramatic Art* [London], 2:276). More recently, Reese has described the rigidly paralleled" action and the redundancy of the "symbolic episodes" (pp. 208, 210).

11. See Roland Mushat Frye, *Shakespeare and Christian Doctrine* (Princeton: Princeton Univ. Press, 1963), p. 151.

12. Virgil K. Whitaker asserts that, except for Marlowe, Shakespeare was "the only dramatist who worked seriously at solving the structural problem presented by the dramatic treatment of English history" (*The Mirror up to Nature* [San Marino: Huntington Library, 1965], p. 16). *Richard III* reflects a "firm architecture of style and construction" (Clemen, *The Development of Shakespeare's Imagery* [Cambridge, Mass.: Harvard Univ. Press, 1951], p. 49). The "cyclical structure" (Rossiter, "The Structure of *Richard III*," *Durham University Journal* [1938–39], p. 46) suggests "a rhetorical symphony of five movements, with first and second subjects and some Wagnerian *Leitmotifs*" (Rossiter, *Angel*, p. 7). Alice L. Birney examines Margaret as a representative of "the satirist at a primitive stage" (*Satiric Catharsis in Shakespeare* [Berkeley: Univ. of California Press, 1973], p. 16).

13. E. K. Chambers, *Survey*, p. 91. Richard "was a sonneteer's king" (G. B. Harrison, *Shakespeare at Work, 1592–1603* [London: Routledge, 1933], p. 90), Shakespeare's first central figure who is "introspective, imaginative, and eloquent" (M. W. Black, ed., *The Tragedy of King Richard II* [Baltimore: Penguin, 1957], p. 15); he lends "to sentimentality the momentary might of passion" (Charlton, *Shakespearian Tragedy* [Cambridge: Cambridge Univ. Press, 1949], p. 45). On the many faces of Richard, see Lois Potter, "The Antic Disposition of Richard II," *Shakespeare Survey*, 27 (1974), 40.

14. While it may be extreme to assert that the queen "is merely a reflector to emphasize . . . the loving-kindness of [Richard's] devotion" (Lionel Aldred ed., *King Richard II* [London: Macmillan, 1935], p. xxxvi), Richard's "relations with his friends and his wife" do, as Ribner writes, "reveal him as not lacking in private virtue" (p. 153). Robert R.

Reid has maintained that Richard's love affair was "with his kingdom"; rejected, he "instinctively turns on himself" ("Richard II: Portrait of a Psychotic," *JGE*, 16 [1964], 63).

15. It is true, as F. E. Halliday observes, that many of Richard's passages are quasi-soliloquies, since he "rarely talks to people; he talks to things, to the earth, to the crown" (*The Poetry of Shakespeare's Plays* [London: Duckworth, 1954], p. 81).

16. J. A. Bryant sees Richard as *"microchristus"* and *"microcosmos,"* as the "Lord's anointed" and as "Everyman" ("The Linked Analogies of *Richard II,*" *Sewanee Review*, 65 [1957], 425) while J. W. Draper analyzes him as the mercurial type ("The Character of Richard II," *PQ*, 21 [1942], 230). Leonard F. Dean argues that Shakespeare depicts an ironic version of the tragic hero, in whom "tragic qualities . . . are constantly undercut and thwarted" ("From *Richard II* to *Henry V:* A Closer View," in *Studies in Honor of De Witt T. Starnes* (1967), rpt. in *Shakespeare: Modern Essays in Criticism*, ed. Leonard Dean [New York: Oxford Univ. Press, 1967], p. 192). To the contrary, both Travis Bogard in the king's suffering ("Shakespeare's Second Richard," *PMLA*, 70 [1955], 208) and P. G. Phialas in the nature of the tragic process (*"Richard II* and Shakespeare's Tragic Mode," *TSLL*, 5 [1963], 344) view Richard as a significant step in Shakespeare's development of tragic character. For a similar view, see Harold F. Folland, "King Richard's Pallid Victory," *SQ*, 24 (1973), 390, 398.

17. Rabkin, p. 81. F. W. Moorman claims that Shakespeare viewed divine right with "mordant irony" ("Plays Attributed to Shakespeare," in *Cambridge History of English Literature*, 5:278), and Kott asserts that to Shakespeare "history has no meaning" in the repetition of "its cruel cycle" (p. 37). To the contrary, Shakespeare utilized the "publicly acknowleged morality" (Robert Langbaum, *The Poetry of Experience* [New York: Random House, 1957], p. 161) to depict the "dichotomies" in the human interpretation of this moral order (Talbert, *Problem of Order*, p. 200). He "develops the political issue in all its complexity, and leaves judgment upon it to the spectator" (J. D. Wilson, ed., *King Richard II* [Cambridge: Cambridge Univ. Press, 1951], p. xxxv); "no one can tell whether Bolingbroke or Richard II is in the right" (Craig, *The Enchanted Glass* [Oxford: Blackwell, 1950], p. 157).

18. In what Leonard Dean describes as a good example of the "theatricality of politics" (*"Richard II:* The State and Image of the Theater," *PMLA*, 67 [1952], 214), Richard is "capable enough . . . in his official role of ceremonialist" (Theodore Weiss, *The Breath of Clowns and Kings* [New York: Atheneum, 1971], p. 210). This "emblematic tableau" (Diane Bornstein, "Trial by Combat and Official Responsibility in *Richard*

II," Shakespeare Studies, 8 [1975], 140) reveals, however, the "nature of Richard's exercise of power" (Norman J. Jeffares, "In One Person Many People: King Richard II," in *The Morality of Art,* ed. D. W. Jefferson [London: Routledge and Kegan Paul, 1969], p. 54); and the unfinished tournament is a "reflection of Richard's character . . . as well as his love of ceremony" (P. G. Phialas, "The Medieval in *Richard II,*" *SQ* [1961], 306).

19. Rossiter (ed., *Woodstock: A Moral History* [London: Chatto and Windus, 1946], pp. 48–49) explains the passage through reference to the older play. A. F. Watt (ed., *King Richard II* [New York: Clive, 1907], p. xix) calls Mowbray Richard's "scapegoat." J. D. Wilson has written that Mowbray's lines are "embarrassed and ambiguous," that the issue of the murder "is left quite obscure" (*King Richard II,* p. 126). Tillyard has observed that Shakespeare "leaves uncertain the question of who murdered Woodstock and never says that Richard was personally responsible" (p. 297), and Black that "Mowbray speaks ambiguously" (p. 32).

20. Shakespeare's intention was "to show Richard playing the part of majesty with a fair efficiency in these first scenes" (Peter Ure, ed., *Richard II* [London: Methuen, 1956], p. lxv).

21. Richmond, p. 124.

22. W. G. Clark and W. A. Wright, eds., *The Cambridge Shakespeare* (Cambridge, 1864), vol. 4, and C. H. Herford, ed., *The Works of William Shakespeare* (London, 1899), vol. 6 (see Black, ed., *The Life and Death of King Richard the Second: A New Variorum Edition of Shakespeare* [Philadelphia: Lippincott, 1955], p. 29)—though not considering the effects on the total scene—have accepted the lines as indicative of Richard's complicity. So also, more recently, have Craig, ed., *The Complete Works,* p. 648, and G. L. Kittredge, ed., *The Tragedy of King Richard II,* rev. Ribner (Waltham, Mass.: Blaisdell, 1966), p. 5.

23. Palmer, p. 130; see also J. D. Wilson, *King Richard II,* p. 139.

24. Richard becomes "man and martyr" (Karl F. Thompson, "Richard II: Martyr," *SQ,* 8 [1957], 160) as the scenes "are played against each other for effect" (W.B.C. Watkins, *Shakespeare and Spenser* [Princeton: Princeton Univ. Press, 1950], p. 80) to force the spectators to "see the unfolding story through the eyes now of one character, now of another" (Francis Fergusson, *Shakespeare: The Pattern in His Carpet* [New York: Delacorte, 1970], p. 94). See also Paul A. Jorgensen, "A Formative Shakespearean Legacy: Elizabethan Views of God, Fortune, and War," *PMLA,* 90 (1975), 232.

25. Sen Gupta brands York, who later supports Bolingbroke as king, a "spineless, vacillating old man" (p. 117). The opposite view, held by J. M.

Murry, is that York's "loyalty (perfect in kind) is to royalty as the fount of Order. . . . For him royalty is divine, only so long as it fulfills a divine purpose" (*Shakespeare* [London: Cape, 1936], p. 147).

26. Samuel Kliger ("The Sun Imagery in *Richard II,*" *SP*, 45 [1948], 197–98) traces Richard's passage from noonday to eclipse, and K. M. Harris ("Sun and Water Imagery in *Richard II:* Its Dramatic Function," *SQ*, 21 [1970], 162) describes the transfer of the sun imagery to Bolingbroke. Other studies stress the imagery of the earth (Richard D. Altick, "Symphonic Imagery in *Richard II,*" *PMLA*, 62 [1947], 339–65), of the crown (Allan S. Downer, "The Life of Our Design," *Hudson Review*, 2 [1949], 242–63), of rise and fall (Jorgensen, "Vertical Patterns in *Richard II,*" *SAB*, 23 [1948], 119–34; Arthur Suzman, "Imagery and Symbolism in *Richard II,*" *SQ*, 7 [1957], 355–70), of negligence, excess, and waste (R. J. Dorius, "A Little More Than a Little," *SQ*, 11 [1960], 13–26), and of trees, plants, and planting (C.F.E. Spurgeon, *Shakespeare's Imagery* [Cambridge: Cambridge Univ. Press, 1935], p. 220). For a general discussion of the image patterns, see Kenneth Muir, *Shakespeare the Professional and Related Studies* (Totowa, N.J.: Rowman and Littlefield, 1973), p. 90.

27. Robert Hapgood, "Shakespeare's Thematic Mode of Speech: *Richard II* to *Henry V,*" *Shakespeare Survey*, 20 (1967), 42.

28. Lacking "the virtue of passive fortitude" (H. N. Hudson, *Shakespeare: His Life, Art, and Characters* [Boston, 1872], I, 55) to control his "consciousness of his own nullity, which descends, at certain times, almost to baseness" (F.P.G. Guizot, *Shakespeare and His Times* [New York, 1852], p. 310), Richard on occasion "reduces tragedy to melancholy" through his juxtaposition of "hysteria, emotional excess, and of true tragedy" (Traversi, *Richard II to Henry V*, pp. 30, 32).

29. Richard's final words have been branded as "the merest of lip-service" (Willard Farnham, *The Medieval Heritage of Elizabethan Drama* [Oxford: Blackwell, 1956], p. 417), his final actions as "boyish . . . impetuosity" (A. C. Swinburne, *Three Plays of Shakespeare* [New York: Harper, 1909], p. 83). To the contrary, Quinn avers that Richard "dies as Somebody, a lion overpowered; a king deposed" (" 'The King Is Not Himself': The Personal Tragedy of Richard II," *SP*, 56 [1959], 184) who has learned to "distinguish in himself shadow from substance" (D. H. Rieman, "Appearance, Reality, and Moral Order in *Richard II,*" *MLQ*, 35 [1964], 40). There is unmistakeably a move "toward self-knowledge, and even repentance" (Ure, p. lxxxii), a "developing away from self-serving despair" (R. L. Montgomery, "The Dimensions of Time in *Richard II,*" *Shakespeare Studies*, 4 [1968], 82). On the significance of Aumerle's

shifting loyalty as a means of creating a compassionate view of Richard, see Warren J. MacIsaac, "The Three Cousins in *Richard II*," *SQ*, 22 (1971), 139.

30. On the one hand, Bolingbroke is seen as "a manifestation . . . of the actual Machiavellian philosophy" (Ribner, "Bolingbroke, A True Machiavellian," *MLQ*, 9 [1948], 178), a "schemer" whose "speeches . . . betray calculation in their over-humility, over-sweetness" (R. F. Hill, "Dramatic Techniques and Interpretation in *Richard II*," in Brown and Harris, pp. 115, 106). On the other hand, he is an "instrument in the hands of Providence" (George A. Bonnard, "The Actor in Shakespeare," *SJ*, 82 [1951], 89), an opportunist (Stirling, "Bolingbroke's Decision," *SQ*, 2 [1951], 30) who thought of deposition only when Richard suggested it to him (French, "Who Deposed Richard II?" *Essays in Criticism*, 17 [1967], 424).

31. *Shakespeare and the Audience* (Cambridge, Mass.: Harvard Univ. Press, 1935), p. 50.

32. Henry immediately crushes the Oxford plot despite "the fact that his own brother-in-law is among the conspirators" (Winny, p. 73). With equal promptness he acts to pardon Aumerle; Hapgood contends that the decision is made "before the elder Yorks arrive but for the sake of public relations [he] goes along with the Yorks as they act out their old-fashioned rite of pardon" ("Three Eras in *Richard II*," *SQ*, 14 [1963], 283). Sheldon P. Zitner, to the contrary, considers Bolingbroke a Lord of Misrule who mocks the legitimate reign ("Aumerle's Conspiracy," *SEL*, 14 [1974], 252).

33. Clemen, *Shakespeare's Imagery*, p. 31.

34. "Each of Shakespeare's histories serves a special purpose in elucidating a political problem of Elizabeth's day" (L. B. Campbell, p. 125). Evelyn M. Albright weaves an elaborate explanation for the play as political allegory ("Shakespeare's *Richard II* and the Essex Conspiracy," *PMLA*, 42 [1927], 686–720; "Shakespeare's *Richard II*, Hayward's History of *Henry IV*, and the Essex Conspiracy," *PMLA*, 46 [1931], 694–719). Alfred Hart claims that a medieval concept of the divine right of kings is "historically false" and that Shakespeare and his colleagues "drew their allusions to the doctrines" from the Tudor-inspired *Book of Homilies* (*Shakespeare and the Homilies* [Melbourne: Melbourne Univ. Press, 1934], pp. 68, 73). J. W. Figgis points out, however, that Wycliffe's writings in defense of imperialism and the general struggle against the papacy did lead Richard to "claim for himself the position of an absolute monarch by Divine Right" (*The Divine Right of Kings* [Cambridge, 1896], p. 73). By contrast, the driving force in the development of divine right during

the Tudor era was not the need for antipapal theory but the desire for an omnipotent crown in parliament (J. W. Allen, *A History of Political Thought in the Sixteenth Century* [London: Methuen, 1928], p. 169).

35. Tillyard writes that *Richard II* is "only the prelude" of a "great new epic attempt" (p. 299), and E. K. Chambers calls it the "first act in the trilogy which leads up to . . . *Henry V*" (*Survey*, p. 89). Recently, John R. Elliott has examined the material in acts 4 and 5 which "look[s] forward to the continuing historical events that Shakespeare is to depict in the remainder of the *Richard II-Henry IV-Henry V* tetralogy" ("History and Tragedy in *Richard II*," *SEL*, 8 [1968], 269).

CHAPTER IV: *KING JOHN, HENRY IV, HENRY V*

1. Bullough, *Sources*, 4 (1962), 5 and Robert Adgar Law ("On the Date of *King John*," *SP*, 54 [1957], 119–27) represent the majority view while E.A.J. Honigmann (ed., *King John* [London: Methuen, 1954], p. xviii), Alexander (p. 99), and William Matchett (ed., *The Life and Death of King John* [New York: New American Library, 1966], p. xxii) claim Shakespeare's priority. Tillyard even suggests that *The Troublesome Raigne* is a bad quarto of *King John* (p. 248); J. D. Wilson demurs, predictably suggesting that the two are derived from a nonextant common source play (ed. *King John* [Cambridge: Cambridge Univ. Press, 1954], p. xx).

2. The play is "a bridge, a transition" (Sidney Shanker, *Shakespeare and the Uses of Ideology* [The Hague: Mouton, 1975], p. 56), "an experimental play between the two historical tetralogies" (Pierce, p. 125). Sen Gupta describes it as "a new type of historical drama, in which the dramatist projects an idea through the interaction of plot and character" (p. 98).

3. *Prefaces to Shakespeare* (Princeton: Princeton Univ. Press, 1946), 1:31.

4. Two distinct concepts of King John coalesced in the mind of the Elizabethan spectator: the medieval image of the tyrant and the Reformation image of the protestant martyr (Elliott, "Shakespeare and the Double Image of King John," *Shakespeare Studies*, 1 [1965], 65–66; Jonathan R. Price, "*King John* and Problematic Art," *SQ*, 21 [1970], 26). Unlike the versions by John Bale and the anonymous author of *The Troublesome Raigne*, Shakespeare's play presents "a situation of profound moral complexity" (J. L. Simmons, "Shakespeare's *King John* and Its Source: Coherence, Pattern, and Vision," *Tulane Studies in English*, 17 [1969], 61), in which "right and wrong . . . are question-begging words" (Reese, p.

284); the "ambivalence of response . . . constitutes the central political and theatrical interest of the play" (Richmond, p. 100).

5. Manheim, p. 131.

6. If it is an exaggeration to call John a tragic figure (Charles Stubblefield, "Some Thoughts about *King John*," *CEA Critic*, 35, No. 3 [1973], 27), it is also misleading to assert that he as a usurper forfeits all sympathy "from the outset" (J. D. Wilson, *King John*, p. xliv). He views the throne as a possession, like a landlord wanting a good yield (Ellis-Fermor, p. 39), falling, as Webster has observed, somewhere between the villainy of Richard III and the sensitivity of Richard II (p. 136).

7. Bromley may correctly brand John merely "a vassal of the Pope" (p. 49), but John Sibley perceptively notes that Shakespeare's emphasis upon John's usurpation also invalidates his submission of the English throne to Rome ("The Anomalous Case of *King John*," *ELH*, 33 [1966], 421).

8. There is no evidence to support the claim that John is "sincerely repentant for his sins" (Ribner, *English History Play*, p. 122), and only slightly more credible is Adrien Bonjour's observation that the final words of Prince Henry and the Bastard are "like a pardon giving lasting rest to a tormented soul" ("The Road to Swinstead Abbey: A Study of the Sense and Structure of *King John*," *ELH*, 18 [1951], 265).

9. Matchett, p. xxxvi; see also Matchett's earlier article "Richard's Divided Heritage in *King John*," *EIC*, 12 (1962), 240. Emrys Jones finds a structural parallel in *Mundus et Infans*, in which the moral innocent must encounter the world of experience (*The Origins of Shakespeare* [Oxford: Clarendon, 1977], p. 235). Julia C. Van de Water sees him as two separate characters, a vice in the first three acts and a patriot in the last two ("The Bastard in *King John*," *SQ*, 11 [1960], 143), and to F. P. Wilson he is a split Shakespearean personality leading to both Falstaff and Hal (*Studies*, p. 38).

10. Calderwood, "Commodity and Honour in *King John*," *UTQ*, 29 (1960), 355; Matchett, ed., p. xxxvii. General estimates of the Bastard's character vary widely: "comic" to William Hazlitt (*Characters of Shakespeare's Plays*, 3rd ed. [London: Templeman, 1838], p. 232), "lovable" to A. C. Swinburne (*A Study of Shakespeare* [London: Chatto and Windus, 1879], p. 74), the Machiavel legitimized to John F. Danby (*Shakespeare's Doctrine of Nature* [London: Faber and Faber, 1949], p. 73), a "high-spirited, brave dare-devil" to Murry (p. 162), the Bastard is branded a "crude materialist" by Gunnar Boklund ("The Troublesome Ending of *King John*," *Studia Neophilologica*, 40 [1968], 177) and realizes, according to Ronald Stroud, that "he must either embrace the erring obsessions of his world or remain a moral 'bastard' " ("The Bastard to the Time in *King John*) *Comparative Drama*, 6 [1972], 155).

11. Clemen notes that Shakespeare masses the reports of Constance's deaths, Elinor's death, the barons' rebellion, and the French invasion to achieve an overwhelming effect (*Dramatic Art,* p. 105).

12. Faulconbridge's function as a chorus has been frequently noted (Sprague, p. 211; Bevington, *Tudor Drama and Politics* [Cambridge: Harvard Univ. Press, 1968], pp. 199, 243; Bilton, p. 67), while O. J. Campbell perceives his role as a satirist (*Shakespeare's Satire* [London: Oxford Univ. Press, 1943], pp. 13–14). Ifor Evans correctly calls him "a commentary, comic, satiric, and eloquent in turn, on all the values that the play suggests" (*A Short History of English Drama* [Boston: Houghton Mifflin, 1965], p. 55). His soliloquies do humanize him, however, by revealing his own bias (Clemen, *Shakespeare's Soliloquies* [London: Cambridge Univ. Press, 1964], p. 14).

13. See Bullough, 4:17; J. D. Wilson, *King John,* p. xxi.

14. "*King John:* The Ordering of This Present Time," *ELH,* 33 (1966), 149. The play, according to John Masefield, "is an intellectual form in which a number of people with obsessions illustrate the idea of treachery" (*William Shakespeare* [New York: Holt, 1911], p. 76; a "struggle of kingly greeds and priestly pride (Edward Dowden, *Shakespeare* [London: Macmillan, 1877], p. 168), it reflects a "mixture of philosophical materialism and machiavellian politics" (Berman, "Anarchy and Order in *Richard III* and *King John,*" *Shakespeare Survey,* 20 [1967], 54).

15. Alan C. Dessen traces the influence on this scene to the psychomachia tradition of the moralities (*Elizabethan Drama and the Viewer's Eye* [Chapel Hill: Univ. of North Carolina Press, 1977], p. 144).

16. This temptation by John, as acted by Herbert Beerbohm Tree, is the first Shakespearean scene on film (Robert Hamilton Ball, "Tree's *King John* Film: An Addendum," *SQ,* 24 [1973], 455).

17. Topical critics are especially attracted to this scene as a parallel to Jesuit equivocation (Reese, p. 272) or the advice to Philip of Spain to await Mary's death before expecting papal support for his cause (L. B. Campbell, p. 147).

18. E. K. Chambers, *Survey,* p. 105; Palmer, p. 321.

19. "The last and most terrible of Shakespeare's wailing women" (Mark Van Doren, *Shakespeare* [Garden City: Doubleday, 1939], p. 91), Constance in her "heart-rending, soul-absorbing grief" (Anna Jameson, *Characteristics of Women* [Philadelphia: Carey, Lea and Blanchard, 1833], p. 168) reflects "the dark background and the pathetic consequences of the struggle" (Fergusson, p. 66).

20. On the predominance of the imagery of heat and fire, see Halliday,

p. 90, and E. C. Pettet, "Hot Irons and Fever: A Note on Some of the Imagery of *King John*," *EIC*, 4 (1954), 128. Spurgeon (p. 245) and Honigmann (p. lxii) discuss the profusion of body images, while Robert D. Stevick ("Repentant Ashes: The Matrix of 'Shakespearian' Poetic Language," *SQ* [1962], 367) focuses on the significance of the imagery in Arthur's plea to Hubert for mercy.

21. Line references to *The Troublesome Raigne of King John* are to Bullough's edition.

22. William Empson describes "three worlds, each with its own hero" (*Some Versions of Pastoral* [London: Chatto and Windus, 1935], p. 43), while Dessen speaks of "dual protagonists" ("The Intemperate Knight and the Politic Prince: Late Morality Structure in *1 Henry IV*," *Shakespeare Studies*, 7 [1974], 157). This absence of a single dominant role as a "star vehicle," according to Webster, has hurt the popularity of the play in the theater (p. 133).

23. The prompt copy from the Smock Alley Theatre indicates the need for at least six different scene settings (Gunnar Sorelius, "The Smock Alley Prompt-Books of *1* and *2 Henry IV*," *SQ*, 22 [1971], 124).

24. Ed., *The First Part of King Henry IV*, Arden Shakespeare (London: Methuen, 1960), p. xxviii.

25. Stephen Gardiner, *De Vera Obedientia, Oratio* (1535); see Allen, p. 126.

26. Allen, p. 127; William Tyndale, "The Obedience of a Christian Man," in *Doctrinal Treatises and Introductions to Different Portions of the Holy Scriptures* (Cambridge, 1848), pp. 179–80; Sir Thomas Craig, *Concerning the Rights of Succession to the Kingdom of England* (London, 1703), p. 16. As Pierce has recently observed, Shakespeare in *1, 2 Henry IV* "displays the quest for political order as fundamentally like the quest for personal order within the family"—the Percies fail while the Lancastrians ultimately succeed (pp. 171, 213).

27. *Richard II to Henry V*, pp. 81–82.

28. The topicality of the *Henry IV* plays has been investigated at length by L. B. Campbell, pp. 218ff. The plays reflect the "delicate equilibrium of late sixteenth-century English society" (Charles Barber, "Prince Hal, Henry V, and the Tudor Monarchy," in Jefferson, p. 68; see also William B. Stone, "Literature and Class Ideology: *Henry IV, Part One*," *CE*, 33 [1972], 894. Hart asserts that *2 Henry IV* was heavily cut by the censor because of the possible parallel between Elizabeth and Henry IV, a king depicted as "refusing wise counsel" and "depressing his nobles" (p. 194).

29. Sir Thomas Hoby, trans., *The Book of the Courtier* by Baldassare Castiglione (London: Dent, 1928), pp. 261ff.; Starkey, *Dialogue Between*

Cardinal Pole and Thomas Lupset, ed. Sidney J. Herrtage, The Early English Text Society (London, 1878), pp. 100–1; Elyot, *The Boke of the Governour* (New York: Dutton, 1907), p. 9.

30. J. H. Walter, ed., *King Henry V,* Arden Shakespeare (London: Methuen, 1954), pp. xvii–xviii.

31. James Hoyle describes the *tableau vivant* as Hal standing "between the two extremes of self-indulgence" ("Some Emblems in Shakespeare's History Plays," *ELH,* 38 [1971], 525); see also Charles Mitchell, "The Education of a True Prince," *Tennessee Studies in Literature,* 12 (1967), 19.

32. P. 109. Recent arguments to the contrary include Daniel Seltzer, "Prince Hal and the Tragic Style," *Shakespeare Survey,* 30 (1977), 20; and Sherman H. Hawkins, "Virtue and Kingship in Shakespeare's *Henry IV,*" *ELR,* 5 (1975), 343. More to the point is Sanders's discussion of the various roles Hal assumes but ultimately rejects ("The True Prince and the False Thief: Prince Hal and the Shift of Identity," *Shakespeare Survey,* 30 [1977], 29–34).

33. Rudolf B. Schmerl reminds us that such a scene would be far funnier to the comically detached spectator than to Hal ("Comedy and the Manipulation of Moral Distance: Falstaff and Shylock," *Bucknell Review,* 10 [1961], 132).

34. P. 186. See also Dean, "From *Richard II* to *Henry V,*" p. 198. Such ambivalence is characteristic of the play as a whole (Cleanth Brooks and Heilman, *Understanding Drama* [New York: Holt, Rinehart, Winston, 1948], p. 384; Anthony La Branche, " 'If Thou Wert Sensible of Courtesy': Private and Public Virtue in *Henry IV, Part One,*" *SQ,* 16 [1966], 381).

35. William B. Hunter, "Falstaff," *SAQ,* 50 (1951), 89; Alan Gerald Gross, "The Justification of Prince Hal," *TSLL,* 10 (1968–69), 28.

36. Sen Gupta, p. 137; Masefield, p. 112; Manheim, p. 166.

37. Elmer M. Blistein, *Comedy in Action* (Durham: Duke Univ. Press, 1964), p. 10.

38. In this respect Bromley aptly notes that Henry is a "wholly public figure" (p. 61), though to call his remorse "nothing but rhetorical posture" (p. 66) and to view him as a subtly drawn hypocrite (Goddard, 1: 162) and a "cynically adept politician" (Winny, p. 87) is to oversimplify the character as it appears on stage.

39. Like Henry IV, writes Riggs, Hotspur is engaged in "the ceaseless accumulation of 'proud titles' unrelieved by moments of social occasion or self-fulfillment" (p. 159). Of a bloody and vicious mind (W. Gordon Zeeveld, " 'Food for Powder'—'Food for Worms,' " *SQ,* 3 [1952], 310), Hotspur's instincts—"informed by the merely negative" (Raymond H.

Reno, "Hotspur: The Integration of Character and Theme," *Renaissance Papers* [1962], p. 25)—are for "rebellion and anarchy rather than for order" (Northrop Frye, "Nature and Nothing," in *Essays on Shakespeare,* ed. Gerald W. Chapman [Princeton: Princeton Univ. Press, 1965], p. 43).

40. A sampling of the diversity of opinion will suggest the large body of criticism. Falstaff has been traced to various literary and folk anteced-ents: the allegorical figures of medieval drama (Bernard Spivack, "Falstaff and the Psychomachia," *SQ,* 8 [1957], 458), the mock king and Lord of Misrule (Frye, "The Argument of Comedy," *English Institute Essays* [1948], 71); the *miles gloriosus* of Plautus (J. D. Wilson, *The Fortunes of Falstaff* [Cambridge: Cambridge Univ. Press, 1943], p. 83); the court fool and soothsayer (Roy Battenhouse, "Falstaff as Parodist and Perhaps Holy Fool," *PMLA,* 90 [1975], 32); the *picaro* of Renaissance fiction (Her-bert B. Rothschild, Jr., "Falstaff and the Picaresque Tradition," *MLR,* 68 [1973], 14). Others find the origins in several characters of *The Famous Victories of Henry V* (D. B. Landt, "The Ancestry of Sir John Falstaff," *SQ,* 17 [1966], 70—in particular in the influence of Richard Tarleton's striking impersonations in the role of Dericke (James Monaghan, "Falstaff and his Forebears," *SP,* 18 [1921], 360); in figures from the London streets of Shakespeare's day (Paul N. Siegel, "Falstaff and His Social Mi-lieu," *Shakespeare Jahrbuch,* 110 [1974], 139); in the degenerate depen-dence upon the feudal order (T. A. Jackson, "Marx and Shakespeare," *International Literature,* 2 [1963], 87).

41. While John Shaw ("The Staging of Parody and Parallels in *1 Hen-ry IV,*" *Shakespeare Survey,* 20 [1967], 64) and Paul A. Gottschalk ("Hal and the 'Play Extempore' in *1 Henry IV,*" *TSLL,* 15 [1973–74], 609) perceive a broad parody and J.D.A. Ogilvy sees a comic attack upon both Euphuism and Arcadianism ("Arcadianism in *1 Henry IV,*" *ELN,* 10 [1972–73], 185), Richard L. McGuire argues that the scene, far from being parodic, is the turning point for the relationship between Hal and Falstaff ("The Play-within-the-Play in *1 Henry IV,*" *SQ,* 18 [1967], 50); see also Fredson Bowers, "Shakespeare's Art: The Point of View," in *Lit-erary Views,* ed. Carroll Camden (Chicago: Univ. of Chicago Press, 1964), pp. 54–55.

42. Shakespeare, according to Norman Council, makes the concept of honor and the major characters' response to it central to the play ("Prince Hal: Mirror of Success," *Shakespeare Studies,* 7 [1974], 144). This em-phasis is "a mark of the secular atmosphere of *1 Henry IV. . . .* In the world of politics and civil war [honor] functions as a substitute for moral principle" (Prior, p. 202).

43. In an interesting article U. C. Knoepflmacher treats Falstaff's coun-

terfeit rising as a parody of Hal's rising to glory at Shrewsbury ("The Humors as Symbolic Nucleus in *Henry IV, Part I*," *CE*, 24 [1963], 501).

44. Tillyard (p. 300), J. D. Wilson (ed., *The First Part of the History of Henry IV*, pp. vii–xiii), Harold Jenkins (*The Structural Problem in Shakespeare's Henry the Fourth* [London: Methuen, 1956], rpt. in *Discussions of Shakespeare's Histories*, ed. Dorius [Boston: Heath, 1964], p. 47), and Leo Kirschbaum ("The Demotion of Falstaff," *PQ*, 41 [1962], 158) support the concept of a single play. Law (p. 223), H. Edward Cain ("Further Light on the Relation of *1* and *2 Henry IV*," *SQ*, 3 [1952], 38), and M. A. Shaaber ("The Unity of *Henry IV*," in *Joseph Quincy Adams Memorial Studies* [Washington, D.C.: Folger Shakespeare Library, 1948], p. 228) argue for two separate plays. G. K. Hunter maintains that the two plays form a diptych, depending more on parallel incidents than narrative continuity ("*Henry IV* and the Elizabethan Two-Part Play," *RES*, NS 5 [1954], 237, 243).

45. "The Comical-Tragical-Historical Method—*Henry IV*," in Brown and Harris, p. 163.

46. David P. Young speaks of the "malaise which envelops the play" (ed., *Twentieth-Century Interpretations of Henry IV, Part Two* [Englewood Cliffs, N.J.: Prentice-Hall, 1968], p. 5); and Leech compares the tone to that of the dark comedies ("The Unity of *II Henry IV*," *Shakespeare Survey*, 6 [1953], 22). L. C. Knights calls the play a satire against statecraft and warfare ("Notes on Comedy," *Scrutiny*, 1 [1933], 366); see also Richard David, "Shakespeare's History Plays: Epic or Drama?" *Shakespeare Survey*, 6 (1953), 137.

47. Both Frank Manley ("The Unity of Betrayal in *II Henry IV*," *Studies in the Literary Imagination*, 5, No. 1 [1972], 91) and Berman ("The Nature of Guilt in the *Henry IV* Plays," *Shakespeare Studies*, 1 [1965], 18) speak of the disease imagery reflecting the sickness at the heart of the play. Other significant patterns of imagery include betrayal (Norman N. Holland, ed., *The Second Part of King Henry IV* [New York: Signet, 1965], p. xxiii), of robbery (Hapgood, "Falstaff's Vocation," *SQ*, 16 [1965], 98), and of noise (Richard Knowles, "Unquiet and the Double Plot of *2 Henry IV*," *Shakespeare Studies*, 2 [1966], 135).

48. While Charles Fish observes that Shakespeare made alterations from Holinshed to render Archbishop Scrope a less favorable character ("Henry IV: Shakespeare and Holinshed," *SP*, 61 [1964], 218), Kelly points out that in actuality Henry tended to lose support from the chroniclers with the archbishop's execution (p. 23).

49. P. 125. Law asserts that Shakespeare's primary source is not Holinshed but *1 Henry IV* ("The Composition of Shakespeare's Lancastrian Trilogy," *TSLL*, 3 [1961–62], 323).

50. Charles R. Forker, "Shakespeare's Chronicle Plays as Historical-Pastoral," *Shakespeare Studies,* 1 (1965), 87; E. Rubinstein, "*1 Henry IV:* The Metaphor of Liability," *SEL,* 10 (1970), 292; Rossiter, *Angel with Horns,* p. 61; the characters "carry about with them a fuller and more complex humanity than is required by the exigencies of their role" (J.I.M. Stewart, *Character and Motive in Shakespeare* [London: Longmans, Green, 1949], p. 118).

51. Ed., *The Second Part of King Henry IV,* Arden Shakespeare (London: Methuen, 1966), p. xlvii.

52. Prince John's action is considered "shameful perfidy" (Ribner, "The Political Problems in Shakespeare's Lancastrian Tetralogy," *SP,* 49 [1952], 183), "a dastardly example of treachery" (G. Wilson Knight, *The Olive and the Sword* [London: Oxford Univ. Press, 1944], p. 27). Jorgensen argues that contemporary spectators, aware of political necessities, would not have been "so obdurately embittered" as later critics ("The 'Dastardly' Treachery of Prince John of Lancaster," *PMLA,* 76 [1961], 492).

53. Forced to ignore Hal's reformation in *Part 1* (Edgar T. Schell, "Prince Hal's Second 'Reformation,' " *SQ,* 21 [1970], 13), Shakespeare again sets the theme of Hal's "redeeming time" (Hugh Dickinson, "The Reformation of Prince Hal," *SQ,* 12 [1961], 33; Jorgensen, " 'Redeeming Time' in Shakespeare's *Henry IV,*" *Tennessee Studies in Literature,* 5 [1960], 102), a phrase according to Bryant intended to remind the playgoers of Ephesians ("Prince Hal and the Ephesians," *Sewanee Review,* 67 [1959], 204).

54. Clearly Shakespeare sacrifices any sign of sorrow in Hal "to obtain his *coup de theatre*" (Bullough, 4:264). If the argument that Falstaff is ritually slain fails to explain the spectators' reactions (Philip Williams, "The Birth and Death of Falstaff Reconsidered," *SQ,* 8 [1957], 364), so does the claim that Hal in the banishment is revealing himself possessed of Christian virtue (Franklin B. Newman, "The Rejection of Falstaff and the Rigorous Charity of the King," *Shakespeare Studies,* 2 [1966], 153). C. L. Barber correctly notes that the problem "is not in justifying rejection morally but in making the process cogent *dramatically*" ("From Ritual to Comedy: An Examination of *Henry IV,*" *English Stage Comedy: English Institute Essays* [1954], 45); we are transferred forcibly from comedy to history (Jonas A. Barish, "The Turning Away of Prince Hal," *Shakespeare Studies,* 1 [1965], 10).

55. Humphreys, ed., *The First Part of King Henry IV,* p. xxxii.

56. Kott predictably proclaims that Falstaff and the cutpurses provide the appropriate training for Hal's first royal action (p. 50).

57. While it is oversimplistic to speak of Falstaff as a "sensitive, self-

conscious man . . . [who] invites our sympathy and forgiveness" (S. A. Small, "The Reflective Element in Falstaff," *SAB*, 14 [1939], 132), the character does continue to exercise an appeal (Samuel B. Hemingway, "The Demotion of Falstaff," *SQ*, 3 [1952], 310; Eben Bass, "Falstaff and the Succession," *CE*, 24 [1962–63], 502; Prior, "Comic Theory and the Rejection of Falstaff," *Shakespeare Studies*, 9 [1976], 171). That appeal itself is dangerous (Samuel Johnson, ed., *The Plays of William Shakespeare* [London, 1765], 4:356), and throughout part 2 progressively "the 'satyr, lecher, and parasite' in Falstaff are uppermost" (E. E. Stoll, *Shakespeare Studies* [New York: Macmillan, 1927], p. 424; Charlton, *Shakespearian Comedy* [New York: Barnes and Noble, 1938], p. 188; Traversi, p. 31). Richmond terms him the "evil genius of the new England" (p. 143).

58. "Counterfeits of Soldiership in *Henry IV*," *SQ*, 24 (1973), 378.

59. Line references are to the edition of J. Q. Adams, *Chief Pre-Shakespearean Dramas* (Boston: Houghton Mifflin, 1924).

60. Cobler, for instance, berating Dericke for his tremendous appetite, suggests Falstaff's favorite pastime: "Why, thou wilt eate me out of doores"; Cobler and Dericke parody the serious scene of Henry's boxing the ear of the Lord Chief Justice and being committed to the Fleet, just as Hal and Falstaff parody the serious confrontation of king and prince.

61. Here is the likely source for Shakespeare's double entendre in *2 Henry IV* (II, i, 14–29); see my note in *AN&Q*, 5 (1967), 69–71.

62. For a tracing of particular borrowings see Humphreys, ed., *The First Part*, pp. xxxii–xxxiv, and Reese, pp. 293ff.

63. "*1 Henry IV*: Art's Gilded Lie," *ELR*, 3 (1973), 138. Ribner describes the plays as the "ultimate peak" in the development of Shakespeare's histories (*English History Play*, p. 193), and Berry describes them as "subtler, more complex, more aesthetically coherent elaborations of dramatic techniques and political insights expressed in the first tetralogy" (p. 104).

64. Alvin Kernan describes the second tetralogy as Shakespeare's epic, *The Henriad* ("The Henriad: Shakespeare's Major History Plays," *Yale Review*, 59 [1969–70], 3), while Battenhouse ("The Relation of *Henry V* to *Tamburlaine*," *Shakespeare Survey*, 27 [1974], 72), Robert Egan ("A Muse of Fire: *Henry V* in the Light of *Tamburlaine*," *MLQ*, 29 [1968], 17), and Ribner (*English History Play*, p. 193) relate the play to Marlowe's heroical tragedy of the Scythian conquerer. An epic version of national heroism (Albert H. Tolman, "The Epic Character of Henry V," *MLN*, 34 [1919], 9), the drama, like all epics, "praises heroes and denounces villainy" (Reese, p. 321).

65. Patterned after the precepts of Renaissance military books (Jorgensen, *Shakespeare's Military World* [Berkeley: Univ. of California Press,

1956], p. 72), Henry is "the copy-book paragon of kingly virtue" (Tillyard, p. 345), conceived *"con amore"* by the playwright (J. D. Wilson, ed., *King Henry V* [Cambridge: Cambridge Univ. Press, 1955], p. xiv). Henry is the supreme leader (Walter, p. xxiii), a "synthesizing Elizabethan genius" (Weiss, *Clowns and Kings,* p. 296), a "Machiavel of goodness" (Danby, p. 90). On the other hand, possessed of "gross vices" (W. B. Yeats, *Ideas of Good and Evil* [London: Bullen, 1903], p. 163), Henry is an "amiable monster" (Hazlitt, p. 206), fit "for whatever is animal in human affairs" (Masefield, p. 122). A Hotspur without charm (Bromley, p. 85), his father's true son (A. C. Bradley, *Oxford Lectures on Poetry,* 2nd ed. [London: Macmillan, 1909], p. 257), a murderer (C. H. Hobday, "Image and Irony in *Henry V,*" *Shakespeare Survey,* 21 [1968], 109), "a dead man walking" (Ellis-Fermor, p. 47), Henry is a consummate Machiavel (Manheim, p. 167).

66. Gareth Lloyd Evans, "Shakespeare, the Twentieth Century and Behaviourism," *Shakespeare Survey,* 20 (1967), 139.

67. Hands, "Notes to the Working Text," *The Royal Shakespeare Company's Production of Henry V,* ed. Sally Beauman (Oxford: Pergamon Press, 1976), p. 232; Rabkin, "Rabbits, Ducks, and *Henry V,*" *SQ,* 28 (1977), 294.

68. Critics have spoken in various ways of the tension between the personal man and the public ruler (W. M. Merchant, "The Status and Person of Majesty," *Shakespeare Jahrbuch,* 90 [1954], 285; Palmer, p. 218; Dean, p. 203), and of the striking diversities between the Henry of the choruses and the Henry of the play (Prior, *Drama of Power,* p. 313; Gail H. Thomas, "What Is a King?" *Ball State University Forum,* 5, No. 3 [1964], 39). Berman describes the "debate between character as a complex of individual motives and character as an emblem" (ed., *Twentieth-Century Interpretations of Henry V* [Englewood Cliffs: Prentice-Hall, 1968], p. 2). On the role of irony in the play, see Battenhouse, *"Henry V* as Heroic Comedy," in *Essays on Shakespeare and Elizabethan Drama,* ed. Richard Hosley (Columbus: Univ. of Missouri Press, 1962), pp. 163–82; and Allan Gilbert, "Patriotism and Satire in *Henry V,*" in *Studies in Shakespeare,* ed. A. D. Matthews (Coral Gables: Univ. of Miami Press, 1953), pp. 40–64.

69. Pierce states that the French king's "unseemly and fruitless squabbles with his son" indirectly reflect glory upon Henry's conduct (p. 232); Haldeen Braddy argues that Shakespeare depicts the French as brave, loyal, and patriotic ("Shakespeare's *Henry V* and the French Nobility," *TSLL,* 3 [1961], 189).

70. Modern text division, usually based on the appearances of the chorus, locates the actions of the first two acts in England.

71. Surely the purpose of the chorus is neither to "admit defeat in

[Shakespeare's] attempt to impose dramatic form upon history" (Whitaker, p. 16) nor to "indicate the perspective from which the events and personalities are to be viewed" (Sen Gupta, p. 140). As Ornstein correctly observes, the chorus is "too imbued with patriotic pride to criticize the great adventure or recognize its tarnished edges" (p. 185). An "abstract of average public opinion" (Goddard, 1:217), the chorus functions as the "verbal creation of pageantry" (Bilton, p. 79) which exudes patriotism and exalts the heroic king (Bullough, 4:351).

72. For the past century, topical references to Essex have been assumed in the choruses (Richard Simpson, "The Political Use of the Stage in Shakespeare's Time" and "The Politics of Shakespeare's Historical Plays," *The New Shakespeare Society's Transactions* (1874), cited in L. B. Campbell, p. 258; Evelyn M. Albright, "The Folio Version of *Henry V* in Relation to Shakespeare's Times," *PMLA,* 43 [1928], 734). A dissenting view by Warren Smith argues for a later, non-Shakespearean authorship of the choruses and a reference not to Essex but to Lord Mountjoy ("The *Henry V* Choruses in the First Folio," *JEGP,* 53 [1954], 38–57).

73. Attention to a "transformation" between the Hal of the *Henry IV* plays and King Henry V is not uncommon. E.F.J. Tucker relates the change to the legal doctrine of the King's Two Bodies ("Legal Fiction and Human Reality: Hal's Role in *Henry V,*" *ETJ,* 26 [1974], 308–9; see also Peter H. Davidson, "Richard and Hal—'Effeminate' Princes," *N&Q,* 12 [1965], 95). Henry's maturation within the play is argued by such critics as Richmond (p. 200), Berry (p. 113), Dorothy Cook ("*Henry V:* Maturing of Man and Majesty," *Studies in the Literary Imagination,* 5 [1972], 111, 113), and Marilyn Williamson ("The Episode with Williams in *Henry V,*" *SEL,* 9 [1969], 281).

74. Now the opportunist of war (Craig and Bevington, *Complete Works,* p. 738), Pistol represents the "new upstart nobility risen from the ranks of trade" (Daniel C. Boughner, "Pistol and the Roaring Boys," *SAB,* 11 [1936], 226). He is appropriately named from the "unruly, blustering weapon" noted for its "astonishing report" (Jorgensen, *Redeeming Shakespeare's Words* [Berkeley: Univ. of California Press, 1962], pp. 71, 74).

75. Phialas, "Shakespeare's *Henry V* and the Second Tetralogy," *SP,* 62 (1965), 158; Winny, p. 181. Manheim's comment that since none of the soldiers overhears Henry's comment the king does not reveal his weakness (p. 179) is simply a perverse defiance of the function of the soliloquy in Elizabethan drama. To Honor Matthews, Henry "cultivates a deliberate 'non-attachment' to humanity" (*Character and Symbol in Shakespeare's Plays* [Cambridge: Cambridge Univ. Press, 1962], p. 54); to Webster, he comes to know "humility and infinite responsibility" (p. 129). His aware-

ness of the hollowness of ceremony is a mark of his maturity (Theodore Spencer, *Shakespeare and the Nature of Man* [New York: Macmillan, 1942], p. 84).

76. Falstaff's failure to return to the stage may have been prompted by Will Kempe's departure from the Lord Chamberlain's Company (J. D. Wilson, *Fortunes of Falstaff*, p. 125), and the report of his death may have been comic (Robert F. Fleissner, "Falstaff's Green Sickness unto Death," *SQ*, 12 [1961], 55) or a satiric attack on Lord Cobham (Alice Lyle Scoufos, "The 'Martyrdom' of Falstaff," *Shakespeare Studies*, 2 [1966], 178). But certainly the juxtaposition of the scene with that in which Henry orders the execution of the traitors at Southampton is intended to reveal the expense of power and responsibility (Robert L. Kelly, "Shakespeare's Scroop and the Spirit of Cain," *SQ*, 20 [1969], 80).

77. Robert P. Merrix argues at some length that the allusion, "by virtue of its structural position and symbolic function, exposes one of several flaws in Henry's character" ("The Alexandrian Allusion in Shakespeare's *Henry V*," *ELR*, 2 [1972], 321). Richard Levin has used the passage to construct an attack upon what he calls "literary criticism by wild analogy" ("On Fluellen Figures, Christ Figures, and James Figures," *PMLA*, 89 [1974], 302–11).

78. "The Humor of Corporal Nym," *SAB*, 13 (1938), 132.

79. Newman, p. 160. Karl P. Wentersdorf notes that Henry does not specify the charges of treason because it would publicly raise the specter of the Lancastrian usurpation; the rebels, on the other hand, hope that their silence will save the lives of their wives and children ("The Conspiracy of Silence in *Henry V*," *SQ*, 27 [1976], 280, 283).

80. George R. Price contends that the scene is not raising a moral issue for Henry but is emphasizing "his common touch, his willingness to understand his men" ("Henry V and Germanicus," *SQ*, 12 [1961], 58). More importantly, however, the "decidedly tragic" moment reveals a troubled conscience which moves beyond the mere celebration of a conqueror (Traversi, *Richard II to Henry V*, p. 188; Harbage, *As They Liked It* [London: Macmillan, 1947], p 12).

81. Ed., *The College Shakespeare* (London: Macmillan, 1973), p. 246. Jorgensen concentrates on Shakespeare's use of the traditional language of the bluff soldier ("The Courtship Scene in *Henry V*," *MLQ*, 11 [1950], 181), while to Brian Vickers the "wit and brilliance of [the] wooing language" look forward to the high comedies which follow (*The Artistry of Shakespeare's Prose* [London: Methuen, 1968], p. 166). Both the view that Hal in this scene "has become like Hotspur" in his crass manipulation of others (Williamson, "The Courtship of Katherine and the Second Tetralogy," *Criticism*, 17 [1975], 334) and that, having begun like Hotspur,

he now is genuinely "honest and peaceseeking" (William Babula, "Whatever Happened to Prince Hal? An Essay on *Henry V*," *Shakespeare Survey*, 30 [1977], 59) miss the rich ambiguity that marks his character from beginning to end.

82. *Character and Society in Shakespeare* (Oxford: Oxford Univ. Press, 1951).

83. Harbage, *Theatre for Shakespeare* (Toronto: Toronto Univ. Press, 1955), p. 48.

84. *The Multiple Plot in English Renaissance Drama* (Chicago: Univ. of Chicago Press, 1971), pp. 16, 116.

CHAPTER V: *HENRY VIII*

1. Both Theobald and Malone believed that *Henry VIII* was Elizabethan in origin, a view more recently supported by E. K. Chambers (*William Shakespeare,* 1:497). Critical consensus, however, dates the play around 1613 when it perhaps celebrated the marriage on St. Valentine's Day of Princess Elizabeth, daughter of James I, to Prince Frederick, the Elector Palatine; "to good patriots the anti-Catholic implications of the marriage offered the best of reasons for great rejoicing" (R. A. Foakes, ed., *King Henry VIII* [London: Methuen, 1957], p. xxxi). Francis A. Yates argues for a general revival in literature of "the symbols of the Elizabethan cult"; in this play Shakespeare uses "a real Tudor king, Henry VIII, to make his contemporary points about his hopes for the youngest royal generation" (*Shakespeare's Last Plays* [London: Routledge and Kegan Paul, 1975], pp. 74, 78). As to authorship, since James Spedding, responding to Tennyson's suggestion, claimed in *The Gentleman's Magazine* in 1850 that *Henry VIII* was a work of collaboration, the argument has never ceased. Principal proponents of Fletcher's hand include (as sole author) Robert Boyle and H. Dugdale Sykes and (as collaborator) A. H. Thorndike, Marjorie H. Nicolson, Law, Halliday, Mincoff, Cyrus Hoy, Ornstein, and J. C. Maxwell; those claiming sole Shakespearean authorship include Alexander, Baldwin Maxwell, Hardin Craig, Thomas Clayton, Schoenbaum, Bullough, and Foakes. The most inclusive summaries of the diverse points of view can be found in Foakes's introduction to the Arden edition (1957) and in J. C. Maxwell's introduction to the Cambridge edition (1962). Tillyard argues that Shakespeare had had material on *Henry VIII* in mind since the earlier tetralogies but had simply never been provoked to putting it into dramatic form ("Why Did Shakespeare Write *Henry VIII?*" *CQ,* 3 [1961], 26).

2. Harbage, *Annals.* As reissues of *Sir Thomas Wyat, Edward IV, Thomas Lord Cromwell,* Marlowe's *Edward II,* Shakespeare's *Richard III, 1, 2 Henry IV,* and Rowley's *When You See Me, You Know Me* would attest, however, there was renewed interest in the history plays around 1612. Felix Schelling has suggested that Shakespeare's play was written to challenge Rowley's frivolous version of *Henry VIII (The English Chronicle Play* [New York: Macmillan, 1902], pp. 248–49), a view endorsed by Bullough (4:442).

3. See my *Tragic Perspective,* pp. 201–65, for a discussion of the significance of multiple choric figures in establishing the social dimensions of tragedy in *Timon of Athens, Coriolanus,* and *Antony and Cleopatra.*

4. Peter Saccio describes the play as "a historical pageant" *(Shakespeare's English Kings* [London: Oxford Univ. Press, 1977], p. 210), and Eugene M. Waith calls it "a series of magnificent shows . . . tending to make the chronicle even more like a masque than like a tragedy" *(The Pattern of Tragicomedy in Beaumont and Fletcher* [New Haven: Yale Univ. Press, 1952], p. 119). The "Tudor forms are Jacobeanized" (Jones, p. 195), utilizing an epic movement (G. W. Knight, *Shakespeare and Religion* [New York: Barnes and Noble, 1967], p. 76) built on "narrative rather than dramatic technique" (F. David Hoeniger, ed., *The Life of King Henry the Eighth,* in *Complete Works,* ed. Harbage, p. 782) and "stressing masquelike effects in the opulent manner of court entertainment" (Bevington, ed., *Complete Works,* p. 1271; Reese, p. 33n).

5. Rabkin, *Common Understanding,* p. 230. Ribner attributes the weakness of the play to the general decline of the history play and Shakespeare's "failure to embody an overall consistent philosophical scheme" *(English History Play,* p. 288); Frederick O. Waage, Jr., argues that Shakespeare, personally distressed with Prince Henry's death, reflects his sense of historical discontinuity ("Henry VIII and the Crisis of the English History Play," *Shakespeare Studies,* 8 [1975], 299).

6. Goddard, 1:269. A critic of the London *Times* spoke in 1811 of the "accumulated *ennui* of *Henry VIII*" (quoted in Goddard, p. 270), and Lytton Strachey accused Shakespeare of being bored *(Books and Characters* [New York: Harbrace, 1922], p. 64).

7. C. K. Pooler, ed., *Henry VIII* [London: Methuen, 1915], p. xxxii.

8. Baker, "Introduction to *Henry VIII*" in *Riverside Shakespeare,* p. 978. Halliday speaks of a "series of loosely related private disasters interspersed with pageants" (p. 190); *Henry VIII* fails, according to A. A. Parker, because Shakespeare was unable "to transform his historical theme into successful dramatic art" ("Henry VIII in Shakespeare and Calderón," *MLR,* 43 [1948], 330).

9. G. W. Knight, *The Crown of Life* (London: Oxford, 1947), p. 326; Charles Knight, *Shakespeare's Works* (London: Routledge, 1840), 2:398.

10. Leech, "The Structure of the Late Plays," *Shakespeare Survey*, 11 (1958), 19, 29; the "total effect . . . of a complex tonal and thematic orchestration" (Schoenbaum, ed., *The Famous History of the Life of King Henry the Eighth* [New York: New American Library, 1967], p. xxxv) is an achievement worthy of Shakespeare's maturity" (Richmond, "Shakespeare's *Henry VIII*: Romance Redeemed by History," *Shakespeare Studies*, 4 [1968], 348).

11. Herbert Howarth, *The Tiger's Heart* [New York: Oxford, 1970], p. 153). The structure, "distinguished by constant and alarming shifts in its perspective on character and action" (Lee Bliss, "The Wheel of Fortune and the Maiden Phoenix of Shakespeare's *King Henry the Eighth*," *ELH*, 42 [1975], 3), represents "true history . . . because in tone and temper it steers a middle course between the lightheartedness—the merry bawdiness—of comedy and the gloom of tragedy" (Sen Gupta, p. 153).

12. Paul Bertram, *Shakespeare and the Two Noble Kinsmen* (New Brunswick: Rutgers Univ. Press, 1965), p. 159. Frank Kermode describes the structure as a pattern of tragic falls in the old *"de casibus"* tradition ("What Is Shakespeare's *Henry VIII* About?" *Durham University Journal*, NS9 [1948], 48–55; rpt. in *Shakespeare: The Histories*, ed. Waith [Englewood Cliffs: Prentice-Hall, 1965], p. 178), while Hardin Craig speaks of an overriding controlling factor of "God's ascertainable purpose" (*An Interpretation of Shakespeare* [New York: Dryden, 1948], p. 357).

13. See, for example, D. Douglas Waters, "Shakespeare and the 'Mistress-Missa' Tradition in *King Henry VIII*," *SQ*, 24 (1973), 459–62.

14. Both Hazlitt (p. 222) and Anna Jameson (*Shakespeare's Heroines* [New York: Burt, n.d.], p. 362) rhapsodize over her patience and self-control. More to the point, as Harbage observes, Shakespeare "goes far beyond Holinshed in giving Katherine virtue and ability, and he movingly dramatizes her distress" (*As They Liked It*, p. 71).

15. Numerous critics have attempted to explain away this inconsistency. Marjorie Nicholson, claiming Shakespeare intended to depict a "later Iago," is typical of those who see collaboration as responsible for the two faces of Wolsey ("The Authorship of *Henry VIII*," *PMLA*, 37 [1922], 500); Ribner describes "basic inconsistencies within [Shakespeare's] sources" (*English History Play*, p. 289). Webster notes that, whatever the cause, on stage the "two sides of the man's nature . . . are not irreconcilable" (p. 201).

16. Berman, *"King Henry the Eighth*: History and Romance" *English*

Studies, 48 (1967), 112; see also A. W. Schlegal, *Lectures on Dramatic Art and Literature* (London: Bell, 1902), pp. 419–22.

17. It is this pattern which has led various critics to describe the structural similarities with the romances: the "sweep of life shaped in a restorative pattern" (Foakes, p. xli), the "forces of spiritual regeneration and reformation" (Howard Felperin, "Shakespeare's *Henry VIII:* History as Myth," *SEL,* 6 [1966], 240), in this instance applied to the nation as a whole rather than to particular individuals. See further Alexander, "Conjectural History or Shakespeare's *Henry VIII,*" *Essays and Studies,* 16 (1931), 113.

18. Yates calls it a theophany (p. 76), and John Cutts argues for Trinitarian overtones in the triple crowning ("Shakespeare's Song and Masque Hand in *Henry VIII,*" *Shakespeare Jahrbuch,* 99 [1963], 192–93). Others emphasize the juxtaposition of Katherine's spiritual with Anne's secular coronation (Bradbrook, *The Living Monument* [Cambridge: Cambridge Univ. Press, 1976], p. 74; Foakes, p. lii). Shakespeare's source for Katherine's vision, as E. E. Duncan-Jones has observed, possibly was a dream experience by Queen Margaret of Navarre shortly before her death ("Queen Katherine's Vision and Queen Margaret's Dream," *N&Q,* NS8 [1961], 142–43).

19. Henry acts consistently throughout the play to secure his throne and establish the succession; to some critics he is a "dummy king" (Van Doren, p. 289) or so vague as to be irritating (Ornstein, p. 211); to another he is one whose wisdom evolves "through a plausible series of historical errors of judgment" (Richmond, p. 347); to another he is the agent of a divine providence who must be judged only in terms of his fruits: "a great queen and the establishment of the reformed church" (Kermode, p. 179); to another he is "the political statesman *par excellence*" (Bliss, p. 15).

Index